TESI GREGORIAN

Serie Filosofia

22

PEDERITO A. APARECE, OSA

TEACHING, LEARNING AND COMMUNITY
An Examination of Wittgensteinian Themes Applied to the Philosophy of Education

EDITRICE PONTIFICIA UNIVERSITÀ GREGORIANA
Roma 2005

Vidimus et approbamus ad normam Statutorum Universitatis

Romae, ex Pontificia Universitate Gregoriana
die 03 mensis februarii anni 2005

R.P. Prof. LOUIS CARUANA, S.J.
R.P. Prof. GEORG SANS, S.J.

ISBN 88-7839-029-1
PRINTED IN ITALY

GREGORIAN UNIVERSITY PRESS
Piazza della Pilotta, 35 - 00187 Rome, Italy

ACKNOWLEDGEMENTS

As this research has been brought to a conclusion, a deep sense of thankfulness overcomes me, primarily to God the Almighty, for the Love that has sustained me through the difficult times of my work. I place on record my sincerest gratitude to the Superiors past and present of the Order of St. Augustine, the Province of Sto. Niño de Cebu, and the Province of Madrid (Escorial), for having given me the opportunity to pursue advanced studies in philosophy. My deep-felt indebtedness to Rev. Fr. Louis Caruana, SJ, the director of this dissertation, for his kind guidance, valuable criticism, and unfailing encouragement. I have drawn so much from the wealth of his scholarship and his knowledge of Wittgenstein. A special word of thanks to Rev. Fr. Georg Sans, SJ, for his thorough examination of my work. To Rev. Fr. George Lawless, OSA and Rev. Fr. Francis Galvan, OSA, who have read and corrected parts of the thesis. I also would like to thank all my confrères in the Collegio Internazionale Agostiniano S. Monica.

I thank in a special way my loving parents, my brother and sister, whose self-transcending love continues to enrich my life at the deepest levels, Uncle Pepe, Auntie Fe, all my relatives for being there for me through thick and thin, and all my friends in the Philippines, in Rome specially the Pundok ni Beato Pedro Calungsod, in the United States, in the U.K. and elsewhere, for their unfailing love, encouragement and support which is a prime font of strength for my life.

GENERAL INTRODUCTION

1. Aim of the Research

It is widely accepted among Wittgensteinian scholars that in the development of Wittgenstein's ideas he possessed no succinct and precise theory regarding the philosophy of education. His interest in the field of education, however, can be seen in his pedagogical approach to the philosophical problems which he tried to solve. In one of his lectures Wittgenstein said that when we discuss about words we always ask how we were taught to use them. His educational approach to the analysis of the reality of language provides a convincing motive to investigate into the major philosophical themes in correlation to the field of philosophy of education specifically what is considered as the three fundamental factors in education, viz. teaching, learning and community.

The present research work intends to examine the following Wittgensteinian themes: the concept of *meaning as use, rule-following* and the idea of *Philosophy as therapy* in relation to the basic educational elements: *teaching, learning* and *community*. The overall argument consists of making evident and defending the claim that Wittgenstein's ideas are valid theoretical foundations for a clarification of the aforementioned educational concepts and that based on this a new perspective of understanding them is offered. Consequently, the claim will attest their significance in the philosophy of education.

Wittgenstein's treatment and analysis of meaning provides valuable insights into the concept of teaching. The work, however, is not aimed at producing proofs of an absolute correspondence between his concept of meaning and teaching but rather presenting how the nature of teaching could be viewed in the context of Wittgenstein's concept of meaning and how his understanding of «meaning as use» contributes to a new model of understanding the teaching practice.

His thought on rule-following, on the other hand, offers significant ideas to the character of the process of learning. His assertion that understanding a language entails that one has properly followed rules in its usage gives more than sufficient ground for an analysis regarding its impact on the problem of learning. The investigation will reveal that the character of the learning process is comparable to following a rule.

Lastly, the proposed research work would attempt to demonstrate that Wittgenstein's idea of «philosophy as therapy» highlights the prevailing interaction between communal practices and the educational system. It is through an investigation of the elements of his thoughts on the therapeutic nature of philosophy which makes evident the particular function and contribution of the community in the sphere of education which directly affects the instructional approach of educators and downgrades the idea that learners come to be educated as *tabula rasa*.

2. Methodology, Scope and Limitation

The work will primarily revolve around the ambit of philosophy of education. Hence, the study would not delve into a detailed investigation of the whole Wittgensteinian philosophy. Areas of his thought such as philosophy of mathematics, ethics, meta-philosophy, and logic will not be discussed save some emphasis that is relevant to the main arguments of this work regarding education. The method of my research is generally expository and critical. I will be engaging in a textual analysis of Wittgenstein's writings and speculative analysis of the basic concepts of education rather than data-analysis of concrete educational phenomena. The major part of the study will principally treat significant ideas in the later stage of Wittgenstein's philosophy, specifically those concerning language and psychology represented mainly by the *Philosophical Investigations*. Nonetheless, this study will also make reference to other important works of Wittgenstein, namely, *Tractatus Logico-Philosophicus, Blue and Brown Books, On Certainty, Culture and Values, Remarks on the Philosophy of Psychology, Philosophical Grammar, Remarks on the Foundations of Mathematics and Zettel*.

Philosophy of education is a branch of philosophy virtually concerned with every aspect of the educational enterprise. In this regard, therefore, this study is focused solely on issues and arguments concerning these three fundamental educational elements: *teaching, learning and the community*. However, this does not mean that other concepts in education outside of this frame of reference would be disregarded.

The understanding of the nature of education involves a conglomeration of ideas hence this work will make infrequent reference to other concepts in education that would serve to elucidate arguments in line with the aim of this work.

3. Originality of the Thesis

Most of the present-day scholars on Wittgenstein pay considerable attention to investigating his ideas in the area of logic, philosophy of language, philosophy of mathematics, ethics, anthropology, philosophy of mind and others but very few show interest with developing his thoughts in the field of philosophy of education. Scholars like Paul Smeyers, Michael Peters, and James Marshall are some of the few who accentuate the significance of Wittgenstein's thoughts in the theme of education. Some studies have been made regarding Wittgenstein and his style of teaching, language learning, the importance of a linguistic community but no specific investigation so far has been done concerning how his analysis about *meaning*, *rule-following* and *philosophy as therapy* could contribute to a novel understanding of the concepts of *teaching*, *learning* and the role of the *community* in education respectively. Hence, the present research may constitute one significant contribution to both fields of philosophy of education and Wittgensteinian scholarship. Furthermore, it would ultimately claim that Wittgenstein's ideas are not only confined to the philosophy of language but also significant in and not alien to the philosophy of education.

4. The Structure of the Thesis

This research, as an application of Wittgensteinian philosophy to philosophy of education, sheds light on a new perspective of the basic educational concepts, upon which educational practice can be based philosophically and didactically. Appropriately, the dissertation consists of five parts: Select Wittgenstein Themes related to Education (Chapter 1); The Basic Concepts of Philosophy of Education (Chapter 2); *Meaning as Use* and the Concept of Teaching (Chapter 3); *Rule-Following* and the Process of Learning (Chapter 4); *Philosophy as Therapy*, Education and the Community (Chapter 5).

In order to make clear Wittgenstein's primary ideas that are related to education, Chapter 1 will primarily concentrate on the elaboration of the fundamental themes in Wittgensteinian philosophy, namely, *meaning as use*, *rule-following*, and *philosophy as therapy*. We aim, by this means, to acquire coherent understanding about these concepts and how they are related to the educational enterprise. Thus, this chapter will serve as the pillar upon which the development of the whole work will rest. In the process of extracting Wittgenstein's major arguments some critical assessments will be made as regards the assertions that he makes about these concepts.

In Chapter 2, we shall discuss the basic concepts of philosophy of education, viz., *teaching, learning, and community*. It is undeniable that education involves interplay between these three elements without which no goal of the process of education could be attained. The rudiments of their respective nature will thus be examined. We shall proceed in our discussion in four sections. First, we shall present a historical sketch of the development of philosophy of education with reference to philosophers regarding its nature and purpose. Second, we shall investigate into the teaching practice. Here, we shall deal with a conceptual analysis of the teaching activity. Third, we shall delve into a study of the learning process. Lastly, we shall examine the role and the importance of the community in the educational enterprise, i.e. the significance of the social environment in education will be demonstrated and the idea that the school as a community is an integral part in the system of education will be explained.

Chapter 3, 4, and 5 will be the central sections of this dissertation because here we shall attempt to relate the fundamental Wittgensteinian themes to the basic concepts of philosophy of education. The main objective of Chapter 3 is to investigate whether the outcome of the philosopher's consideration of meaning offers a coherent adherence to the established comprehension of the concept of teaching or provides an innovative outlook that would lead us to reconsider our present conception of it. We shall approach this problem by first elaborating on the rationale behind utilizing the concept of teaching in his investigation. Second, we shall make an exposition of the character of *teaching* by extracting its features from his later works. In order to achieve this aim, emphasis will be made to his use of *training* and *explanation*. Third, after describing his use of teaching in his writings, we shall engage in an illustration of the *logical connection* between the concepts of *meaning* and *teaching*. Fourth, having examined the character of teaching in his works and established the logical relation we shall demonstrate its impact in Wittgenstein's analysis of meaning and then his comprehension of the concept of teaching taking into consideration the impact of his notions of language-games, family resemblance and form of life.

Finally, based on our argumentation, we shall make an appraisal whether Wittgenstein's treatment of teaching in his analysis of meaning deviates or adheres from the accepted view of teaching.

Chapter 4 shall attempt to develop a conceptual investigation of the *process of learning* in the light of Wittgenstein's idea of rule-following. The contention that we shall defend here can be described in two points. First, the dynamism of rule-following provides an understanding *sui generis* of the process of learning, i.e., the fundamental features of rule-following, such as practice and training (teaching); provide a considerable contribution to the emerging paradigm of learning. Wittgenstein's notion of rule-following is of major importance in our investigation to provide backing for our contention and thus will highlighted here. Second, based on our arguments we will discover that Wittgenstein was neither a cognitivist nor a behaviorist in the strict sense of the word but one who incorporates both camps in his philosophical analysis. Thus, our main claim bridges, in a way, the gap between the cognitivist and behaviorist theories of learning and consequently dissolves the dichotomy.

In Chapter 5 we shall deal with an investigation of the relevance of his thought regarding the nature of *philosophy as therapy* in the field of education. We shall demonstrate in this section that Wittgenstein's idea of philosophy as therapy highlights the prevailing interaction between communal practices and the educational system. It is through an investigation of the elements of his thoughts on the therapeutic nature of philosophy, for instance, philosophical problems as specific forms of intellectual illnesses, perspicuous representation as a way of restoring health, and the image of the philosopher as therapist, and others, that we make evident the particular function and contribution of the community in the sphere of education which directly affects the instructional approach of educators and downgrades the idea that learners come to be educated as *tabula rasa*.

CHAPTER I

Select Wittgensteinian Themes Related to Education

Many philosophers, from ancient to contemporary times, have shown interest in dealing with the phenomenon of education. Some have even gone to the extent of assigning it pride of place and prominence in the discipline of philosophy. John Dewey, for example, in his thought went so far as to claim that education is philosophy. However, due to the evident development in the terrain of education and philosophies of education, most present day thinkers on education, narrow the gap that exists between educational theory and practice. One such effort consists in improving both the concepts about education and the ways in which these concepts are used, that is, helping educators, and particularly educational philosophers, deal with some of the vague and confusing terms and concepts which exist in the field of education. It is in this area where Wittgenstein's thoughts assume considerable significance.

It is widely accepted among Wittgensteinian scholars that in the development of Wittgenstein's philosophy he possessed no succinct and precise theory regarding education. However, his interest in education in his pedagogical approach to philosophical problems is beyond dispute.[1] His educational reflections on the analysis of language permit us to select fundamental themes which are relevant to education, specifically, his concepts of *meaning, rule-following and philosophy as therapy*.

Educational discourse is permeated with concepts and ideas. Such is the reality which provides *language* with an indispensable role in education. Language is a salient part of the educational process. It is not a

---

[1] M. PETERS – J. MARSHALL, *Wittgenstein*, 152-191.

static structure.[2] It is a social and dynamic institution,[3] which affects both students and teachers. Teachers teach primarily with language (understood as a formal system of human syntactico-semantic structures, i.e., the use of signs/symbols, sounds, gestures, or marks having understood meanings), and students, after having accustomed themselves to the educational atmosphere, use language to eventually adjust to their everyday life. The relation of Wittgenstein's ideas to education practically lies not only in their educational characteristics, that is, the manner or way they are presented, but also in their capability to clarify the complexities of language and its potential.[4] Wittgenstein's investigation into the inner workings of language, which formed his thoughts on *meaning, rule-following and philosophy as therapy*, can be considered as a fundamental tool in clarifying the statements and propositions of educational thought and practice.

In the first Chapter, we shall present an elaboration of select Wittgensteinian themes that are relevant to education. No particular claim to originality is made with respect to this since a vast number of books have already been written which critically evaluate each particular theme. In spite of that, we aim, by this means, to acquire coherent ideas about Wittgenstein's conception of *meaning, rule-following, philosophy as therapy* and how these concepts are related to the educational enterprise.

1. The Concept of «Meaning» in the *Philosophical Investigations*

Linguistic analysis is central in Wittgenstein's philosophy. In both his early and later philosophy, he aimed to provide precision to understanding the nature of language. He endeavored to clarify our understanding of language, i.e., «to help us work ourselves out of the confusions we become entangled in when philosophizing»[5]. One way of obtaining a clear comprehension of language is to have a distinct concept of meaning. A frequent feature of philosophical writings during this past half-century involves uncertainties about meaning.[6]

---

[2] P. RAO, *A survey*, 71.
[3] P. RAO, *A survey*, 71.
[4] H. A. OZMON – S. M. CRAVER, *Philosophical foundations of education*, 290.
[5] A. CRARY, *The New Wittgenstein*, 1.
[6] B. RUNDLE, «Meaning and Understanding», 94.

Wittgenstein in the preface to the *Philosophical Investigations*[7] wrote that he had committed grave mistakes in what he wrote in his first book – the *Tractatus*.[8] He considered language-world ties as name-object relations while in the *Investigations* he affirms that these relations are maintained by certain rule-governed human activities. Hans-Johann Glock, in the Preface of the book *Wittgenstein: A Critical Reader* says that both the *Tractatus* and the *Investigations* contain two fundamentally different and self-contained outlooks of Wittgenstein.[9] Despite the fact that the two evident phases of Wittgenstein's thought appear to be disconnected, there is an implicit unity between them. Wittgenstein, throughout his work, maintains that language is a totality of a finite number of symbols with syntactical and semantical structure.[10] Thus, it is from these two books that we can trace back how Wittgenstein viewed the reality of meaning. However, since we are concerned in developing Wittgenstein's later philosophy, his earlier theory of meaning shall not be investigated. This section will be wholly devoted to a description of both the general and the specific aspects of Wittgenstein's thought regarding *meaning* as presented in the *Philosophical Investigations*.

The definition contained in *PI* §43[11] has been considered as the «hallmark of Ludwig Wittgenstein's later philosophy».[12] It states that, «for a large class of cases – though not for all – in which we employ the word "meaning" it can be *defined* thus: the meaning of a word is its use in language» [*PI* §43; *emphasis added*].

The concept contained in this passage plays a crucial role in the development of his later view regarding language and meaning. This obviously underlies the evident shift from his former outlook in the *Tractatus*, i.e., from a representational view of meaning to one that consid-

---

[7] L. WITTGENSTEIN, *Philosophical Investigations* (German-English parallel text). Hereafter cited as *PI*.

[8] L. WITTGENSTEIN, *Tractatus Logico-Philosophicus* (German-English parallel text). First published 1922. Hereafter cited as *TLP*.

[9] H.J. GLOCK, ed., *Wittgenstein: A Critical Reader*, preface.

[10] P. RAO, *A survey*, 71 ff.

[11] There have been a number of various readings of Wittgenstein's definition of meaning. However, Garth Hallett in his book *Wittgenstein's Definition of Meaning as Use* successfully provides a detailed study of this definition. Contrary to objections raised against his thesis, he effectively defends his view by limiting his arguments to what this particular statement really asserts. For further discussion regarding this issue, cf. G. HALLETT. *Wittgenstein's Definition of Meaning as Use*, 172, 3n.

[12] G. HALLETT, *Wittgenstein's Definition of Meaning as Use*, 1.

ers *use* as vital in the understanding of meaning. This transformation obviously expresses Wittgenstein's attempt to counteract the growing dogmas of traditional theory of meaning, which claims that meaning points to *something* (situated either in factual space or inside the recesses of the mind as an image) exterior to the proposition, which endows it with sense. Wittgenstein develops this offset starting with a quotation from St. Augustine's *Confessions I, 8.* He characterizes Augustine's theory as a classic example of the misdirection of effort to search for a common set of characteristics or some essence for the use of the general term *language.* We should note that Wittgenstein does not claim that Augustine's theory of language is erroneous. On the contrary, Wittgenstein regarded the *whole pursuit* of finding the common, fixed essence of language that is flawed. He attempted to solve this predicament with an appeal to use.

However, contrary to his intention in the *Tractatus*, ascertaining the use of words does not commit Wittgenstein to constructing any explicit theory of meaning, i.e., *meaning is use*, which is sometimes attributed to him. While his new method leads him to emphasize the use of words in his discussion, he never proposed a *use theory* to substitute the *picture theory.* He is hesitant to state that the meaning of the word is *always* its use since his criticism regarding the determinateness of meaning implies the awareness of the diversity of the uses of words in different circumstances. His positive account of meaning intends to act as an antidote to mistaken or misleading conceptions of meaning.

The fundamental import of Wittgenstein's view about *the meaning of the word is its use in a language* is that to understand the meaning of a term it is necessary for us to consider how it is used in a language. This simply posits that use completely exhausts meaning. We should not even think that Wittgenstein, with this claim, insists on identifying *something* that could be labeled as the *meaning* of a certain expression. The use of an expression is not to be considered as something merely going along with the utterance and somehow providing it with meaning. «He is not pressing the question "what is the meaning of the word?" in the sense of "what is that thing that is a word's meaning?"»[13] His definition does not refer to an object of any kind or an inner process. Utterances and signs are said to be meaningful when they possess a distinctive *use* in a system of signs – in a language. According to Wittgenstein, use comes before meaning. The establishment of language

---

[13] B. STROUD, «Mind, meaning, and practice», 300.

can only be made clear by paying attention to the *use* of words and sentences in the flow of life.

If this contention would be taken at face value, it would be tantamount to saying that no meaning would be understood unless one can identify the word's use or to a more radical claim - without use there is no meaning. Albeit this might seem highly plausible based on Wittgenstein's line of reasoning, we still need to refine these crucial concepts, viz., meaning and use, in order to have a clear understanding of what Wittgenstein really intends to purport. Even though various Wittgensteinian scholars present diverse interpretations regarding Wittgenstein's definition of meaning, a significant number of authors would retain the dominance of the practical character of these concepts. With the purpose of indicating their affinity to the educative process, i.e., a purely non-idealistic activity, the reader will notice that major stress will be given upon their pragmatic feature in the course of elaboration.

During the twentieth century, there was a cornucopia of literature that tackled not only Wittgenstein's view of meaning but also the concept of meaning in general. To consider all of them in this section is a task too arduous to undertake. It is important for our purposes to specify that we are trying neither to trace Wittgenstein's lexical treatment of the word *meaning* nor to develop the intricacies that other commentators present in their interpretation of his arguments. We shall rather endeavor to elaborate the framework of Wittgenstein's general treatment of the notion of meaning, i.e. that language-world ties as name-object relation holds no ground and that the use of the word takes center-stage. Hence, we shall limit our discussion to what we consider as central – to assess the arguments that support Wittgenstein's definition of meaning in *PI* §43 and how it leads to a distinctive conception of meaning.

The *Blue Book* opens with the question, «What is the meaning of a word?» [*BB* 1][14]. According to Garth Hallett, for Wittgenstein «meaning was merely the "important thing" about a word»[15]. This implies that when we deal with a word what we primarily would strive to know or understand before anything else is the meaning of that word. How then do we explain the meaning of the word? Wittgenstein tells us «"the meaning of a word is what is explained by the explanation of meaning." I.e.: if you want to understand the use of the word "meaning", look for what are called "explanations of meaning"»[*PI* §560].

---

[14] L. WITTGENSTEIN, *The Blue and Brown Books*. Hereafter cited as *BB*.
[15] G. HALLETT, *Wittgenstein's Definition of Meaning as Use*, 74.

With this statement, Wittgenstein is not advancing an *explanation theory of meaning,* but rather one of the various methods that he employs in order to highlight the explanation of words and how they are taught. The emphasis that he puts on the explanations of meaning serves to stress the significance of ordinary linguistic practices of communities. Nonetheless, the passage shows that the meaning of the word is not something more abstruse and theoretically multifaceted than what is evident in the normal practice of explaining the word. Wittgenstein points to the customary way for determining the truths about the meaning of a word and that is through an examination of explanations. He was interested in the dynamics of teaching language as part of his analysis of meaning. Wittgenstein focuses on the use of the word in language, i.e., how one would actually carry out in explaining the meaning of the word to someone else. If to understand the meaning of a word is to attend to the explanations of meaning, then teaching the meaning is practically the same as providing an explanation of the meaning.

Nevertheless, two evident predicaments confront us. On the one hand, if meaning is to be found in the explanation of meaning, how does Wittgenstein account for the existence of different explanations of meaning? On the other hand, if there are diverse explanations of meaning, are there satisfactory explanations of meaning? For Wittgenstein one explanation of the meaning of the word is just as justifiable as another.[16] Mark Addis asserts that «Wittgenstein thought that maintaining that meaning can be explained in a variety of ways helps to stress the need for the philosopher to pay attention to the community's ordinary linguistic practices when he is troubled by questions about meaning»[17]. Wittgenstein opposes the idea that there must be something behind what we actually say and think that gives it a determinate sense via a discussion of cases of how we actually use words. Regarding the second question, Addis affirms Wittgenstein's insistence that reasonably definite practices of explanation with respect to the *explanandum* besides the supposition that there are adequately explicit practices of using linguistic elements is sufficient to distinguish correct from incorrect

---

[16] There obviously exist other explanations regarding the meaning of a word, which are not acceptable to any linguistic community. However, Wittgenstein does not deny the fact that, considering a change of usual practices of explaining a word, these now unacceptable explanations of the meaning of a word will soon be accepted. *Cf. PI* §83.

[17] Cf. M. ADDIS, *Wittgenstein*, 50.

explanations. This entire endeavor can be encapsulated in what Garth Hallett calls Wittgenstein's rejection of the conception of unitary meanings - that meaning is not an object, not to be the subject of inner state or process, not an image and not a feeling.[18] Aside from treating meaning as referring to an object in the *Tractatus*, Wittgenstein had never assumed any position supporting the idea that the meaning of a word is an image or a feeling. In fact he was occupied with investigating and destabilizing the views that meaning consists in mental processes and meaning as consisting of explicit rules.[19]

It has been established by Wittgenstein's use-based semantics that meaning is not «something (an object) beyond the sign and corresponding to it, in the way Smith corresponds to the name "Smith"» [*AWL* II §2][20]. «You say: the point isn't the word, but its meaning, and you think of the meaning as a *thing* of the same kind as the word, though also different from the word» [*PI* §120; emphasis added]. The idea that *the meaning of a word is the object, for which it stands*, as apparently affirmed by the passage from the *Confessions* turns up to be one aspect of meaning that Wittgenstein rejects.[21] However, this does not imply that words can never be said to stand for objects since «a word may or may not stand for an object, but, when it does, that object is not its meaning»[22]. *Meaning* is not used in the fashion wherein an object corresponds to a word. «Here the word, there the meaning» [*PI* §120]. Wittgenstein considered this as an ill-natured view of meaning that needs therapy. Wittgenstein's post-*Tractatus* position clearly demonstrates that there are words like *expectation*, *wish*, *meaning*, and the like which do not have reference to any object in the world. Linguistic representation does not entail a complete correspondence between words and things (objects). Glock confirms that for Wittgenstein «there is no such thing as *the* name-relation»[23]. The point made in *PI* §39-40 clearly illustrates the need to caution ourselves against the temptation of treating meaning as an object.

---

[18] G. HALLETT, *Wittgenstein's Definition of Meaning as Use*, 33-75. See also J.F.M. HUNTER, *Wittgenstein on Words as Instruments*, 27 ff.

[19] Cf. D. STERN, *Wittgenstein on Mind and Language*, 121.

[20] A. AMBROSE, ed., *Wittgenstein's Lectures Cambridge 1932-1935*, 44, text added. Hereafter cited as *AWL*.

[21] *PI* §40.

[22] B. RUNDLE, «Meaning and Understanding», 97.

[23] H.J. GLOCK, *Wittgenstein: A Critical Reader*, 18.

Another criticism of Wittgenstein regarding the concept of meaning is directed to the claim that meaning involves a sort of inner process in one's mind.[24] Wittgenstein notes this contention in his ideas contained in *BB* 47 - 48. He maintains that our tendency to consider the mind as some sort of a depot whence diverse activities (including speech) are derived is one basis of error. A major part of the *Investigations* is devoted in battling this usual tendency to ascribe meaning as involving the dimension of the *inner*. Wittgenstein tried to remove what Hallett calls the «gratuitous and ill-founded»[25] preconceived conviction that there must be mental activities prior to or accompanying words, i.e., the consideration on which concurrent psychological experience present to consciousness at the moment is identified with the meaning of the word. He rejects any determinateness of meaning by referring to *something* going on inside oneself. According to Stern, «for Wittgenstein, this remained a crucial misunderstanding of the nature of mind and meaning: in thinking that something in the mind must determine what we mean by our words, we commit ourselves to a theory of these mental processes»[26]. As a reaction to this contention, Wittgenstein maintained that it is only by looking at how we explain the use of words are we able to understand the meaning, which is not *something* behind what we say and think that provides words with determinate sense.

Connected with the concept of meaning as a mental event, is the view of meaning as an image, a picture or what he specifically calls something that *comes before our mind* [*PI* §§139-140]. What he is rejecting is the conviction that meaning depends on some entity coming before one's mind, i.e., having an *image* before our mind's eye. Wittgenstein was aware of the working necessity of images. If they were necessary then it implies that images *must* go together with words for without them, words would become futile and lifeless. It is precisely this *necessity* that Wittgenstein was criticizing. He was convinced that it is neither a *necessary condition* nor a *sufficient basis* in understanding the meaning of the word that particular items come before our minds when a word is uttered because on the one hand, as McGinn states, «introspection cannot be relied upon to produce any kind of ex-

---

[24] Hallett contests that Wittgenstein regarded that William James was wrong in identifying meaning as a process accompanying the statements we mean; for meaning what we say is not an activity of the same logical form as saying the words. Cf. G. HALLETT, *Wittgenstein's Definition of Meaning as Use*, 55.

[25] G. HALLETT, *Wittgenstein's Definition of Meaning as Use*, 40.

[26] D. STERN, *Wittgenstein on Mind and Language*, 106.

perience when a sign is understood»[27]. On the other hand, it is not sufficient «because the picture does not in itself *determine* the correct use of the associated word; we cannot read off the associated picture how the word is to be applied»[28], i.e., an image *per se* does not suffice, it still needs something besides itself in order to have meaning – it still requires its meaning being fixed. Hallett suggests that «finding an image does not end the search for meaning»[29]. Wittgenstein finally disproves this concept of meaning as an image by claiming that mental images do not *determine* the use of the word since they are themselves merely signs disposed to an array of interpretations – they are semantically stagnant.

Still arguing around the psychological ambit, Wittgenstein also impugns the idea of assimilating the concept of meaning to the concept of sensation (feeling) or other mental *experiences*.[30] This idea of meaning posits that a word has meaning precisely because some special feeling or experience accompanies it. If this were the case, each user of a word, having a different feeling for a word, could mean something different by it. Wittgenstein indicts this tendency with these statements: «When longing makes me cry "Oh, if only he would come!" the feeling gives the words "meaning". But does it give the individual words their meanings?» [*PI* §544]; «But when one says "I *hope* he'll come" - doesn't the feeling give the word "hope" its meaning? (And what about the sentence "I do *not* hope for his coming any longer"?) The feeling does perhaps give the word "hope" its special ring; that is, it is expressed in that ring. – If the feeling gives the word its meaning, then here "meaning" means *point*. But why is the feeling the point?» [*PI* §545].

Wittgenstein emphatically confronts this emotive theory of word meanings in his reply, «when we understand a statement we often have certain characteristic experiences connected with it and with the words it contains. However, the meaning of a symbol in our language *is not* the feelings it arouses or the momentary impression it makes on us. The sense of a sentence is neither a succession of feelings nor one definite feeling. To know the meaning of a symbol (e.g., a word) is to know its

---

[27] C. McGINN, *Wittgenstein on Meaning*, 6.

[28] C. McGINN, *Wittgenstein on Meaning*, 7; cf. *PI* §73.

[29] G. HALLETT, *Wittgenstein's Definition of Meaning as Use*, 46.

[30] Fur further discussion regarding this objection about feeling as constituting the meaning of a word cf. G. HALLETT, *Wittgenstein's Definition of Meaning as Use*, 48-73.

use» [*AWL* I, § 25][31]. «The meaning of a word *is not* the experience one has in hearing or saying it, and the sense of a sentence is not a complex of such experiences»[*PI*, p. 181e; *emphasis added*]. However, it is worth noting that he never denies the possibility of inner feelings as attributes of meaning nuanced in some expressions or that these expressions are sometimes associated with these feelings. What Wittgenstein definitely opposes is the idea that psychological-feeling or mental experiences *constitute* meaning. With the same criteria, Wittgenstein censured the view that feeling or mental experiences determine the meaning of a word. Furthermore, he disabuses us of the idea that *meaning* is ontologically situated in the mind or in the brain. It is undoubtedly clear from his arguments that Wittgenstein contravened the view that it is possible to give a *locus* to *meaning* other than *in language*. This *locus* of language may seem indistinct except insofar as language is part of our *practices*. If we mean things by using language then meanings are in the language that we share in common. Meaning is understood, according to Wittgenstein, only in the context of our shared practices and not some occult, essentially *inner* (mental processes, images, experiences or feelings) faculty. The following passage astutely reveals his criticism about this misguided notion of meaning: «If God had looked into our minds he would not have been able to see there whom we were speaking of» [*PI*, p. 217e].

After dismantling the commonly mistaken notions of meaning, Wittgenstein can now without hesitation, claim that the meaning of the word is its use. However, one of the fundamental predicaments that an investigation into meaning encounters, accentuating the significance of use, is the challenge of context. The importance of *context* or *system* in the workings of language is manifested by two decisive factors: Wittgenstein's negation of the idea of elementary proposition and the establishment of the concept of language-game.[32] If Wittgenstein contends that for a word or a sign to have meaning it must be incorporated into a system (context), then this implies that a meaningful word essentially belongs to a system.[33] It is its use in a language that allows a word to have its meaning and this is based on a broader context. The meaning of a word is characterized by its role in the system of language. In view

---

[31] *AWL*, p. 29 text and emphasis added.
[32] F-N. TING, *Wittgenstein's Descriptive Method*, 58.
[33] Cf. «Wittgenstein' Lectures in 1930-31», in G.E. MOORE, *Philosophical Papers*. Hereafter cited as *MWL*.

of the fact that without a context words would become lifeless, i.e., without meaning [*BB* 5], this would give us reason to confirm that a word has meaning only when it is *used* within a certain context. Hence, in Wittgenstein's later philosophy, context is of cardinal importance to meaning. [34] By dealing with contextual contingency, we hope to have demonstrated how contexts also become the *source* of meaning.

This particular claim is relevant to education in the sense that if Wittgenstein places meaning within a social context, as was discussed earlier, then he asserts that language-games are the primary agent in motivating the learning of speech. This implies that in language training should come first before explanation. It is on this assertion that Wittgenstein bases his criticism regarding the ostensive definition or teaching of words.

In the course of his investigation regarding the concept of meaning, Wittgenstein did not discard the problem that ostensive definition poses. In fact, if we look at the first part of the *Investigations* we will notice his explicit preoccupation with the paradigmatic view of language learning as portrayed by St. Augustine in his *Confessions,* i.e., through ostension. [35] Here are a few passages which reveal Wittgenstein's concern about ostensive definitions in language learning: «An important part of the training will consist in the teacher's pointing to the objects, directing the child's attention to them, and at the same time uttering a word» [*PI* §6]; «One thinks that learning language consists in giving names to objects» [*PI* §26]; «Someone coming into a strange country will sometimes learn the language of the inhabitants from ostensive definitions that they give him; and he will often have to *guess* the meaning of these definitions; and will guess sometimes right, sometime wrong» [*PI* §32]. Earlier in the *Philosophical Grammar,* [36] we find Wittgenstein paying attention to ostensive definition. He investigates whether ostensive gestures could be the primary marks, which are applied when learning to speak. [37]

---

[34] Cf. *AWL,* p. 34-36.

[35] Wittgenstein says parenthetically «I do not want to call this "ostensive definition", because the child cannot as yet ask what the name is. I will call it "ostensive teaching of words"» [*PI* §6]. Wittgenstein's point here seems to be grammatical rather than substantial. He takes into consideration the incapacity to ask questions about language. He prefers to use *teaching* rather than *definition* since in this case he is convinced that the former seems to perform the same job as the latter.

[36] L. WITTGENSTEIN, *Philosophical Grammar.* Hereafter considered *PG.*

[37] Cf. *PG* §88.

Ostensive definition is fundamentally characterized by pointing (with a finger) at the referent (object) which the word to be learned designates. This model of language learning, as Wittgenstein saw it, manifests a hard-to-dispel attraction of conceiving ostension as the ultimate basis of meaning. As Kerr observes, «the first 60 or so remarks in the *Investigations,* although at one level a satire on logical atomism which can be appreciated only by its former partisans, may also be read, more accessibly, as an exploration of the temptation to equate meaning with pointing to objects»[38]. This is perhaps the principal origin of the idea that what one points at in ostensively explaining the meaning of a word is its meaning. Others find this the natural way in which language gets in touch with reality [*PG* §89], i.e., it can be illustrated as a rule for teaching gesture-language into word-language to connect an articulated word with the help of an ostensive movement to the object being shown [*BB* 90].

It is this natural tendency of understanding language learning that Wittgenstein tries to eliminate. He does not specifically take objection to the fact that we sometimes use ostensive definition when we talk (for we obviously apply ostensive gestures in everyday speech). Failure to recognize this would be to misunderstand his critique. He is attacking rather the idea that meaning can be employed to a word *simply* through an act of ostensive definition. No matter how useful ostensive definition might be in ordinary communication, according to Wittgenstein, it cannot by itself account for language learning – it has its limitations. If this were the case, then ostensive definition by itself could never fix the meaning of a word since it «can be variously interpreted in *every* case» [*PI* §28]. When I point to a clock and say, «that is a clock» the person to whom I am ostensively defining the word *clock* could take me to be defining the shape, color, quantity, or any number of other things.

In this regard, Wittgenstein says, «the ostensive definition explains the use – the meaning – of the word when the overall role of the word in language is clear» [*PI* §30]. This means that ostensive definition can only become useful if we already have a language, i.e., a person does not understand the meaning of a word unless he can use it correctly in regular discourse, which is outside the ostensive definition. Wittgenstein emphasizes that ostensive definitions do not teach us language *ex nihilo* as if our minds were like the Lockean *tabula rasa.* With this assertion, he is not trying to bring ostensive definition into disrepute since

---

[38] F. KERR, *Theology after Wittgenstein,* 70.

it can obviously be an effective educational tool. He is rather emphasizing that the name-object relation is *not* a fundamental relationship in language, i.e., teaching someone the meaning of a sign does not entirely consist in establishing an association between the sign and such content. Ostension as a way of teaching a student the meaning of a word will only be successful if the student already knows the place of the word in its language, its *grammar*, i.e., it only helps the student because he already knows how these names can be used.

We terminate this discussion regarding Wittgenstein's criticism of ostensive definition with Robert Fogelin's assertion, «if we take ostensive definition as the *fundamental* method of assigning meanings to words, we have failed to realize that the activity of giving an ostensive definition makes sense only within the context of a previously established linguistic framework. Such an account of language acquisition presupposes that the learner already possesses a language; that is, it presupposes the very phenomenon it is intended to explain»[39].

Earlier in the *Blue and Brown Books*, Wittgenstein reveals the inception of his preoccupation with use by stating that, «If we had to name anything which is the life of the sign, we should have to say that it was its use» [*BB* 4]. This observation about use being essential to meaning is later on accentuated in §43 of the *Investigations*. We have seen in the previous sections that Wittgenstein repudiates the idea that meaning is an object, image and feeling. This led him to affirm that the meaning of the word is its use since it is immune to the arguments presented against objects and mental states. However, *use* is not simply a concept arbitrarily chosen by Wittgenstein as the basis for his semantic investigations since it entails the crucial concept of intentionality. Nor is it a literal counterpart for *meaning* but it allows us to get away from the coercion of meaning's misconception. Nevertheless, there have been various readings regarding the concept of use in Wittgenstein's definition. Some attempt to discuss use in the sense of *usage* and some in the sense of *practice*.[40] A general picture of vagueness, nonetheless, remains over the precise significance of Wittgenstein's treatment of «use». In this case, if uncertainty exists over the exact sense of *use*, then we would need to explore the variety of interpretations in order to probe what Wittgenstein really wanted to convey regarding such a notion. For this purpose, we shall consider the readings of use as *usage*

[39] R. J. FOGELIN, *Wittgenstein*, 118.
[40] See M. B. HINTIKKA – J. HINTIKKA, *Investigating Wittgenstein*, 217-218.

and *practice*. It is crucial for us to make this distinction here since both these terms, being directly associated, could straightforwardly be confused.

Usage is generally defined as the act or the manner of using (e.g., a word). If we try to substitute this description for Wittgenstein's definition of meaning, we have an account of meaning as the *act or manner of using a word in a language*. What is the implication if we maintain this understanding of use? One nuance would be that *use* would appear to be a repeated action done in one way or another in a specific manner. This repeated activity - a single manner may be considered as a model or a rule. Consequently, this gives rise to a regular pattern of usage. Such a view of use places more emphasis upon the aspect of *frequency* (pattern) rather than *utility*. A ten-euro bill, for example, becomes valuable specifically because of an established usage – a constant use of money. Hallett describes such *usage* as the formal aspect of use.[41] He maintains that this formal aspect is sometimes apparent by itself in the *Investigations*.[42]

Based on the aforementioned arguments, we observe that usage is characterized by *regularity*. If we consider *use* in terms of usage, then we take it to mean that whenever we use a word we are held within the confines of following an established structure. Wittgenstein seems to regard use in the sense of usage when he said that «If he *used* the words "if" and "but" as we do (i.e., as we regularly do), shouldn't we think he understood them as we do?» [*PI* p. 182e; *text added*] However, we notice that if we apply the sense of use solely to usage, we get the impression that Wittgenstein was merely emphasizing on the accepted regular pattern or manner of using as a decisive factor for determining meaning. According to Wittgenstein, there is more to meaning than just regularity. Too much stress on regularity shrouds the usefulness of words. Utility, in fact, constitutes the criterion for whether a rule (in this sense, usage) belongs to the meaning of a word. We shall not discuss this point in great detail because we might deviate from our original purpose. What is important here is to stress that Wittgenstein, taking into consideration his suggestion that the game has not only rules but a point, did not wholly accentuate the concept of use as usage even if the «general characteristic of a word's use is compatible with a

---

[41] G. HALLETT, *Wittgenstein's definition of Meaning as Use*, 104.
[42] Cf. *PI* §§151, 182, 197, 555, 557, 558, 565 and p. 147e (b).

merely formal notion of use»[43]. If a game had nothing but formal rules for the manipulation of signs, if there is no extralinguistic application to words, they would become meaningless. Utility must not be left out of account. As Hallett affirms, «if meaning were defined as rules of use (as usage), and merely this were meant [...] then the definition would differ from Wittgenstein's thought in a number of ways»[44].

Just as *use* can be viewed in terms of its formal aspect (usage), so too we can take into account its practical dimension – *utility*. This characteristic is apparently manifested by the term *practice*. Here are some passages in the *Investigations,* which indicate this aspect of use: «Thus the point here is what we call the "goal"» [*PI* §88]; «If the feeling gives the word its meaning, then here "meaning" means *point*» [*PI* §545]; «And it is the service which is the point» [*PI*, p. 178e]. These sections tell us that Wittgenstein's understanding of *use* connotes more than just regularity or should we say *rules of use*. Indeed, practice also incorporates the idea of repetition or regularity. However, aside from this, it primarily suggests, as what is mentioned in the cited passages, a *goal* a *point* or a *role*.[45] In practice, one intends to achieve mastery of *a* technique by repeated activity. Now this practice is not an isolated phenomenon. It is rooted within a situation, in human customs and institutions. Imagine one engaging in a game of chess without practice. Could we consider him using the chess pieces correctly? On the other hand, could we ever say that he is playing chess? If there does not exist a technique for the game of chess, no one could intend to play the game of chess. «To understand a sentence means to understand a language. To understand a language means to be a master of a technique» [*PI* §199]. Such technique is evidently obtained through practice. If we apply this to the definition of meaning, then we have the idea that in order to understand the meaning of a word we need to have mastered a technique in the use of words through practice - «The substratum of this experience is the mastery of a technique» [*PI* p. 208e].

With this concept of practice, Wittgenstein has incorporated use into a much wider context, i.e., pulling it out from the view of regimented occurrences and weaving it into the textile of social affairs. Another important element compatible with practice is *training*. It is important to note that we need *training* in order to engage ourselves in practice

---

[43] G. HALLETT, *Wittgenstein's definition of Meaning as Use*, 104.
[44] G. HALLETT, *Wittgenstein's definition of Meaning as Use*, 106, text added.
[45] Cf. *PI* §182.

[*PI* p.185e].[46] With practice, we can see not only how we use signs but also what we actually do with these signs.

We have seen that use in the sense of *usage* possesses a very limited context in its application. More importantly, Wittgenstein's treatment of use implies a much wider application, i.e., concerning not only the regularity of use (of words) but also its goal, point, role, and function immersed within the framework of the community – of a form of life. Albeit Wittgenstein did not deny the fact that we can consider use in terms of usage, it would be much more reasonable, based on our evaluation, to regard him as favoring use as practice in his definition of meaning. Furthermore, this concept ties in with other factors, viz., language-games, family resemblance and form of life.

Language-games, family resemblance and form of life are other important concepts within Wittgenstein's investigation on language, in general, and meaning, in particular. Language-games practically came from his reflection that in language we play games with words. «We can think of the whole process of using words…as one of those games by means of which children learn their native language. I will call these games "language-games" and will sometime speak of a primitive language as a language-game» [*PI* §7]. «Here the term "language-*game*" is meant to bring into prominence the fact that the *speaking* of language is part of an activity, or of a form of life» [*PI* §23].

He employs this concept in order to introduce thought experiments to help explore the workings of language, to help shed light on existing language uses and to stress the relevance of the contextual dependence of the meaning of linguistic expressions. It serves as a major analytical device to which Wittgenstein appeals in examining the complex phenomena of languages. Language-games are thought of merely as (artificially) constructed simplified models, which are useful as objects of comparison with natural languages.

In the *Blue Book* Wittgenstein develops the idea of language-games in order to prove his view that there are no general fixed rules that apply to every part of language. In examining a series of language-games, Wittgenstein demonstrates the different uses of words in a variety of contexts. If there exist diverse contexts of using words, this would account for what Wittgenstein describes as a variety of language-games [*PI* §24].

---

[46] See J. SCHULTE, *Wittgenstein: An Introduction*, 106ff.

In Wittgenstein's later philosophy we can see a development in the idea of language-games from mediating basic language-world ties to obtaining a primacy over the concept of rules.[47] Wittgenstein stresses the primacy of language-games over their rules because it is by virtue of them that complexities regarding rule-following are clarified. It is precisely with reference to language-games that we can understand what it is to follow a rule and not vice versa.

We do not need to go into further details regarding this subject since many of its basic characteristics have already been presented. We should not forget, however, to point out its relevance to Wittgenstein's view of meaning. Language-games are closely intertwined with the appeal to use as a major key in the analysis of meaning. To explain the meaning of a linguistic utterance is to point to the use it has and this, in turn, can be clarified by studying that use under its appropriate language-game.

Wittgenstein, in his later philosophy, was patent about his position against our propensity to look for the essence of things or for a common characteristic mark. He maintained that propositions are not united by a common essence, i.e., a general propositional form as he sustained in the *Tractatus*. Accordingly, we have a misguided attempt to search for a single, common, general, and basic defining feature that unites all propositions (along with an associated disdain for the particular case [*BB* 18] and a similar lack of concern for the differences among cases). This is evident in his attack on the insidious *craving for generality*. This tendency to yearn for generality, according to Wittgenstein, is a sort of illusion that disorients us to think that «the answer to these questions (e.g., "*What is* language?" "*What is* a proposition?") is to be given once and for all; and independently of any future experience» [*PI* §92]. It is in opposition to this kind of exaggerated conception that Wittgenstein directs his arguments. Words cannot be definitely defined by clear and specific attributes; usage presents a train of associations, which pass through one similarity after another. This reveals no hard core of meaning – an essence.

Like a *game*, we only find a complex network of overlapping and criss-crossing similarities [*PI* §67]. The levels of similarity are certainly significant enough for all members to be identified as such; but the sort of similarity involved does not lend itself to any easy answer to the question, «what defines a member of family *x*?» There may be no

---

[47] Cf. *PI* §§654, 656.

single trait which all members of the family hold in common yet an answer can be given, so long as we are prepared to receive different answers, listing different overlapping sets of predicates in different cases. His employment of family resemblance demonstrates the lack of margins and the distance from precision that characterize different uses of the same concept, e.g., *games*. Wittgenstein invoked the thought of family resemblance to be consistent with the philosophical method that he is introducing, i.e., the descriptive method of philosophy.[48] It not only helps us elude a Platonic view about essences and objects, but also enables us to compare and contrast cases in order to know how words are used in ordinary life.

Consequent upon his pragmatic understanding of meaning, Wittgenstein introduces another concept which, among others, constitutes a fundamental role in his investigation into the understanding of meaning. This is what he calls *form(s) of life*.[49] Finch describes it as all phenomena of human behavior, and activities, which accompany the speaking of language as far as they are meaningful.[50] Albeit Wittgenstein mentions this phrase only five times in the *Investigations*[51], nonetheless it demonstrates the importance that activities and customs, i.e., the entirety of practices within a linguistic community, have in human understanding of how language works.

By positing a *form of life*, Wittgenstein was obviously no longer concerned with a consideration of language from the point of view of mental conjecture. He was rather preoccupied with the basic patterns of social intercourse, which, according to Fergus Kerr «are the kind of activities out of which human life is formed no matter what language is spoken or what the social structure is»[52]. He intended to underscore the social and conventional aspects of our lives as possessors of language. It is within these characteristic activities of human life that language resides, i.e., language is interwoven in them.

---

[48] See F-N. TING, *Wittgenstein's Descriptive Method*, 1-61.

[49] James Peterman explains the difference between the terms *form* and *mode*. Although Wittgenstein speaks of both terms, e.g., *modes of thinking, modes of living, form of life*, we need to make a distinction in order to be able to grasp the weight that Wittgenstein puts upon both of these terms respectively. Cf. J. PETERMAN, *Philosophy as therapy*, 107.

[50] H.L.R. FINCH, *Wittgenstein – The Early Philosophy*, 90.

[51] Cf. *PI* §§19, 23, 241, pp. 174e & 226e.

[52] F. KERR, *Theology after Wittgenstein*, 30.

As we noted earlier, Wittgenstein insisted that *context* is crucial in our dealing with meaning. Context (form of life) – specifically, our practices, on the one hand and the facts of nature on which our practices depend, on the other – make up the background within which it is possible to give a precise description of the nature of language and meaning. On this account, Wittgenstein contends that if we detach our understanding of what we say and think from its everyday context, i.e., our ordinary use of them in our daily life (in our form of life) we would be committed to a misunderstanding of grammatical truism. This argument underlines the significance of agreement in language – «"so you are saying that human agreement decides what is true and what is false?" – It is what human beings *say* that is true and false; and they agree in the *language* they use. That is not agreement in opinions but in form of life» [*PI* §241]. We do not agree on the mental level but practically on the words we use in spite of changes in language, i.e., agreement in human actions. This clearly demonstrates Wittgenstein's assertion of the value of the socio-cultural dimensions of the usage of language. For Wittgenstein, it is hard to dispel a form of life from our activity of speaking. It is certainly incorporated into a variety of human activities. In this sense, according to Ting, «language can no longer be explained by the requirement of the *a priori order*, instead, by the *a posteriori actual surroundings of the human order, i.e., the forms of life*»[53].

2. Rule-following Considerations

Another important issue inevitably associated with the later Wittgenstein is rule-following. According to Esfeld, «when it comes to accounting for meaning, we face the problem of rule-following»[54]. Rules in Wittgenstein's sense play a role in a host of pedagogic and critical activities, some of which are institutionalized, e.g., education: the teaching of language, explanation, correction of mistakes, and others. These issues are of great interest to Wittgenstein and to education since rule-governed activities play an important part in the teaching and learning process.

---

[53] F-N. TING, *Wittgenstein's Descriptive Method*, 51.
[54] M. ESFELD, «Rule-Following», VII (1), 191.

We find in some parts of the *Investigations* as well as in his *Remarks on the Foundations of Mathematics*[55] his discussion regarding the problem. Wittgenstein was interested in such questions concerning the essential feature(s) of rules and how they are related to other concepts, e.g., language-games [*RFM* VI: 15].[56] He insisted that rules are fundamental to language, and that language comes into being when rules are adopted for the use of signs and terms.

The main question of following certain rules is obviously connected with his effort to clarify the nature of meaning and understanding. The latter is a special case of rule-following in the sense that understanding an expression reveals ability to follow a rule for its correct application. Many of Wittgenstein's deepest observations on meaning are embedded in terms of what following a rule signifies. The rule-following problem becomes another point of discussion regarding the query of what it is that can apply to all the uses of a word. But before we proceed in our appraisal of Wittgenstein's view concerning rule-following, it is fitting that we must first of all examine how the term *rule* is understood and used.

2.1 *What is a rule?*[57]

Through *language-games* and *meaning as use*, Wittgenstein has initiated an approach towards a productive development of the concept of rules. Games and language depend on our ability to abide by rules – the notion *rule* is one of the main links in the analogy between languages and games. When we speak, we follow the rules of grammar and pronounciation while games necessarily involve rules. However, Wittgenstein notes that rules and their applications are varied.[58] The concept of

---

[55] L. WITTGENSTEIN, *Remarks on the Foundations of Mathematics*, G.H. von Wright – R. Rhees – G.E.M. Anscombe, ed., translated by G.E.M. Anscombe, [Oxford: Blackwell, 1978]. Hereafter cited as *RFM*.

[56] See also *RFM* I: 1-5, VI: 16-17, 19-47.

[57] Using the interrogative as the title of this section mainly aims to delineate a description of the use of the word and how the term *rule* is understood in the *PI*. For Wittgenstein the concept of a *rule* is applied more broadly than just to explicit rules, i.e., Wittgenstein's discussion of rules is meant to apply to all rule-governed activity.

[58] Passages from *PI* §185-197 present Wittgenstein's observation that, on the one hand, a rule seems to have a determinate application and conversely, that rules are speculatively capable of a multitude of applications. A clearly intended metaphor for rules can be found in *PI* §§193-194 where Wittgenstein considers the movements of a kinetic machine. He reached the conclusion that though it is not wrong to discover

a rule is a *family resemblance* concept, which indicates that there is no fundamental nature to rules[59], only common characteristics or similarities. In this section, however, wer are not searching for a stipulated definition of *a* rule but rather how Wittgenstein himself viewed what a rule is and how he presents his observations in the *Investigations*.

Wittgenstein begins his exposition on the subject of rules in *PI* §185.[60] He proceeds (from *PI* §§185 – 243) in answering questions such us: How do we learn rules? How do we follow them? Where are the criteria which decide whether a rule is followed correctly? Are they socially and publicly taught and enforced? In a distinctive Wittgensteinian manner, the answers are not directly forthcoming in the sense that the philosopher was aware that these types of questions underlie Platonic forms and ideas. He endeavored to eliminate any external or internal authority beyond the actual applications of the rule. The question remains: how can we qualify a rule?

Baker and Hacker in *Wittgenstein: Rules, Grammar, and Necessity* present a detailed account about the nature of rules and of understanding that seems to be sketched in the *Investigations*. They claim that identifiable characteristics about rules are revealed in the *Investigations*, i.e., «our calling anything a rule is governed by certain criteria for anything's being a rule – criteria that are part of our linguistic practice, part of the grammar of "rule"»[61]. These conditions of a rule may be summed up in three points: rules are known publicly,[62] rules have a

---

that the machine is performing according to its design, it is nevertheless useful not to forget that there is also a possibility that the machine will go kaput, thaw out, etc. This means that it is possible that *in an actual case* of a machine's operation a different sequence of movements can occur other than those projected by the design. In the same way, *in the actual case* of rule-following it is possible for someone to have a different reaction and to still be in accordance with the rule.

[59] What a rule is cannot be learned by searching for the essence of *rule*, for it does not possess an essence, nor can it be clarified by formulating an analytic definition. In search for *a* definition of a rule, one may attempt to look further, not realizing that the rule is understood in the process by which it is followed.

[60] Other Wittgensteinian authors indicate that the arguments from *PI* §138, regarding meaning and understanding, are related to the problem of rule-following. See B. HALE, «Rule-following, Objectivity and Meaning», 370, 392 fn.1; see also D. BOLTON, *An Approach to Wittgenstein's Philosophy*, 137.

[61] R. ELDRIDGE, *Leading a Human Life*, 204.

[62] I prefer to use the word *public* rather than *transparent* (as used by Eldridge, p.204) because the latter somehow does not intimate the nuance of Wittgenstein's claim in *PI* §202 regarding the connection between rule-following and practice. Furthermore, the term *transparent* hardly explains the fact that rule followers cannot al-

normative character, i.e., the term normative here refers more to the prescriptive character rather than the coercive/descriptive connotation of the word basing on Wittgenstein's claim in *PI* §198 and rules manifest an objective agreement[63] between the rule and its extension.

Rules are publicly known. They derive this particular characteristic from their predisposition of being expressed.[64] It is insinuated in the *Investigations* as suggested by Eldridge that, «a rule is *expressible* by those whose practice the rule describes, and such that expressions of the rule are *recognizable* by those whose practice it describes»[65]. Most definitely, the idea that rules are public derives from Wittgenstein's claim that «"obeying a rule" is a practice» [*PI* §202]. Practice affirms that rules are part of a *form of life*. Hence, they are publicly known. It is evident from *PI* §190 onwards that the meaning of a rule *determines which steps are to be taken*. The criterion for following a rule – for successfully understanding the meaning of such a rule, is found in *the way we use it* and *the way we were taught to use it* [*PI* §190]. This statement confirms the idea that the meaning of rules lies in their use, i.e., when one is given a rule, its use is not present as that of a shadow nor is it predetermined so that the steps to be taken in following a rule are logically necessary. According to Baker and Hacker, «there is no such thing as a rule-governed practice the rules of which cannot be tabulated, and no such thing as rules of a practice which nobody is in a position to formulate»[66]. According to Wittgenstein, «a rule *qua* rule is detached, it stands as it were alone in its glory; although what gives it

---

ways cite the rule that justifies their actions, nor can they always recognize formulations of the rules when they are offered. It is also in this sphere where a discussion regarding the social character of a rule is relevant. A. McHoul in his book *Wittgenstein on Certainty and the Problem of Rule in Social Science* develops a very interesting investigation on the problem of whether rules are knowable or not and whether rules are social based on an exegetical reading of Wittgenstein's works. However, in this work, major emphasis has been laid upon Wittgenstein's *On Certainty*.

[63] R. ELDRIDGE, *Leading a Human Life*, 204. The author uses the expression *objective accord-conditions*. Again, it is a better option to use a more familiar term *agreement*. It nevertheless manifests the same idea concerning the relationship between a rule and its extension. According to Wittgenstein, the word *agreement* and the term *rule* are related [*PI* §224].

[64] There is nothing in the expression of the formula which causes a rule follower to act in some behavioralistic way. The expression is embedded within an existing *custom* and *uses* and for this reason a rule follower knows how to react to the formula upon seeing them. See *PI* §198.

[65] R. ELDRIDGE, *Leading a Human Life*, 204.

[66] G.P. BAKER – P.M.S. HACKER, *An Analytical Commentary*, II, 62.

importance is the facts of daily experience» [*RFM*, VII: 3]. Thus, rules are public, i.e., they are embedded in custom – practice.

Rules have a normative character. They are «standards of correct-ness and guides to action. For an activity to be rule-governed at all is for rules to have a role in justifying or criticizing performances, in teaching or explaining»[67]. This normativity of a rule is associated with Wittgenstein's idea of *obeying a rule*. By a commonplace definition, to *obey* means to *follow* something having an outside authority, whether of a person, of a rule, or of a history of use. Orders, instructions, com-mands and protocols offer examples of situations to which one owes obedience. In *PI* §198 Wittgenstein claims, «A person goes by a sign-post only in so far as there exists a regular use of sign-posts, a custom». Here, he is delineating the normative aspect of rule-following based on the regularity of use, i.e., rules must be grounded in a custom wherein we are trained to obey. A rule is normative in the sense that rule-following anticipates a multiplicity of performances in a *regular pat-tern* and hence «it is not possible that there should have been only one occasion in which someone obeyed a rule» [*PI* §199]. In Wittgenstein's view, we participate in, build and present ourselves to be guided by this normativity as we take part in our language-games. When we follow an arrow indicated by a street sign, we are not confused whether to follow the direction of its point or of its tail, we simply act as we have been taught to do. Rules are characteristically obeyed. However, obeying a rule is not based upon reasons,[68] i.e., we do not apply words to things from reason by thinking that it is the correct application, something that we can remove from our pockets as a justification of our application when faced with a skeptical challenge. Thus, we are seldom plagued

---

[67] G.P. BAKER – P.M.S. HACKER, *An Analytical Commentary*, II, 63 quoted by El-dridge, p. 204. Although Wittgenstein considers the notion of an ultimate ground of correctness as incoherent and misleading he does not claim that a rule is not solid or definite, i.e., not normative. If it were not normative, how could one account for one's reaction to a rule, i.e., obeying it or going against it? The passage from *PI* §231 indi-cates that a rule has the ability to put one under its compulsion. G.P. BAKER – P.M.S. HACKER, *An Analytical Commentary*, II, 63 quoted by R. ELDRIDGE, *Leading a Hu-man Life*, 204.

[68] Wittgenstein's treatment of rule-following asserts that obeying a rule is not based on reason since reason itself is constituted by rules – rules form an individual's reason for doing things. If following a rule is not a consequence of a process of rea-soning or logical deduction but is characterized as customary or untheoritical, this means that the beginning and persistence of obeying a rule depend upon facets other than reason.

with doubt about the proper way to follow them. Following a rule involves a spontaneous capacity, which is irreducible to judgments about what is the case or to awareness of conventions or conditions.[69] Thus, it is plausible to affirm that rule-following should not be treated as a mere passive action.[70]

Rules manifest an objective agreement, i.e. between a rule and its extension(s). This criterion stems from Wittgenstein's discussion concerning the distinction between the intention of following a rule and the actual act of obeying it. According to Baker and Hacker, «it is always possible to distinguish someone's trying to follow a rule from his actually following it; the first issue turns primarily on his intentions but the second depends primarily on what he actually does. An individual sincerely believing that he is following a rule never logically certifies that he is following the rule; whether he really follows the rule requires that his action conforms with it, and this is settled not by his believing himself to have followed it»[71]. The differentiation is reflected in *PI* §202 where *thinking* of following a rule is distinguished from *actually obeying* a rule. What Wittgenstein would mean by this is that consciously (intentionally) thinking one is following a rule, by definition, is not to obey a rule since an ordinary extension of a rule would be to proceed spontaneously, straightforwardly, and without any preoccupation of

---

[69] J. SKORUPSKI, «Meaning, use, verification», 50.

[70] Notable inquiries can still be formulated regarding the active-passive participation of the follower in obeying the rule. How can a rule, with its normative character, invoke passivity on the part of the follower? Neither the presence or absence of intention nor the cognitive state of the person is crucial in rule-following, for there is no gap between the rule and its correct application for mental acts to fill. Considering this we affirm that a person in obeying a rule in an actual situation does not demonstrate any active attitude towards the application of the rule, i.e., one obeys the rule «blindly» [*PI* §219]. Certainly, we can say that *interpreting* (determining the application of the rule) is a form of non-passive response to a rule. However, interpretation as determining a rule's application was clearly demolished by Wittgenstein since «an interpretation of a sign is simply *another sign*, and by interpreting he in effect means *translating* one sign into another» [C. MCGINN, *Wittgenstein on Meaning*, 14] and it would lead one to an *argumentum ad infinitum*. In saying that we follow rules blindly, Wittgenstein does not mean that we follow the rules passively; it rather means to obey it without guidance of reasons. This seeming observance in rule-following underlies a committed participation of one who follows a rule. This particular commitment can be seen in the fulfillment of the demands of learning and understanding how the rule applies before one can obey it.

[71] G.P. BAKER – P.M.S. HACKER, *An Analytical Commentary*, II, 156 also 62 quoted by ELDRIDGE, *Leading a Human Life*, 204.

confirming whether a rule is being followed correctly, i.e. following the rule blindly [*PI* §219]. Baker and Hacker argue for the internal relation between a rule and its extension,[72] i.e., each one is a necessary condition for the other. What gives sense to an extension is the rule and a rule makes sense when a specific practice, which is in accord with it, is carried out, i.e., in the absence of social interaction, no such internal relation between a rule and its extension could exist. As we noted above, neither the cognitive state of a person nor the presence or absence of intention is crucial in following a rule. What matters is how we learned to apply the rules taught to us in our custom, in practice.

Here Wittgenstein introduces the problem regarding the *interpretation* of a rule. If we accept that to follow a rule means to interpret it, we are then considered to have fallen into the same predicament as that of Wittgenstein's interlocutor [*PI* §198]. Wittgenstein argues that interpretations *do not fix* the application of a rule, i.e., «any interpretation still hangs in the air along with what it interprets» [*PI* §198]. This means that any interpretation of a rule is equally subject to a cornucopia of interpretations as was the original rule. Maintaining this would lead into an infinite regress, we can never reach 'bedrock'. Interpretations, like justification and explanation, are helpful devices that we seldom utilize to eradicate misunderstanding; however, they do not function as the ultimate reason for making a definition more precise than the rule being explained. Hence, acting in accordance with a rule is *not* by any means an interpretation but via an agreement between the rule and its extension(s).

2.2 *Rule-following and Practice*

In the preceding sections, we have seen how *practice or custom* plays an essential role in the understanding of what constitutes rule-following. This perspective is considered as one of the positive insights and the most distinctive view that Wittgenstein offers in his rule-following considerations. Passages containing the idea of custom and practice, found in the *Investigations*, are among the most straightforward in Wittgenstein's consideration of meaning and rule.[73] The inter-

---

[72] However, Eldridge challenges their claim by saying that «the emphasis that Baker & Hacker place on internal relations between rules and their accordants suppresses the odd respect in which rule-following and understanding language are inherently social phenomena». R. ELDRIDGE, *Leading a human life*, 211.

[73] See *PI* §§198, 199, 202.

play between rule-following and practice posits the need for education. How can we ascertain this? An example is furnished by the deviant behavior of children concerning the rule. They either act in accordance with it or not. In both cases, i.e., necessity of correction or the lack of it, (communal) practice is highly important in what is required to learn and follow a rule.

We should note that when Wittgenstein speaks of *practice*, it is fundamentally identical with his use of *custom*. He does not appeal to *practice* as a way of indicating a constructive application about what rule-following consists in.[74] Rather, for there to be such correctness and incorrectness of performance there must be some practice or pattern of behavior or custom with which an individual's actions either do or do not conform. When I follow a rule, I am obeying a practice. Thus, Wittgenstein says, «and hence "obeying a rule" is a practice» [*PI* §202].

What does Wittgenstein aim to achieve in his description of rule-following as a *custom* or *practice*? Practice obviously suggests a usual and ordinary way of doing things.[75] If following a rule is a practice, then it involves an accepted way of following and applying it. Colin McGinn identifies three inter-linked ideas of what Wittgenstein intends to demonstrate by *custom* and *practice*. They are as follows: that rule-following takes place in the area of actual behavior and not in the inner recesses of a person's consciousness or mental mechanism; that rules can be understood only if they are actually obeyed repeatedly; and finally that using and reacting to signs is properly seen as regular and unreflective, not as the consequence of ratiocination.[76]

Wittgenstein insists in the *Investigations* and elsewhere that understanding a rule does not signify a process that accompanies our overt actions of following a rule. The proof that one understands a rule and its application is found in the actual behavior and not in the action-translated internal process. If rule-following is something one can observe, then it is not a hidden process at all. Practice manifests the connection between the rule and a specific form of behavior. Wittgenstein's insistence on the overt manifestation of rule-following helps us

---

[74] M. McCullagh, «Wittgenstein on Rules and Practices», 84.

[75] McGinn believes that it is based on tradition that a custom or practice is established. He says, «Traditions and customs become established and entrenched by dint of regularities in behavior in which people come to acquiesce». C. McGinn, *Wittgenstein on Meaning*, 39.

[76] C. McGinn, *Wittgenstein on Meaning*, 36ff.

to evade the twofold picture of the inner and outer operations in which the former is considered as the authentic locus of rule-following and the latter its materialization. As McGinn claims, affirming rule-following as a practice is to say «that it is nothing other than what it appears to be, though it is difficult to resist trying to get behind the appearances…we should not think of rule-following as what explains practice, since rule-following is nothing over and above (or behind) practice, i.e., use»[77].

The affirmation that following a rule is a practice, according to Wittgenstein, entails that doing what the rule tells us to do allows us to be guided by such rules. Furthermore, what the rule tells us to do is demonstrated in a practice, i.e., a standard series of actions that has become institutionalized as a correct application of the rule. To engage in such a practice is brought about by training and because of this, we follow (obey, apply) the rule in a spontaneous manner, indubitably and without necessarily appealing to any interpretation of it [*PI* §190]. We simply do it.

Having elaborated on the key points underpinning Wittgenstein's thoughts concerning rule-following, let us proceed with our discussion of another fundamental theme – Wittgenstein's view of *philosophy as therapy*.

3. Philosophy as Therapy

3.1 *Logical Clarification: Wittgenstein's Early Conception*

Throughout the early period of his philosophical thought, Wittgenstein, together with Frege, Russell and Moore, maintained that philosophy aims at providing a true explanation of things, its purpose being to arrive at some essential knowledge about reality and the universe that can be formulated or at least made known. This obviously led to Wittgenstein's development of the say-show distinction. For him, logical analysis is the most crucial task that philosophy should undertake since it is an activity and not a body of doctrine or a theory [*TLP* 4.112]. This method is aimed at a clarification of the logic of our language, which has been clearly misunderstood in traditional philosophy. This goal is achieved, he claims, through a critique of language itself.

Wittgenstein's claim that *philosophy is not a theory* aims to put our concept of philosophy as a system of doctrines, complete in all main respects, under the guillotine. His emphasis in *TLP* 4.112 on philosophy

---

[77] C. McGinn, *Wittgenstein on Meaning*, 36.

as an activity demonstrates that Wittgenstein wanted to detach philosophical method from the methods of science since the former does not offer a corpus of knowledge similar to that presented by the latter [*TLP* 4.113]; «Philosophy is not one of the natural sciences» [*TLP* 4.111]. The activity of philosophy consists in providing the correct analysis of language and hence in lingering within the ambit of pure logical formality. If such were the case, then philosophy would not have content, i.e., a realm of its own since, for Wittgenstein, the contingent exhausts the meaningful. It only *indicates* what is speakable - «it will mean the unspeakable by clearly displaying the speakable» [*TLP* 4.115]. With this statement, even if Wittgenstein is convinced that language mirrors the world, he believes that the way in which language represents the world cannot be expressed in language. In distinguishing between saying and showing, he demarcated all 'useful' language (in the sense that it states - or says for that matter - facts of natural science) from the quotidian elements of everyday speech. *Saying*, on the one hand, fundamentally describes or provides information[78] while *showing*, on the other hand, refers to logic that makes language possible. Stern argues that «the distinction between saying and showing arises out of the conviction that there is a fundamental difference between the information that can be communicated in language and those aspects of language that make communication possible»[79]. Hence, metaphysical or philosophical propositions were considered by Wittgenstein, according to Anscombe, «as nonsensical (*pseudo-propositions*): perhaps simply nonsensical, perhaps attempts to say the inexpressible»[80].

With such a consideration, Wittgenstein asserted that philosophy offers a critique of language in as much as it aims at a logical clarification of thoughts – «Philosophy should make clear and delimit sharply the thoughts which otherwise are, as it were, opaque and blurred» [*TLP* 4.112]. Its goal, therefore, is to single out the determinate logical form of every proposition, to distinguish the unspeakability-unthinkability of propositions, to prevent the evidence of what can be *shown* from being confused with the evidence of what can be *said* and to indicate for each sphere the relevant and pertinent criteria of clarity. Briefly, philosophy

---

[78] This refers to natural science according to Wittgenstein in *TLP* 6.53. Wittgenstein was obviously not in favor of equating philosophical problems to problems of natural science. See J. SCHULTE, *Wittgenstein: An Introduction*, 41.

[79] D. STERN, *Wittgenstein on Mind and Language*, 49.

[80] G.E.M. ANSCOMBE, *An Introduction*, 79, 150 texts added.

prompts us to see what cannot be said and to make us realize the sense-lessness and emptiness of metaphysical speculation. Although Wittgenstein realized in 1930-31, according to Bohl, that his doctrine on saying and showing is untenable and merely *plain nonsense*, it forms part of his quest to answer the question «what is philosophy?» in the *Tractatus*.[81]

3.2 *The therapeutic project: Wittgenstein's later view of Philosophy*

Wittgenstein, after having laid his groundwork in the *Tractatus*, thought that he already had solved all the main philosophical problems. Consequently, he was determined to abandon philosophy. However, this was not the case. In 1929, after a decade of intense work Wittgenstein returned to Cambridge and again initiated his academic activity, this time putting former ideas into question and subjecting them to rigorous criticisms to the extent of repudiating some of them, e.g., the *picture theory*. This prefigures his new way of viewing at language and meaning. It was during this period that Wittgenstein exercised an intensive revision of his former estimate of philosophy.

From a perspective that seeks the logical clarification of thoughts, Wittgenstein now considers philosophy to be purely *descriptive*. It seeks to describe the workings of our language – «We must do away with all *explanation*, and description alone must take its place» [*PI* §109]. «Philosophy may in no way interfere with the actual use of language; it can in the end only describe it» [*PI* §123]. This shows that philosophy in the eyes of Wittgenstein was no longer concerned about the disclosure of the logical structure of the world, the language-independent essence of all things, since it does not exist. Rather it seeks «to bring words back from their metaphysical to their everyday use» [*PI* §116]. It describes the common rule-governed relations between words, and does so in order to untangle the knots in our understanding due to the ill-treatment of our concepts in the framework of philosophical consideration.

By focusing his attention on the significance of ordinary (everyday) language [*PI* §494], Wittgenstein underlines the idea that philosophy does not engage in any discovery since «philosophy simply puts everything before us, and neither explains nor deduces anything. Since everything lies open to view there is nothing to explain. For what is hid-

---

[81] R.F. BOHL, JR., «Something in the *Tractatus*», 217- 219. Cf. *TLP* 6.53 – 6.54.

den, for example, is of no interest to us. One might also give the name "philosophy" to what is possible *before* all new discoveries and inventions» [*PI* §126]. The trouble with the *Tractatus* was that it had tried to penetrate things. It was as if the essence of things was hidden from us, and we had, by means of analysis, to excavate what lay within it. Wittgenstein was not interested in "what is hidden" obviously because *what is hidden* can play no role in our rule-governed use of words. This tells us that if «nothing is concealed» [*PI* §435], then philosophy should not preoccupy herself with formulating theses for if there were, everyone would agree with them and it would be preposterous to dispute them [*PI* §128]. Philosophy just «leaves everything as it is» [*PI* §124].

It is a tangle, i.e., confusion of language, which most people experience. Wittgenstein wanted to unravel such an entanglement. What led Wittgenstein to affirm that we pitifully fail to understand? According to him, we make these errors because «we do not *command a clear view* of the use of words» [*PI* §122]. «A philosophical problem has the form: "I don't know my way about"» [*PI* §123]. And the only way to attain clarity in our understanding is to have a *perspicuous representation* since it «produces just that understanding which consists in "seeing connexions"...It earmarks the form of account we give, the way we look at things» [*PI* §122]. How do we achieve this type of representation? Since Wittgenstein claims in §126 that everything lies open to view, it follows therefore that philosophy should not explore that which is beyond plain view, but rather engage in an activity which involves destroying «houses of cards» and clearing up the ground of language [*PI* §118], disclosing the pieces of plain nonsense in philosophical theories [*PI* §119 & §464], bringing words back from their metaphysical to their everyday use [*PI* §116] and develop «reminders for a particular purpose» [*PI* §127]. According to Mark Addis, «the goal of perspicuous representation is to show the rules which govern appropriate employments of a word»[82]. These approaches reflect mainly the methods of *therapy*. Philosophy, as practiced out by the later Wittgenstein, is primarily directed towards showing that such philosophical problems are nonsensical instead of providing solutions to them. It is principally therapeutic, the aim of which is to treat an illness, the dissolution of philosophical problems, i.e., to exorcise philosophical confusion instead of constructing new theories thus giving philosophy peace [*PI* §133].

---

[82] M. ADDIS, *Wittgenstein*, 113.

The therapeutic aspect of Wittgenstein's later philosophy treats philosophical problems as forms of illness [*PI* §255] or a philosophical disease [*PI* §593] that are supposed to be cured. The general form of the illness is «"I don't know my way about"» [*PI* §123]. This highlights the need for clarity. Peterman states that «this lack of clarity gives rise to *deep* disturbances, sometimes referred to as mental cramps»[83]. Wittgenstein is emphatic about his claim that «philosophy is a battle against the bewitchment of our intelligence by means of language» [*PI* §109]. This implies that, for him, philosophical confusion and bewitchment are consequent upon our misconception of the workings of language – these disorders arise when our concepts and ideas are not at work, i.e., «when language *goes on a holiday*» [*PI* §38]. He considers any philosophical problem that arises from our erroneous view about meaning, logical necessity, rule-following, etc., as an illness in need of treatment. We should take note, however, that Wittgenstein characterizes such an illness as intellectual and not psychological.

Philosophical problems (conceptual entanglements) have a variety of causes and some of these include kinds such as misleading analogies – influence of surface grammar and bewitching and confusing myths and pictures.[84] The ones mentioned are only representative samples of causes that are found in the *PI*. The cure for both of these causes of philosophical illnesses and others not identified here lies in the new method applied by Wittgenstein. This method aims at disentangling the constituent threads of the problem and making that problem disappear, thus giving philosophy peace [*PI* §133]. This involves the breaking of the hold of the obsessive, illusory models by forcefully and effectively reminding us of the reality, i.e., of the actual employment of the words and concepts concerned. The method Wittgenstein used was *philosophical* therapy. This will be the subject matter of the next segment.

Evidently, there are motley of methods available to cure illnesses. However, regarding the treatment of philosophical (problems) illnesses Wittgenstein states, «There is not *a* philosophical method, though there are indeed methods, like different therapies» [*PI* §133]. The analogy conveyed in the passage, says Peterman, «is designed to indicate one

---

[83] J. PETERMAN, *Philosophy as therapy*, 17.

[84] There are other causes of this illness such as man's craving for generality, fascination of science, considering only one sort of example – «A main cause of philosophical disease – a one-sided diet» [*PI* §593] and the like. Cf. R. P. MOLLANEDA, *Concrete Approach and Therapeutic Activity*, 116-142.

respect in which philosophy is like therapy: there are different methods of both enterprises»[85]. Let us proceed with our elaboration of this topic by raising three fundamental questions. What kind of therapy did Wittgenstein employ? What are its goals? Furthermore, how does one proceed with such a therapy?

What sort of therapy did Wittgenstein consider? It is evident that when we talk about therapy, we certainly come up with varied types of therapies aside from medical treatment as the most obvious type of therapy, e.g., religious therapy, psychological therapy, ethical therapy, cultural therapy and philosophical therapy. In Wittgenstein's view, however, therapy refers to philosophical therapy - the most legitimate candidate. Therapy operates from a notion of health and illness. Its aim is to present some means to bring an individual back from sickness to health. Peterman claims that «if philosophical confusion is likened to a disease, then the goal of philosophy must be to remove the disease and bring about health»[86]. Each kind of therapy reveals a practice designed to realize some ideal of health in a particular situation in which an ideal is not achieved. The therapy that Wittgenstein uses is characteristically philosophical since he insists on the importance of clarification of key ideas and claims, which have been confused by our bewitchment of language. Since there is no mechanical, easy cure, philosophical therapy should place fundamental importance on the question of the nature of the illness at hand and its cause and not pretend to treat an individual simply by eliminating the cause of the illness. Philosophical therapy, in contrast to psychological therapy, does not depend on any theory of the mind because if it were the case, then the problem would become subservient to such a theory. Rather Wittgenstein seeks, by such therapy, to teach a skill that is critical and destabilizing. He endeavors to fracture the false unities we construct in our minds, so that we will be able to see distinctions and differences, which are missed because «we are dazzled by the ideal» [PI §100].

The primary objective of Wittgenstein's philosophical therapy is to obtain «complete clarity» [PI §133], i.e., «to pass from a piece of disguised (*latent*) nonsense to something that is *patent* nonsense» [PI

---

[85] J. PETERMAN, *Philosophy as therapy*, 19.
[86] J. PETERMAN, *Philosophy as therapy*, 19-20. Cf. *RFM*, V: 53 and *CV*, 57. L. WITTGENSTEIN, *Culture and Value*. Heretofore considered as *CV*.

§§464, 594; *text and emphasis added*].[87] It aims at unmasking philosophical theories to make evident particular instances of nonsense, destroying «houses of cards» and clearing the ground of language [*PI* §118], restoring language to its everyday use [*PI* §116] and showing the fly the way out of the fly-bottle [*PI* §309]. We will not delve into a detailed account of the process involved in achieving these goals since we might deviate from our main line of argument. It is sufficient to note that by realizing these goals, health will be restored and philosophical problems will disappear [*PI* §133]. With the help of such therapy, we will achieve an understanding of grammatical articulations that will prevent those problems from recurring. If this is the case, then there will be no need for explanations because everything will lie open to view [*PI* §126]. Consequently, we could stop doing philosophy when we want to and give philosophy peace [*PI* §133].

As in any other kinds of therapy, varied devices are employed in Wittgenstein's philosophical therapy to attain its aim. This includes kinds like, focusing our attention on the question before attempting to formulate an answer, analyzing expression by means of *perspicuous representation* and finding immediate cases. There are still other forms of devices that could be used in philosophical therapy. However, the aforementioned therapeutic devices are the ones prevalent in Wittgenstein's writings.

«To show a man how to get out you have first of all to free him from the misleading influence of the question» [*BB* 169]. Wittgenstein was aware that we are entangled in the web of philosophical confusion when we answer apparently well-formed question with hastiness. Our not paying attention to the questions is the one that leads us to many misunderstandings. Hence, a therapy that seeks to clear out philosophical problems, according to Wittgenstein, should, first, elucidate the mistakes that prompt confusing and misleading questions. «If you do not keep the multiplicity of language-games in view you will perhaps be inclined to ask questions such as: "What is a question?"» [*PI* §24] Thus, in this type of therapy we need to examine questions carefully and then expose whatever fallacy has led to misleading analogies.

---

[87] Some authors consider this position as Wittgenstein's negative view of the philosophical enterprise. «Instead of providing solutions to philosophical problems - the mind-body problem, the problem of other minds, the problem of skepticism, of the external world, the problem of universals, and the like – Wittgenstein tries to show that such problems are nonsensical». R. SUTER, *Interpreting Wittgenstein*, 5.

Another important therapeutic device is the investigation of language by way of *perspicuous representation*. Wittgenstein considers the development of a perspicuous representation as an antidote to philosophical conflicts, e.g., «A simile that has been absorbed into the forms of our language produces a false appearance, and this disquiets us. "But *this* isn't how it is!" – we say. "Yet this is how it has to *be!*"» [*PI* §112]. It is by means of this technique that one achieves clarity. As mentioned earlier, for Wittgenstein, the only way to attain clarity in our understanding is to have a *perspicuous representation* since by means of this we make conceptual connections that have been overlooked and gradually identify the rules for the correct employment of our words, thus enabling us to get a clearer view of what troubles us – to visualize the actual landscape of language we are treading. «Don't think, but look!» [*PI* §66]

If we successfully apply these aforementioned therapeutic devices, philosophical therapy as Wittgenstein presents it would certainly be able to eliminate integrally philosophical illness and free our intelligence from its bewitchment - thus, providing us with the most needed clarity in how language works and how words are used. Such *complete* clarity serves us in dissolving philosophical problems by means of highlighting the effective practicality of the grammar of our language. An autonomous control of the reflections of philosophy does not exist anymore. «What is your aim in philosophy? – To show the fly the way out of the fly-bottle» [*PI* §309].

In this chapter we have endeavoured to elaborate on the fundamental Wittgensteinian themes, which are relevant to philosophy of education. Our attempt has been primarily motivated by the desire to acquire a coherent understanding of his ideas in order to establish firm grounds upon which to base our arguments when we shall undertake to relate these central themes to the basic concepts of education. This project will be tackled later on in this work. However, before we proceed on this venture, let us first deal with elucidation of the elemental understanding of the basic concepts of philosophy of education, namely, teaching, learning and community.

CHAPTER II

Basic Concepts of Philosophy of Education

«Education may be thought of as having two important and comple-
mentary facets: the one is concerned with education as a process of
growth or development, and the other is concerned with education in
relation to purposes and goals»[1]. These aspects comprise further basic
elements, viz., *teaching, learning* and *community*, which contribute to a
better understanding of what education is. The aforementioned concepts are basic in the standard educational discourse because without
them the general purpose and function of education become incompre-
hensible.

In this chapter, we shall discuss these basic concepts of philosophy
of education. The rudiments of their respective nature will thus be examined. We shall proceed in our discussion in four sections. First, we
shall present a historical sketch of the development of philosophy of
education with reference to philosophers regarding its nature and purpose. In this section, we will consider three historical periods of philosophy of education, namely, the *traditional philosophy of education*,
which consists of the ancient and the medieval times, the *modern philosophy of education*, and the *contemporary philosophy of education*.
Second, we shall investigate into the teaching practice. Here, we shall
deal with a conceptual analysis of the teaching activity. Other issues
related to such activity, viz., its aim, the relation between teaching and
learning and the diverse methods involved in the process would also be
discussed. Third, we shall delve into a study of the learning process. A
discussion regarding theories of learning will also be done to present

---

[1] N. L. BOSSING, *Teaching in Secondary Schools*, 9.

disagreements about its nature. Lastly, we shall examine the role and the importance of the community in the educational enterprise.

1. Philosophy of Education: A Historical Overview

1.1 *Philosophy of Education Qualified*

One of the problems that confront those who write on the history of philosophy of education is that many of the thinkers identified in the standard treatment of philosophy of education are unlikely to be included in standard history of philosophy. Quite the opposite, many if not most of the great philosophers have had little to say directly about education and if they do have something to say, it is of little significance. In spite of this, we cannot jettison the fact that educational discourse does elicit essential philosophical questions. However, before we proceed it is suitable that we should first have an idea of what philosophy of education entails.

Questions such as «is philosophy of education an applied branch of philosophy?», «Does it mean philosophical reflections on education?» or «does it mean forming a *philosophy of education* as one might perhaps form a *philosophy of life?*» persist as a challenge for those who endeavor to specify a definition of philosophy of education.[2] It is not our intention here to enter into a detailed discussion on the meaning and scope of philosophy of education. Nor do we intend to offer any definition or prescribe rules of procedure for such a project. One is too well aware of the hazards involved in any such attempt and the futility of any search for an objective, universally acceptable definition. The purpose of the present discussion is to highlight the prevalent and accepted views about the nature of philosophy of education.

The difficulty in tracing the development of the term *philosophy of education* is that throughout most of Western thought what might be regarded as philosophical reflections on education were never regarded as constituting a distinct discipline or branch of philosophy. The great thinkers of the Ancient world generally melded their reflections on education with their accounts of epistemology, ethics, politics, or human nature. Philosophy of education as a developed elaboration of purely philosophical themes may not have occurred to them.

---

[2] Cf. J. DOLHENTY, *Philosophy of Education*, http://www.radicalacademy.com/philapplied2.htm.

What is ordinarily viewed as philosophy of education (or educational philosophy) has characteristically been regarded as a quest for the philosophical foundations of education. This view connotes an application of speculative theses, viz., metaphysical, epistemological, axiological, etc. – of the different philosophical schools of thought to education in order to derive directives and recommendations on educational curriculum and methodology. Although this point of view is certainly not wrong, it definitely does not encompass the whole idea of what philosophy of education is all about.

Today, *philosophy of education* is regarded as essentially an activity or a method, a disciplined, systematic way of thinking about problems leading to illumination of conceptual meaning and understanding and appraisal of issues and concepts in the educational enterprise, i.e., as a process in which educational practitioners or reformers develop thoughtful, and to varying degrees systematic or coherent justifications for their educational practices and commitments. It is contrasted with *educational theory* since building theories of education is not doing philosophy of education.[3] Nor is it a study of the history of educational thought.[4] Furthermore, it is not a matter of drawing conclusions, making extrapolations, and eliciting implications from bodies of systematic and doctrinaire thought of a metaphysical, social-political, or religious nature.[5] According to Ozmon, «in one basic sense, we can say that philosophy of education is the application of philosophical ideas to educational problems. A philosophy of education becomes significant at the point where educators recognize the need to think clearly about what they are doing and to see what they are doing in the larger context of individual and social development»[6].

Having said this, let us now initiate with our enquiry regarding the historical development of philosophy of education. We shall proceed in our investigation by considering the following issues: the aim of education, the character of teaching, the methods used, the role of the teacher and the nature of the learning process.

---

[3] C. M. HAMM, *Philosophical Issues in Education*, 2.
[4] C.M. HAMM, *Philosophical Issues in Education*, 2.
[5] C.M. HAMM, *Philosophical Issues in Education*, 3.
[6] H. OZMON – S. CRAVER, *Philosophical foundations of education*, xii.

1.2 *Traditional Philosophy of Education*

In this section, we shall be concerned with the philosophical thoughts of distinguished classical philosophers and the application of these ideas to educational problems. Our discussion will primarily revolve around the ancient and medieval periods. However, we must be selective. We shall limit our discussion to the thoughts of Plato, Aristotle, Augustine and Thomas – four prominent figures in their respective intellectual spheres.

The very problem of the relation of philosophy to education is one, which has interested many thinkers of the past.[7] It certainly did not escape the notice of one of the great minds of the western world – Plato. He was clearly engaged in philosophical reflections about the nature, purposes, content, means and ends of education. This is forcefully demonstrated in his works specifically in the *Republic*.[8] Here, he considers education as a means in order to attain a just and perfect society – an ideal state. Nettleship claims that education is treated «as an integral and vital part of the wider subject of the well-being of human society»[9]. For Krentz the aim «is supported by the philosophical search for the *Good*, the protection of the just city from dangers that would threaten to bring about its decline and fall, and the educational means most likely to make the construction of such a just city possible»[10]. For Plato, the good life is characterized rather by a general turning towards what is good and true outside of us and independently of us. This is consistent with his major philosophical views of the world (the world of ideas or forms and the world of matter) and of knowledge and with his ethical and political doctrines. It is through a process of externally directed discipline and thought (education) that enables us to recover the traces of the external good hidden deep within us. This particular activity of transcending matter to advance toward the *Good* is done using dialectic in which one moves from mere opinion to true knowledge. It is for this reason that Plato thought preparation in dialectic should involve a lengthy period of education.

---

[7] See P. HOGAN – R. SMITH, «The Activity of Philosophy», 165-180.

[8] Some ideas regarding education are found in his other works, such as the *Meno, Theaetetus, Protagoras,* and *Laws*. See S. M. CAHN, *Classic and Contemporary Readings*; S. KRAMER, «Education and Digressions», 26 (4), 1976.

[9] R.L. NETTLESHIP, *The Theory of Education*, 1.

[10] A. KRENTZ, «Play and Education», http://www.bu.edu/wcp/Papers/Educ/Edukren.html.

In the *Republic*, Plato presented the kind of education that would assist in achieving a world wherein individuals and society are moved to the degree that they are capable of moving toward the *Good*. His belief in the search for the absolute truth, i.e., genuine universal truth, which is the *Good*, affirms education's emphasis on the movement from a concern with concrete data to abstract thinking – the unchanging and universal.[11]

Plato was concerned to understand matters such as what can be taught, what virtue is and how it can be acquired, how a just system of education should address differences in ability, and so on. This is by no means to suggest that Plato's answers are correct and uncontroversial; but he represents a model of philosophical investigation of educational methods and aims that is undoubtedly relevant in today's educational discourses.[12]

Having thus seen the basic points underpinning Plato's thoughts on education, let us now turn our attention to another renowned theorist, teacher and scientist of the ancient world – Aristotle.

While Plato upheld the primacy of ideas over the non-lasting reality of matter, Aristotle conversely maintained that though ideas are important in themselves, a proper study of matter could lead us to ideas that are more distinct. This position is what we now know as realism. It is based on this doctrine that Aristotle develops his philosophy and consequently his views on education.

There are scant sources of his views on education; however, with reference to his surviving works we can get the gist of his ideas. Aristotle believes that education was central to human existence.[13] Since he considers virtue as a life principle of the state, the teaching of intellec-

---

[11] This shows the consistency of Plato's thoughts for it certainly reflects the idea purported in the Divided Line. See R. S. BRUMBAUGH, «Plato's Ideal Curriculum», 177.

[12] Robert S. Brumbaugh says, «This is what I take Plato's plan for education to be and to involve: it must have multiple aims to be effective; it must have different levels and methods to be "realistic", because of the metaphysical structure of reality. There is a natural sequence of learning, running from fine art to philosophy, which parallels human development of mental power and intellectual maturity». See R.S. BRUMBAUGH, «Plato's Ideal Curriculum», 174.

[13] It is only in the *Politics* wherein Aristotle gives considerable attention to the issue of education specifically in books VII and VIII. Here, he sets forth in detail his philosophy of education. *See* Aristotle, «The Politics» 1260b15, 1266b30-38, 1277a16, 1283a24, 1310a12, 1313b1, 1332b10, 1333b5, VII, 7 – VII, 17.

tual and moral virtues[14] necessary for right reason becomes the goal of education and it is the function of the state to educate people, i.e., to make them virtuous. In this sense, education should be guided by legislation to make it correspond with the results of psychological analysis, and follow the gradual development of the bodily and mental faculties.

Congruent with his realism and his theory of knowledge, education and teaching are always about an object and should have content. Education involves more of a disciplined inquiry into some aspect of reality rather than an interpersonal relationship or expression of feeling between the learner and the teacher. Thus, the school endeavors to promote and develop each person's rationality.[15]

The family and the state are the two basic institutions involved in the educational process. On the one hand, the parents have the primary rights and responsibilities over the education of their children. This is especially true with regard to moral training. If such is the case, teachers' authority is a delegated authority and the school is to be considered an extension of the home. On the other hand, the state exercises some rights about the education of children. This is in view of the future incorporation of children to the society and their contribution to the common good. To this end, the state has an interest in seeing that children will receive the basic skills they need.

The fundamental thoughts sustaining Aristotle's philosophy of education include several points that are of perennial value. He recognizes that the family and the state have an interest in education. The other point is that there are several different goals in education, viz., a man must be trained both at the level of appetites and at the level of reason and that a man must be trained in the exercise of reason.

There are books that treat the issue at hand in much detail. However, our interest in this section is to locate the fundamental ideas regarding education in Plato and Aristotle and how these are representative of the traditional philosophy of education. Essentially, Plato and Aristotle end up at the same place, but the method of getting there is different. Plato believed that one acquires knowledge of ideas through contemplation

---

[14] Moral virtue including practice, excess and defect, pleasure, actions producing virtue, state of character, the mean, particular virtues, extremes, difficulty of holding to the mean. See *Nichomachean Ethics*, Book II, 181-197. The study of Intellectual virtue, contemplative and calculative intellect, science, art, practical wisdom, intuitive reason – knowledge of first principles, philosophic wisdom, practical wisdom and political science. See *Nichomachean Ethics*, Book IV, 223-233.

[15] A. ORNSTEIN – al., *An Introduction to the Foundations of Education*, 112-113.

of ideas (dialectic); Aristotle believed that one could acquire knowledge of ideas or forms through a study of matter. The value of Plato's ideas, on the one hand, is that they have stimulated a great deal of thinking about the meaning and purpose of man, society and education. Aristotle's thoughts, on the other hand, have been of immense importance and include such things as recognizing the need to study nature systematically, using logical processes in thought and emphasizing the rational aspects of human nature. Both, however, highlight the importance of the state in the process of education. In this case, their ideas on community are built around education since all manners in their society are given form through education.

Having thus explored in this section, albeit briefly, the view of education in the context of the Greek civilization through the ideas of Plato and Aristotle, let us now proceed with our investigation into the development of philosophy of education. We now situate our discussion within the ambit of the medieval period. Here, we will be dealing with the ideas of Augustine and Thomas Aquinas that are pertinent to philosophy of education.

Like Plato and Aristotle, Augustine's views about teaching, learning and other thoughts on education are scattered among his various works.[16] However, few of his writings, viz., *De Magistro* (On the Teacher)[17], *De Doctrina Christiana* (On Christian Teaching)[18], and *De Catechizandis Rudibus* (On Catechizing the Uninstructed)[19] contain

---

[16] See G. HOWIE, *St. Augustine: On Education*, viii-ix (Chronological Table).

[17] «This work belongs to the corpus of Augustine's early dialogues». Aside from dealing with the problem of the use of signs, it is obviously considered as pertaining to the educational enterprise in that here St. Augustine introduces the issue of teaching and culminates with the doctrine of the «inner teacher». Cf. D. KRIES, «De Magistro», 519-520.

[18] «The title of this work renders itself in English too easily as *On Christian Doctrine*. The proper sense is less specifically religious and might better be expressed as *On the Form of Teaching Suitable for Christians*». Its relevance to education is obviously understandable from the title itself. It offers a solid foundation for much of the best of Christian preaching. For further discussion regarding this book, cf. J. J. O'DONNELL, «De Doctrina Christiana», 279-280. I prefer to use O'Donnell's translation, i.e., *On Christian Teaching* for *De Doctrina Christiana*.

[19] This specific work deals with the way in which it is possible to communicate the revealed truth to the catechumens, i.e., those who lack the truth, that truth which must be communicated to them to make them worthy to be baptized. This work is considered pedagogical in character along with the *De Doctrina Christiana* since they are both designed for the instruction of catechists, teachers of Scripture and preachers. Cf. B. RAMSEY, «De Catechizandis rudibus», 144-145.

significant discourses regarding education, e.g., aims and methods of teaching, and as such have exerted a considerable influence on teaching process up until contemporary times.

It is accepted by most Augustinian scholars that Plato has had a profound influence on the thoughts of Augustine,[20] i.e., according to Rist, «his "Platonism", as we shall call it, runs deep»[21]. While Plato's exposition of the ideal of a universal, absolute Truth was cosmocentric, i.e., consistent with his view of the world, Augustine's was obviously theocentric, i.e., his arguments are rooted in Christian doctrines. He believed that the source of such Truth was a creator and as such, an inner knowledge of the good (as held by Plato) is implausible since man's soul is not devoid of sin.[22] For Augustine, Truth was possessed only by the Creator, and it was only the «inner teacher», who could reveal this truth unto man. Hence, this accentuates our enquiry into truth (*veritatis inquisitio*)[23] and our need for God. It was the realization of this need that became the focal point for Augustine's idea on education and teaching in particular.[24] According to Kevane, «the role of truth in Augustine's philosophy reflects his life-long connection with the field of education, which exists to teach, a process which is impossible without a truth to be taught»[25]. Indeed, Augustine conducts his procedure at Cassiciacum in terms of a truth-centered education. Thus, Augustine, as Howie confirms, «places education within the context of a personal re-

---

[20] «In Augustine's first work, *Contra Academicos*, as well as in *De Civitate Dei*, finished almost forty years later, Plato's name figures prominently. In the *Retractationes* Augustine renders his final, evenhanded judgment on his previous use of Platonism. He regrets the excessive praise bestowed upon Plato and his followers in his early works, but he still thinks many Platonic doctrines are consonant with Christianity or can be relatively easily harmonized with it». Cf. F. VAN FLETEREN, «Plato, Platonism», 651-654. «It was from Platonism that Augustine understood both the aim and the method of education», G. HOWIE, *St. Augustine: On Education*, 47. The most recent appraisal of Augustine's Platonism and an excellent one at that is Robert Crouse. See R. CROUSE, «Paucis Mutatis Verbis: St. Augustine's Platonism», 37-50.

[21] J. RIST, *Augustine: Ancient Thought Baptized*, 8.

[22] Truth for St. Augustine does not belong to the sensible order but to the intelligible order. See L. R. PATANÈ, *Il Pensiero Pedagogico*, 70.

[23] AUGUSTINE, *Against the Academics (Contra Academicos)*, Bk. I, Ch. 2-4.

[24] In *The Teacher*, Augustine suggests that teachers enable their students to apprehend created truth in preparation for the revelation of uncreated truth. For further discussion regarding this issue see R. M. JACOBS, «Augustine's Pedagogy», 111-123.

[25] E. KEVANE, *Augustine the educator*, 96.

lationship between God, who is the Truth, and man, His beloved creation»[26].

However, Paffenroth observed that «in Augustine's experience, education is debasing in its goals, its practice, and its content. Its goals are only to advance one in an earthly career, to bring success, not wisdom, and it fosters as well as stems from human pride»[27]. This affirmation highlights Augustine's belief that the danger of education lies in the supposition that it is by man's own effort in his studies that he is able to attain an understanding of his surroundings and gaining insight into the eternal.[28] At this point, the role of education dramatically shifts from a means to conquer and order the society into a way used to instill discipline and limit sin, giving one the chance to mediate on God and realize their need for Him.[29] Thus, Augustine viewed education as a process of inquiry focused on God, in order to lead to a realization of one's own need. Augustine's educational program is aimed at theistic conviction in intellectually cultivated Catholic youth through the instrumentality of Christian philosophy. In this context, the discipline (of education) is valued more than the topics (in education) since it is that which is necessary for salvation. In this sense, we take Howie's suggestion that for Augustine «education is therefore a process in which thought and belief, reason and faith, work together towards the goal of understanding»[30].

We have seen that Augustine's philosophy of education is strongly linked with Christian philosophy. This is evidenced by his application of Christian philosophy to the human formation of youth. According to

---

[26] G. HOWIE, St. Augustine: On Education, 10.

[27] K. PAFFENROTH, «Bad Habits and Bad Company», 8.

[28] «He never wrote with admiration or gratitude about any of his teachers». Cf. H. CHADWICK, Augustine, 7. The peril of education is expressed more dramatically when Augustine says, «If anyone were offered the choice of suffering death or becoming a child again, who would not recoil from the second alternative and choose to die?» [City of God 21, 14]. Cf. AUGUSTINE, City of God (De Civitate De). He has been commenting on the corporal punishments meted out in elementary schools and this statement perfectly demonstrates Augustine's concern about the educational methods of his time.

[29] «Augustine holds the educational system partially responsible for the moral helplessness into which he fell and for his concomitant and resulting gradual alienation from God. Worst of all was the fateful fall into the common attitude of spiritual and intellectual pride with which the system was imbued». Cf. KEVANE, Augustine the Educator, 37.

[30] G. HOWIE, Educational Theory, 52.

E. Kevane, he «rejects the very idea of an educational system resting upon and functioning in terms of an autonomous theoretical basis, as it is called, separate from philosophy as such»[31]. It is in Christian philosophy where the significance and practical values of Augustine's philosophy of education rests.

Throughout the middle of the second and eleventh century A.D., Platonism and Neo-platonism, respectively, were the main philosophical influences on Christian theology. However, during the beginning of the twelfth century the Western world was reintroduced to Aristotle's works. The first thorough Christian critique and assimilation of Aristotle's philosophy into Christian theology was provided by Thomas Aquinas.

While Augustine calls Plato «almost a Christian»,[32] Thomas found no conflict between the ideas of Aristotle and the ideas of Christian revelation. [33] His incorporation of Aristotelian philosophy into the Christian faith at first met with serious consternation and criticism among his disciples. It seemed clear to the saintly doctor that «Aristotle's thought must be assimilated into Christian philosophy»[34], and thus he espoused Aristotelianism as a means for the expression of his [thoroughly Christian] system. Obviously, Thomas' thoughts are stamped with Aristotelian influence.[35]

As in the previous sections, we will not make a detailed investigation of Thomas' educational theory. The aim, which we have before us in this section, is to consider the most representative doctrines of Thomas, which are relevant to his philosophy of education, and to leave aside the innumerable applications of those doctrines, which may be found scattered among his extensive works.

---

[31] E. KEVANE, *Augustine the Educator*, 290-291.

[32] G. HOWIE, *Educational Theory*, 15.

[33] This is obviously manifested by his defense of Aristotle in his work *De unitate intellectus contra Averroistas*. Aside from this, he further showed his preference for Aristotle by writing commentaries about some of his works, for instance, *In libros Perihermeneias expositio, In libros posteriorum Analyticorum expositio, In octo libros Physicorum expositio, In libros de caelo et mundo expositio, In libros de generatione et corruptione expositio* and others.

[34] J. MARÍAS, *History of Philosophy*, 164.

[35] The recognition that Thomas is fundamentally an Aristotelian is not equivalent to the claim that Aristotle is the only influence on him. It is the claim that whatever Thomas takes on from other sources is held to be compatible with what he already holds in common with Aristotle.

There are not only insights or suggestions regarding education in the works of Thomas but there is also a precise philosophical principle on the concept of education. We will find it presented especially in *Quaestiones Disputatae*, vol. 1, (*De Veritate*), q. 11[36] and in *Summa Theologiae*, Ia, *quaestio* 117, art. 1. The views regarding education presented in these works are Thomas' solution to the philosophical problem, which focuses on the question regarding the transmission of determinate knowledge and attitudes, and science in particular, which is «certain knowledge through causes» in the strict and rigorous sense.[37]

Thomas' ideas about education are clearly woven within his epistemology. The problem of knowledge, for Aquinas, ultimately concerns how we come to know God. If this were the case, then to know (seek) God is the ultimate end of education. However, as indicated earlier, Thomas' theory of knowledge as noted by Howie «is founded on the belief that all rational understanding originates in sense perception»[38]. This is undoubtedly a manifestation of the Aristotelian maxim - all our knowledge starts from sense experience. Since experience is the starting point of all learning, it becomes the function of the mind, through what Aquinas terms the «active intellect» (*intellectus agens*), to abstract the universal idea from the particular example. This illustrates that Thomas affirms learning to be a continuous development from particulars to general ideas through abstraction. Thus, knowledge comes to human beings through the activity of the human intellect working upon the raw materials found in the sensible world.[39] It is an autonomous cognitive process, which moves from the senses and consumes itself in the interiority of the individual. In this sense, the method of instruction proposed by Aquinas is inductive; such approach stresses the real importance of sense data. His philosophy of education accentuates the cultivation of both the practical and the speculative knowledge since he believed that proper education should take into account the spiritual and the material natures of the individual. Nevertheless, he strongly favors the primary emphasis on the education of the soul since it is that which is higher and more important.

---

[36] For a more comprehensive exposition of this work, see H. JOHNSTON, *A Philosophy of Education*, Ch. 7.

[37] R. COGGI, *S. Tommaso D'Aquino*, 167.

[38] G. HOWIE, *Educational Theory*, 285.

[39] This undoubtedly expresses St. Thomas' firm faith in the efficacy of secondary, or instrumental, causes. See H. OZMON – S. CRAVER, *Philosophical Foundations of Education*, 54.

Question XI of the *Quaestiones Disputatae* (*De Veritate*) concerns the Teacher. In the first article, Thomas confronts the question whether a man may teach and be a teacher, or whether God alone is the teacher.[40] Aquinas defends the view that one man may truly teach another. Some of the objections he deals with stem from a literal interpretation of biblical passages, «Let no man call you rabbi (teacher)» [*Matthew* 23, 8] and some are *semiotic* in the sense that one man cannot show others his knowledge except through signs, but to know a sign is not the same thing as knowing the thing signified by the sign.

The teacher, according to Aquinas, is actually the cause of learning when he intervenes to give systematic instruction. In doing this, he actualizes the learner's active potentiality for knowledge.[41] This implies that for Thomas the natural process of learning occurs when the mind applies common principles that are self-evident (*per se nota*) to the particular circumstances (*ad determinatas materias*). In schooling (*disciplina*), the teacher guides the learner along the steps in the movement of reason. The teacher employs signs, symbols and the techniques of encouragement, which serve as tools in order to motivate and direct the student.

Since the light of reason is required in learning and since God is the source of this light, thus it follows that God alone teaches us from within. God is the primary teacher. However, with the above-mentioned arguments, Thomas affirms that teachers, as part of the stimulus of the physical environment, effectively play an important role in providing systematic instruction. The appeal of Thomas' views on teaching and learning lies in the fact that they are consonant with the commonsense view that learning begins with particulars and advances by a continuous investigative advancement without any need for a transition from learning through sense perception to the process of pure thought.

With the views of Augustine and Aquinas regarding education we have seen how Christian philosophy and Christian doctrine played a crucial role in shaping the medieval philosophy of education. We have

---

[40] «Et primo quaeritur, utrum homo possit docere et dici magister, vel solus Deus». *Quaestiones Disputatae*, 1, (*De Veritate*), q. 11, art. 1.

[41] According to Thomas, knowledge is built upon previous knowledge, and he recognizes that there is within our minds the beginning of the so-called "seeds of knowledge" (*scientiarum semina*) – these are the first conceptions of the mind (*primae conceptiones intellectus*). These are known right away by the light of the active mind when it is first presented with mental images abstracted from the senses.

also observed that although Augustine and Thomas used different approaches in the development of their educational views. While Augustine leaned heavily on the Platonic, spiritual side in the development of his educational views, Thomas, on the contrary, favored the Aristotelian dualistic doctrine of reality with his recognition of the material and the spiritual side of humankind. However, their ultimate end was the perfection of the human being and the ultimate reunion of the soul with God. Thus, we can conclude that it is mainly the growth of Christian philosophy, which enriched the distinctively theocentric character of medieval educational philosophy.

Having determined the nature of the educational enterprise during the Middle Ages let us now extend our enquiry about the development of philosophy of education from the sixteenth to the eighteenth centuries – the age of Enlightenment.

1.3 *Modern Philosophy of Education*

The conventional inception of the so-called *modern* period in the history of philosophy can be arbitrarily identified with the rise of the scientific revolution in the fifteenth and sixteenth centuries. The Modern era is viewed as having demolished of the assumptions, the methods, and the language, which had been the common property of philosophers since the early Middle Ages. This period is also commonly known as the age of enlightenment. Modern philosophy seeks for the meaning of nature and experience. It tries to elude from the authority of tradition and to avoid involvement in ecclesiastical dogmas and religious belief, i.e., philosophy nursed in the fire of science. This noticeable change in the intellectual climate has impacted upon the current society, which obviously includes the field of education.

Here, we shall consider the character of educational philosophy in the period of enlightenment with reference to the views of John Locke and Jean-Jacques Rousseau. These thinkers have written seminal works, which provide valuable insights into the sixteenth-to-the-eighteenth-century educational spectrum.

John Locke is considered the foremost English philosopher of the early period of post-Cartesian philosophy. He wrote extensively – not only on diverse branches of philosophy but also on education, economics, theology and medicine. He is famous for his works *Treatises of Government* (1690) and *An Essay Concerning Human Understanding* (1690). However, it is in his book entitled *Some Thoughts Concerning*

Education (1693)[42] that we find Locke's noteworthy views. Consequently, our enquiry into Locke's philosophy of education will be taken from the ideas presented in this book.

As one of the proponents of British empiricism, John Locke was primarily interested in the extent and certainty of human knowledge. His epistemology is rooted in the concrete, practical, rather than abstract idealisms. In *An Essay Concerning Human Understanding*, he set out to defend a naturalistic account of mental life and a reductionistic strategy for studying and explaining that life. He developed arguments against theories of innate ideas, insisting that the mind becomes furnished solely by way of experience. He believed that the mind was a *tabula rasa* (a blank slate) upon which ideas are imprinted. Hence, what we know is derived from experience by way of sensation and reflection. Based on this line of argument, Locke affirmed that perception is the only mode of knowledge by which we are able to know the natural world and things that have real existence. Neither intuition nor demonstration can provide such knowledge.[43]

The aforementioned arguments indicate why Locke considered education an important activity that deserved careful attention: education helped to fill the blank slate with knowledge and morals. He is convinced that moral education is more important than other kinds of education. In *Some Thoughts Concerning Education*, the goal of education, according to Locke, is to create a virtuous man, i.e., a person who obeys reason instead of passion. Education should aim to instill what he calls the principle of virtue. According to Locke, the *principle of virtue* is the capacity to deny one's own desires, where reason does not authorize them. If someone has this, and exercises this capacity, he will be virtuous, and if one lacks this capacity or fails to exercise it, he cannot be virtuous. Education should cultivate this quality. He wanted such an education to create the archetype of a gentleman: a rationally think-

---

[42] This book originated from a series of letters, which he wrote (ca. 1684) from the Netherlands to advise a friend, Edward Clarke, on his son's education. After his return to England, Locke expanded this material into the book, which first appeared in 1693.

[43] Some things that are known are known immediately, without deliberation, and are known not only to be true but to be universally and necessarily true; e.g., the law of contradiction. Such knowledge is by way of *intuition* (intuitive knowledge). Some things are known to be universally and necessarily true, but this is ascertained only after developing the required arguments leading to this conclusion, e.g., the major proofs in Euclid's geometry. Such is called demonstrative knowledge – it requires *demonstration*.

ing, morally dependable, socially capable person. Here, we begin to see the shift from the theocentric attitude of the Middle Ages to the anthropocentric character of education of the modern period.[44]

As both empiricist and realist, Locke supports the lecture method and other formal ways of teaching. He insists that in teaching the method used should be characterized by the integrity that comes from systematic, organized, and dependable knowledge since through it an efficient, structured, and orderly process that education can accomplish its goals.

He places considerable importance on the role of the teacher (or the tutor) in the educational process. Locke claims that the most important qualities in a teacher are virtue, good breeding, and knowledge of the world. The teacher, according to Locke, need not be a scholar. He only needs to give his student the tools and the inclination that will allow him to study further on his own. The teacher should not bombard the child with rules because it is counterproductive. Locke stresses instead the importance of habit and example in education.[45]

For Locke learning should be enjoyable. His treasure-trove of advice contained in the book is almost single-mindedly geared toward making the experience of education as pleasant as possible for the child. The practical reason for this type of education is that it makes the learning process much more effective. The key to making learning pleasant is to make sure that it is never seen as a task or duty. If children are not forced to learn, but come to it of their will, then they will apply the same high-spirited energy that we see in their play, to their learning. The only sad thing is that Locke allows little importance to school learning. Nevertheless, he emphasized the importance of environment and conditioning in the formation of youthful character and capacity,

---

[44] During the age of enlightenment, much attention was directed towards the human condition. Locke continues to move within this sphere of attention and tries to answer questions such as what is a human being? How does it differ from other species? What are the limits of human potential? He admits that one becomes moral through education – humans have no innate ideas of God, no innate moral truths, no natural inclination towards virtue. He defined man as both rational and moral. See J. W. YOLTON, *John Locke and the Way of Ideas*, 26, 27. Locke's denial of innate ideas puts a premium on individual effort, on the labor necessary to gain knowledge from experience. See N. TARCOV, *Locke's Education for Liberty*, 83.

[45] Locke points out that children rarely understand rules, and that they cannot remember too many at a time. The child either will end up being punished constantly, then giving up on the attempt to be good, or else the rules will not be enforced, and the child will lose his respect for authority. See M. CRANSTON, *John Locke*, 16.

views that may well be taken for granted today, but which impressed some of Locke's adverse critics as innovative.

Another prominent figure in the eighteenth century whose philosophical views held great importance for education was Jean-Jacques Rousseau. His ideas have influenced subsequent generations of educational thinkers. They have even permeated the practice of informal educators. Rousseau is better known for his contributions to political philosophy in his *Social Contract*,[46] which is considered his masterpiece. However, his principal views regarding education are found in *Emile*. It is a middle way between a novel and a pedagogical treatise. It speaks about the formative journey of Emile from infancy to the adult age. He is guided by a preceptor, the same Jean-Jacques, who starts from the presupposition that the child is not a small man obtained almost differently from an adult, an imperfect being, an empty vase to be filled up with knowledge and ideas. He is instead a being in itself already complete who possesses, in potency, a series of particular characteristics, which the master will have to help develop, being careful not to interfere directly and authoritatively on its experiences. The fulcrum of the educational action moves therefore from the master to the student, who becomes a subject, not anymore an object of the formative process.[47] Thus, we shall limit our discussion to his proposals for education contained in the book.

The focus of *Emile* is upon the individual instruction of a boy in line with the principles of natural education. Rousseau made, it can be argued, the first comprehensive attempt to describe a system of education according to what he saw as nature.[48] He stresses wholeness and harmony, and a concern for the person of the learner. Central to this was the idea that it was possible to preserve the «original perfect nature» of

---

[46] «In that he argues for a version of sovereignty of the whole citizen body over itself, expressing its legislative intent through the general will, which is supposed to apply to all equally because it comes from all alike. The "general will" tends to promote liberty and equality, in Rousseau's view, and it both arises from and promotes a spirit of fraternity». N. DENT, «Rousseau, Jean-Jacques», 780.

[47] The essential spirit of Rosseau's project is to ground Emile's education in Nature and to aim it toward freedom, a freedom to enter with others into social and civic association, a freedom to obey self-imposed laws. A method of education that would minimize the damage by noticing, encouraging, and following the natural proclivities of the student instead of striving to eliminate them. For further discussion regarding the contents of this book see *Emile*, translated by Allan Bloom; see also M. NICHOLS, «Rousseau's Novel Education» and WILLIAM BOYD, *Emile for Today*.

[48] Cf. W.A. STEWART – W. P. MCCANN, *The Educational Innovators*, 28.

the child by means of careful control of his education and environment, based on an analysis of the different physical and psychological stages through which he passed from birth to maturity. This emphasis was essential. Rousseau argued that the impetus for learning was provided by the growth of the person and that what the educator needed to do was to aid opportunities for learning. He however promoted a personal, loving bond between the teacher and the student.[49]

One of Rousseau's major contributions is the link he establishes between nature and experience.[50] His «emphasis on the place of naturalism in education», Ozmon notes, «has affected the way pragmatic educators view the child. Children are no longer seen as miniature adults, but as organisms going through various stages of development»[51]. The attention given by Rousseau to the nature of child growth and his conviction of the intrinsic goodness of people set the stage for the present-day child-centered education. His pedagogy is developmental and follows nature since he believed that it dictates a sequence of development for children. Education practically aims at developing the interests of children - their innate propensity to discover the world in which they live. It strives to help secure the ultimate goal of human life - happiness. In this sense, education should cultivate the physiological, psychological, and social developmental stages of childhood. It must eventually prepare the child for society, although not as society is presently structured.

It is evident that in the educational philosophy of the modern era, particularly that of Rousseau and Locke the ideal of the individual person (be it an adult or a child) is established. Education based on their proposed ideas should strive to bring about concrete development of the power of human reason, especially when linked with empirical methods of inquiry, in order to achieve the improvement of the human condition. Enlightenment writers on education tended to look away

---

[49] This bond will be the bedrock, the indispensable prerequisite, for any real education. Rousseau was willing to go further in cultivating this bond: the tutor takes as his job the raising of one child from infancy to adulthood. This implies that for Rousseau students must be tutored at home rather than sent to school, given the corrupted condition of French social institutions, that the natural order of human development dictated that attention to reflective thinking must not come too soon.

[50] «Certainly, his connection of nature and experience has influenced many educational theorists, including Johann H. Pestalozzi, Friedrich Fröbel, Francis W. Parker, G. Stanley Hall, and John Dewey». H. OZMON – S. CRAVER, *Philosophical Foundations of Education*, 124.

[51] H. OZMON – S. CRAVER, *Philosophical Foundations of Education*, 124.

from the rigor of ecclesiastical ideals for the advancement of education. They had little faith in the capability of the religious establishment to provide the kind of education they thought appropriate to modernity. The mindset that posed questions about natural laws of human nature and society tended to turn attention away from traditional theological accounts of the human condition and focused attention rather on questions concerning the observable environments in which people lived. However, this view is obviously tempered by the presence of the Catholic School movement spearheaded by the Jesuits during this period.

This kind of discourse, rooted in the Enlightenment of the eighteenth century, has determined the outlook of education and the educational system to the present day. Even the diversity of reactions provoked by this debate in the course of the nineteenth and twentieth century, can only be fully understood when seen in the light of Modernism. According to the Enlightenment ideal, education entailed developing one's natural aptitude. This could be realized by controlling the instincts of nature and focusing on reason. Modern philosophy of education moved away from purely religious teaching to an emphasis on the individual and the development of one's ideas and knowledge.

1.4 Contemporary Philosophy of Education

We have demonstrated that during the Age of Enlightenment in the eighteenth century, through the ideas of John Locke and Jean-Jacques Rousseau, important changes in education and educational theory emerged. Educators believed that people could improve their lives and society by using their reason and their powers of critical thinking. The significant impact of these ideas is still present in our current educational practice.

The years that followed the *Age of Reason* manifested numerous developments in the field of education.[52] There are many implications of these advances in educational theory and practice, but space permits us to outline only a few of noteworthy ones. Thus, we shall limit our discussion to the novelties of the twentieth century educational philosophy

---

[52] These developments are represented by the ideas of the nineteenth and twentieth century educational thinkers such as Heinrich Pestalozzi, Johann Herbart, Friedrich Fröbel, Montessori and others. See J.H. PESTALOZZI, *How Gertrude Teaches her Children* and F. FRÖBEL, *The Education of Man*.

particularly those contained in the ideas of John Dewey and Paulo Freire.[53]

John Dewey was an American philosopher and educator whose writing and teachings have had a profound impact on education especially within the United States. His philosophical orientation can be characterized as a kind of pragmatism or more specifically a naturalistic empiricism. His books *Democracy & Education* and *Experience & Nature* contain the bulk of his fundamental philosophical notions. Dewey formed a view of experience wherein action, enjoyment, and what he called *undergoing* were integrated and equally fundamental. This notion of experience is closely connected to his idea of nature. He conceived nature as a developing system of natural transactions admitting of a tripartite distinction between the physiochemical level, the psychophysical level, and the level of human experience. Here, Dewey followed Rousseau's lead in assessing the significance of nature in education. In this sense, although the object remained the individual, Dewey's philosophy of education takes a practical orientation. His chief concern was with the growth of practical knowledge in the development of critical knowledge.[54] He considers ideas as instruments in the solution of human problems; philosophy is thus designated as instrumentalism.[55] This is focused on *learning-by-doing* rather than rote learning and dogmatic instruction, which was the current practice of his day.

The major aim of education, according to Dewey, is to encourage children, as individuals, to continue their lifelong education as cognitive and overall growth.[56] Education is a social necessity.[57] It con-

---

[53] For a biography of John Dewey see G. DYKHUIZEN, *The Life and Mind of John Dewey*. For Paulo Freire see E. COLLINS, *Paulo Freire: His Life, Works and Thought*.

[54] This is described clearly in his work *How We Think*. Cf. J. DEWEY, *How We Think*.

[55] H. OZMON – S. CRAVER, *Philosophical foundations of education*, 131-132.

[56] «Growth for him was not growth in *any* direction which would be consistent with his claim that desirable growth is that which permits more growth; it is rather growth in practical critical thought, which opens up the possibility of more control of the environment». See R.S. PETERS, «John Dewey's philosophy of education», 106. J. DEWEY, *Democracy and Education*, Ch. 4.

[57] «Although Dr. Dewey's philosophy of education is consistently naturalistic, it is most widely known for its emphasis on the social. Many consider Dr. Dewey's social interpretation of education his most distinctive contribution to educational theory. This suggests that a thoroughgoing naturalistic point of view is wholly compatible with high regard for the distinctively human, or social. Indeed, Dr. Dewey's emphasis

stitutes a natural and social process that permits human society to maintain and transmit its beliefs, ideas and knowledge. Dewey views education as guidance.[58] It fosters the continuous reconstruction of growth of experience.[59]

John Dewey's focus on education constituted a unique element in his philosophical thinking and writing. Although he did not coin the phrase progressive education, it has come to be associated with him.[60] He believed that schools should teach students how to be problem-solvers by helping them learn how to think rather than simply learning by rote lessons about vast areas of information. The main task of the teacher (adult educator) is to evaluate the experience of the young, i.e., to understand both their attitudes and tendencies and the directions that such tendencies are taking. He must see to it that the maximum potential number of ideas acquired by children and youth are obtained in such a fundamental way that they become seminal ideas with the force of movement in the guidance of conduct.[61]

In Dewey's view, schools should focus on judgment rather than knowledge so that schoolchildren become adults who can, according to Campbell, «pass judgments pertinently and discriminatingly on the problems of human living»[62]. In this sense, methods in education are considered arrangements of subject matter, which make it most effec-

---

on the social is the correlative of his emphasis on the natural. The social, according to Dr. Dewey, provides the natural bridge from behavior that is organic to behavior that is distinctively human. We can better appreciate the significance of his social theory of education when we view it as the natural out-growth of the empirical view of man and nature». P.A. SCHILPP, ed., *The Philosophy of John Dewey*, 435.

[58] D. M. DELANEY, SDB, *The Philosophical Presuppositions*, 121.

[59] J. DEWEY, *Democracy and Education*, Ch. 1.

[60] During most of the twentieth century, the term *progressive education* has been used to describe ideas and practices that aim to make schools more effective agencies of a democratic society. The education of engaged citizens, according to this perspective, involves two essential elements: (1) *Respect for diversity*, meaning that each individual should be recognized for his or her own abilities, interests, ideas, needs, and cultural identity, and (2) the development of *critical, socially engaged intelligence*, which enables individuals to understand and participate effectively in the affairs of their community in a collaborative effort to achieve a common good. These elements of progressive education have been termed *child-centered* and *social reconstructionist* approaches, and while in extreme forms, they have sometimes been separated, in the thought of John Dewey and other major theorists they are seen as being necessarily related to each other.

[61] J. DEWEY, *Moral Principles in Education*, 2.

[62] J. CAMPBELL, *Understanding John Dewey*, 215-216.

tive in use and not something outside of the material. His concept of participation lies at the bottom of this claim.

Dewey's contribution to the development of education in the twentieth century has been incalculable. His greatest contribution has been to liberate the education of children from traditional education and forged a philosophy of education that emphasizes the merging of the individual with contemporary industrial and social progress.[63]

Another important figure in the contemporary educational ambience is the Brazilian educator Paulo Reglus Neves Freire. He advocated a novel idea, which has impressed informal educators: emphasis on dialogue and his concern for the oppressed. His philosophy of education, as presented in his famous work *Pedagogy of the Oppressed*, is not viewed as a simple method but rather an organic political consciousness.

Freire is best-known for his attack on what he called the banking concept of education, in which the student was viewed as an empty account to be filled by the teacher.[64] He considers education as a deeply political project oriented toward the transformation of society. It is to be the path to permanent liberation. The first stage is that by which people become aware of their oppression and through praxis transform that state. The second stage builds upon the first and is a permanent process of liberating cultural action. For Freire, authentic education is always a practice of freedom rather than an alienating inculcation of skills. He believed that education could improve the human condition, counteracting the effects of a psychology of oppression, and ultimately contributing to what he considered the ontological vocation of humankind - humanization. With this conception of education, Freire promotes the dialogical approach, while neutralizing the teacher-student dichotomy.[65]

---

[63] See D. DELANEY, *The Philosophical Presuppositions*, 123.

[64] The *Banking Concept* is more hurtful than helpful to those involved both teachers and students. In this system, where students are the depositories of knowledge and teachers are the depositors, students memorize instead of understanding concepts. See P. FREIRE, *Pedagogy of the Oppressed*.

[65] The dialogical approach to learning is characterized by co-operation and acceptance of interchangeability and mutuality in the roles of teacher and learner, demanding an atmosphere of mutual acceptance and trust. In this method, all teach and all learn. Without dialogue, there is no communication, and without communication, there can be no liberatory education. Such dialogue, in Freire's approach, centers upon the learners' existential situations and leads not only to their acquisition of liter-

Regarding the nature of learning, Freire describes the fallacy of looking at the education system like a bank, a large repository where students come to withdraw the knowledge they need for life. Knowledge is never a fixed commodity that is passed from teachers to students. Students must construct knowledge from whatever knowledge they already possess. Teachers must learn how the students understand the world so that the teacher understands how the student can learn. Thus, in this sense, teaching is conceived of as a political process. It must engage in a democratic process to avoid teaching authority dependence. The teacher must learn about (and from) the student so that knowledge can be constructed in ways that are meaningful to the student. Teachers must become learners and the learners must become teachers. What Freire advocates here is the idea of a *liberatory* education.

This kind of education is mutually supported learning for empowerment. Whatever its formal structure or precise purpose, such education is a component of and subordinate to a *liberatory* praxis which seeks to transform the social order. This is one of Freire's renowned contributions to twentieth century philosophy of education. Transforming actions in aggregate comprise a revolutionary stance, which simultaneously announces an egalitarian, participatory, and democratic social order and denounces hierarchical, authoritarian, and alienating systems of organizations. The content of this type of education is both critical consciousness[66] and the development of appropriate skills and competencies related to praxis. Its process is dialogical, affirming the mutual and coequal roles of teachers and learners. The governance of liberatory education reflects and anticipates the social order announced by its vision.

Contemporary philosophy of education evidently highlights the integration of the individual within the social context. The emphasis on the significant role of the socio-political system in the field of education

---

acy skills, but also, and more importantly, to their awareness of their right as human beings to transform reality. See P. FREIRE, «The Adult Literacy Process», 480-498.

[66] This is a level of consciousness characterized by depth in the interpretation of problems, through testing one's own findings with openness to revision, attempting to avoid distortion when perceiving problems and preconceived notions when analyzing them, receptivity to the new without rejecting the old because it is old. In striving toward critical consciousness, the individual rejects passivity, practicing dialogue rather than polemics, and using permeable, interrogative, restless, and dialogical forms of life. Critical consciousness is brought about not through an individual or intellectual effort, but through collective struggle and praxis.

has made a number of important theoretical innovations that have had a considerable impact on the development of the twentieth century educational practice.

After our investigation, albeit a concise one, we were able to trace historically the prevalent characteristics of philosophy of education, viz., the cosmocentric, theistic (theocentric), anthropocentric, and the social features. With this fact, we are now going to elaborate on the three basic concepts of education, viz., teaching, learning and the community.

2. The Teaching Activity

2.1 The Concept of Teaching

Educational discourse embodies instances of teaching. We, therefore, shall attempt in this part of the chapter to develop a descriptive rather than a normative concept of teaching. We shall also consider other themes that pertain to such activity, such as, its relation to learning, its aim, and its application of various methods in order to attain such goal.

In any conceptual analysis, it might seem natural, even compulsory, to commence with a definition. John Passmore, however, points out that, «the word "teaching", like most other words in regular daily use, does not have sharply defined limits». He further adds that it «is a deeply-rooted word, with a long history; it has a multitude of idiomatic applications; these cannot be summed up in a definition which will give us the "essence" or the "real meaning" of teaching»[67]. In Wittgensteinian terminology, the concept of teaching is «a blurred picture».[68] Though this may be the case, we should not discount the fact that we need to have a working definition if we want to talk sensibly and clearly about teaching. We need to stress, however, that our concern here is not to provide an explicit definition but only to investigate certain elements of the accepted meaning in order to understand the concept better.

Israel Scheffler offers a particularly plausible description. Accordingly, «teaching may be characterized as an activity aimed at the achievement of learning, and practiced in such a manner as to respect

---

[67] J. PASSMORE, *The Philosophy of Teaching*, 19-20.

[68] The concept of teaching is broad and general. It has different modes, e.g., training, imparting, explanation and different methods, e.g., lecture, discussion, or demonstration. See C.J.B. MACMILLAN, «Rational Teaching», 418.

the student's intellectual integrity and capacity for independent judgment»[69]. This definition does not claim to exhaust the meaning of the concept. However, it provides us with key ideas, viz., it is an activity,[70] it involves an interaction between a teacher and a learner and it aims for the attainment of learning. In our enquiry, let us pose two questions: How do we qualify the activity of teaching? Is it an activity reducible to professional teaching? These questions will serve as guidelines in order for us not to miss the wood for the trees.

There are diverse approaches to the idea but in ordinary usage, the term *teaching* or *to teach*, implies a certain mode of action, which is characterized by a particular intention.[71] The standard teaching claim appears like this: Alex teaches Latin to Mary, or to put it in a philosophical quasi-algebra: X teaches A to Y. X and Y slots usually take words for people while A carries the *subject* or the *content* of what is taught. In this case, such activity is characterizable as intentional, i.e., it is undertaken with the purpose of bringing about learning.[72] A fundamental requirement then in teaching is intentionality – a goal-oriented activity;[73] any person who claims to be teaching must intend to achieve learning in the one he claims to teach.[74] John McNeill asserts, it «is cor-

---

[69] I. SCHEFFLER, *Reason and Teaching*, 67, italics added.

[70] It is a concrete and particular activity in the sense that the process of teaching constitutes sequences of acts and events, which may have datable beginnings or ends. It is an enterprise, which we undertake or in which we are engaged. See P. KOMISAR, «Teaching: Act and Enterprise», 168-193. T.W. Moore opposes to this idea when he says, «For one thing, the word "teaching" is not the name of any one activity. Teaching may involve many different kinds of activities: talking, asking questions, writing on blackboard, setting up situations in which pupils can learn, and many others». T.W. MOORE, *Philosophy of education: an introduction*, 67.

[71] G. FENSTERMACHER – J. SOLTIS, *Approaches to Teaching*, 1-49.

[72] «Teaching necessarily involves the intention that someone should learn as a result of what one does». T.W. MOORE, *Philosophy of education: an introduction*, 67. See also D. P. ERICSON – F. S. ELLET, JR., «Teacher Accountability and the Causal Theory of Teaching», 277; D. KERR – J. SOLTIS, «Locating Teacher Competency: An Action Description of Teaching», 6.

[73] Scheffler underlines «teaching, as normally understood, is an activity, requiring effort and allowing for the exercise and development of proficiency, and oriented toward a goal that may lie beyond any segment of it». Israel Scheffler, «A concept of Teaching», 22. See also I. SCHEFFLER, «The Concept of Teaching», 261.

[74] Some have tried to argue, contrary to this ordinary understanding, that a teacher's goal of bringing about learning is but one desire of teaching and, as such, is not essential to teaching. For further discussion on this position see P. KOMISAR, «Teaching: Act and Enterprise», 168-193.

rectly understood as activity done with the intention to bring about learning, and that for some teaching acts though learning doesn't occur, fulfillment of intention does»[75]. This indicates that the necessary and sufficient condition of the activity is the intention to attain learning on the part of another.[76] J. Passmore claims, «"teaching", it would seem, sometimes means "aiming at achieving learning" and sometimes means "actually achieving learning", is sometimes an attempt-word and sometimes a success-word»[77]. Thus, we must be careful not to equate and reduce teaching to a mere «intention to teach».[78] We need to stress here that «as an activity, teaching can be best understood not as a single activity, but as a whole family of activities within which some members appear to be of more central significance than others»[79]. If this were the case, then *teaching*, contrary to the presupposition of most twentieth century educational literature, is not an activity that exclusively takes place inside the classroom.[80] Having thus qualified the activity, let us now discuss another blurring topic, i.e., concerning the teaching act and professional teaching.

Since *teaching* is not exclusive to classroom setting, it is also not restricted to professional teachers. Although it can become an occupation, the professional teacher is not the sole person responsible for such an activity. Passmore claims, «"anybody can teach" is a true statement;

---

[75] J. McNeill, «Recognizing Teaching», 93.

[76] Cf. G. Moran, *Showing How*, 35. See also N.L. Gage, *The Scientific Basis*, 20.

[77] J. Passmore, *The Philosophy of Teaching*, 20.

[78] «If teaching is reduced to intention, then the verb *to teach* and the noun *teaching* are left without any intrinsic connection. That is, what one intends as teaching (the verb), is not necessarily what results as teaching (the noun)». G. Moran, *Showing How*, 37; Moran claims that the way to this equation is «to say that teaching is the showing how in the process of teaching-learning». *Ibid.*, 41.

[79] Training and instruction are included among these activities, i.e., they are not considered equal to teaching but form part of the teaching process. T. F. Green, «A Topology of the Teaching Concept», 30, 57. For an analysis of the concept *training* see H. Schofield, *The Philosophy of Education*. See also M. Uljens, *School Didactics and Learning*, 15.

[80] Current literature that deals with teaching usually treats it only within the classroom. If we maintain this, a discussion on teaching cannot draw upon a contrast of what teachers do in classrooms and what they do in other settings for teaching. For instance, the dichotomy between parents and teachers is, according to Moran, «the denial of a central activity of the parent, namely, to teach». G. Moran, *Showing How*, 5. «When teaching is equated with classroom instruction in a school, what disappear are not only most kinds of teaching but also the language, imagery, and techniques in improving classroom instruction itself». *Ibid.*, 3.

little though professional teachers may like to admit that fact. Not only can anybody try to teach, but anybody can succeed in teaching, something to somebody»[81]. However, we need to distinguish two propositions «everybody can teach something to somebody» and «everybody can teach anything to anybody». The second proposition is false and that is what justifies the existence of the profession in education. Though this is the case, McNeill posits, «it is not the uniqueness of the pre- and post-assessment acts to the teaching profession that constitutes them as teaching acts. Some teaching acts may be unique to professional teachers, but teaching acts are not»[82]. Thus, it is not reducible to professional teaching. It follows from our arguments that the subject of the act *per se* is not necessarily a human being.[83]

We have indicated previously that such an activity intends to achieve learning. This means that, although there are other goals of teaching the principal aim of teaching is learning.[84] In this case, we could say that nobody is supposed to be teaching if what he was doing were in no way connected with the aim of teaching. It is not our intention here to elaborate on the topic of learning. This issue will be dealt with in the next part of this chapter. Nonetheless, we need to discuss the relationship between teaching and learning. This will be the subject of the succeeding section.

---

[81] J. PASSMORE, *The Philosophy of Teaching*, 25.

[82] J. MCNEILL, «Recognizing Teaching and some Related Acts», 99.

[83] The terms *to teach* and *teaching* need to be situated as the activities of *teachers*. But one should not presume without hesitation that the *teacher* is necessarily an individual human being. Cf. G. MORAN, *Showing How*, 7, 43-50. Passmore claims, «When we see somebody performing a complex task, we tend automatically to presume that someone has taught him to do it; if we cannot find a human teacher we substitute "nature"». J. PASSMORE, *The Philosophy of Teaching*, 24.

[84] The objectives of teaching extend far beyond the subject matter being taught. Essentially, teaching aims at developing well-integrated people who are capable of undertaking a responsible, independent, and active role in society. Teaching objectives extend from intellectual abilities and cognition (social insight) to psychomotor learning (learning practical skills) and affective learning (development of emotions, attitudes, morals, and values).

2.2 Teaching and Learning

Although the tradition of studying teaching and learning as separate disciplines results in knowledge that fails to capture the reciprocal and interactive influence that each has on the other, both are of central importance to education.[85] The belief that teaching necessarily entails learning is widely held.[86] We frequently assimilate it to learning. However, the supposed links between these two events remain controversial. Learning is conceptually independent of teaching. This is evidenced by the fact that learning can occur outside the teaching situation.[87] If this is the case, then we can say that teaching, although it aims to obtain learning, is an activity that does not necessarily result in learning, i.e., there is no logical relation between both concepts.[88] Nonetheless, successful teaching does imply learning.[89] The fact that there is a logical relationship between successful teaching and learning, however, does not allow us to conclude crudely that there is a logical relation between teaching and learning.[90] Aside from the problem of logical relation, teaching and learning also solicit the predicament of causal relation. Regarding this issue Allen Pearson provides a plausible analysis.[91] He says, «to talk about the logical relation between teaching and learning is, then, to talk about relations that might exist between the concepts of teaching and learning. To talk of a causal relation between teaching and learning is to talk about relations that might exist between specific instances of

---

[85] Cf. T. J. SHUELL, «Toward an Integrated Theory», 291-311. See also A. PEARSON, *The Teacher*, 78ff.

[86] Like the famous adage, «teaching and learning are two sides of the same coin». Cf. A. S. LARDIZABAL – A. S. BUSTOS – *al.*, *Principles and Methods of Teaching*, 19. See also J. BROPHY – C. EVERTSON, *Learning from Teaching*.

[87] To learn our native language is a great intellectual achievement. Yet this is typically not an outcome of a teaching situation. A child picks up language through interaction and practice within a linguistic community.

[88] This is what is known as the *standard thesis* presented by Israel Scheffler and B. Othanel Smith. See N. NODDINGS, *Philosophy of Education*, 46.

[89] Successful teaching is characterized when students do in fact learn what is being taught by one who teaches. This can be attributed to one's teaching.

[90] D. P. ERICSON – F. S. ELLET, JR., «Teacher Accountability», 286. See also A. T. PEARSON, *The Teacher*, 78-85.

[91] I consider his analysis between the logical and causal relation as well as the ontological relation between teaching and learning, as suitable for the understanding of the polemic that lies between teaching and learning. Cf. A. T. PEARSON, «Teaching, Learning and Ontological Dependence». See also J. A. POPP, *Naturalizing Philosophy of education*, 113-127.

teaching and learning. The point to note is that in the two cases we are talking about different things. To the question, then, of whether relation between teaching and learning is logical or causal, my simple answer is: Yes»[92]. We agree with this point based on the arguments presented. Hence, the concepts of teaching and learning, though they may be independent activities, do entail a certain relation. In the classroom and other instructional settings, teaching and learning occur simultaneously and are experienced by students as an integrated unit with cognitive, affective, motivational, and developmental factors all contributing to the educational experience.

2.3 *The Question on Method(s) in Teaching*

Teachers who stress on the technical nature of teaching tend to emphasize on the science of teaching. Although there are diverse ways in which a scientific approach is vital, too much emphasis on the science of teaching would depersonalize the teaching and learning process. In this sense, a consideration of teaching methods is significant.

We have stressed in the preceding sections that there are three important factors in the educative process, viz., the teacher, the learner and the subject matter. The teacher is necessary to guide the learner. He employs a method (or methods) in order to achieve the goals of teaching. Here, method is understood as the teacher's systematic procedure of getting the subject matter across to the learner.[93] The importance of method lies in the fact that it is indispensable in the attainment of the aim of the teaching activity. The status of a method in some sense will cause or bring about the state of affairs that constitute the goal, which is learning.[94]

Just as there are many ways people learn, e.g., attention, memory, perception, concept formation, etc., there are many different teaching methods. It is the task of the teacher to choose what methods are suitable for a particular goal, i.e., they should be chosen carefully to fit the activity. Thus, the method applied is determined by the goal, which it aims to achieve. In doing so, the teacher can utilize the aid of devices. Although teachers can use the same method and devices, they may differ in their techniques.

---

[92] A. T. PEARSON, «Teaching, Learning and Ontological Dependence», 285.
[93] P. HIRST, «The logical and psychological aspects», 58.
[94] Cf. D. KERR – J. SOLTIS, «Locating Teacher Competency», 7-9.

The fact that there exists a variety of teaching methods indicates that teachers have recognized that there is an increasing diversity of ways of approaching their task. It provides teaching with a degree of flexibility that could be utilized in cases of epistemological changes. Thus, a scientific approach to teaching and the wise use of different teaching methods are important factors in teaching.

3. The Learning Process

3. 1 *What is learning?*

In this section, we shall investigate into the learning process. Our enquiry, however, will be delimited to a conceptual analysis of learning.

It becomes evident in recent literature that there is little agreement about what learning actually is. A definition of learning as «knowledge acquired by study» has raised notable reactions from most psychologists because of the imprecise terms it contains.[95] After years of attempting to synthesize learning theory, Kidd went so far as to suggest, «there is no answer to the question "What is learning?" any more than there is to the question "What is electricity?"»[96]

In ordinary use, however, we usually mean by learning one or all of three things: (a) the act of gaining knowledge – «to learn something» (b) the knowledge gained by virtue of that act – «that which is known» and (c) the process of gaining practical knowledge – «learning how»[97]. Here, learning is linked with knowledge. This is the most obvious level of learning - gathering knowledge relevant to a subject in such a way as to be able to use that knowledge from memory. If this were the case, then we can say that the problem of learning is evidently related to epistemology.[98] However, due to the complex nature of the learning process, the appreciation of what it means to know and how we come

---

[95] Cf. R. SMITH, *Learning How to Learn.*

[96] J. R. KIDD, *How Adults Learn*, 23.

[97] Rodney P. Riegle offers another classification of the concept of learning. He classifies learning into propositional learning (following Israel Scheffler's analysis of propositional knowledge), performative learning, and dispositional learning. For further discussion, cf. R. P. RIEGLE, «The Concept of "Learning"», 77-85.

[98] The history of learning is one of the oldest branches of psychology, beginning with the ancient Greeks and epistemology. See B.R. HERGENHAHN – M. OLSON, *An Introduction to Theories of Learning,* 31; MICHAEL ULJENS, *School Didactics and Learning*, 130-132.

to know remains the only significance of the epistemic dimension of learning.

Gregory Kimble defined learning as «a relatively permanent change in behavior potentiality which occurs as a result of reinforced practice»[99]. Here, learning is indexed by a change in behavior, i.e., the results of learning must always be translated into observable behavior. However, not all human changes are considered learning changes[100] nor are they observable. This behavioral change is relatively permanent, i.e., it is neither transitory nor fixed. The change in behavior need not occur immediately following the learning experience. In bringing out *behavior potentiality*, the idea that learning is not merely a change in behavior is underlined. The change results from experience or practice.[101] This experience must be reinforced, i.e., only those responses that lead to reinforcement will be learned. Learning is treated as a fundamental process. According to Lehman, «it is an "intervening variable" between observable stimuli and observable responses»[102]. Kimble's definition clearly does not encompass the whole idea of learning. Nonetheless, it provides a convenient frame of reference for discussing a number of important issues that must be confronted when attempting to understand such a phenomenon.

That learning invokes complex processes of the whole self has been the source of general agreement. According to Smith, it is possible that learning defies precise definition because it describes a product, a process or a function.[103] John Dewey viewed learning in its broadest sense

---

[99] This definition, however, excludes from consideration changes in behavior due to motivational fluctuations, maturation, and various physical and physiological factors. It argues that a distinction between learning and performance must be made. Moreover, it proposes that reinforcement is necessary for learning to occur. GREGORY A. KIMBLE, *Hilgard and Marquis Conditioning and Learning*, 6. Hergenhahn gives a detailed analysis of the elements of Kimble's definition and notes that this popular definition, albeit popular, is not accepted universally. For further details, see B.R. HERGENHAHN – M. OLSON, *An Introduction to Theories of Learning*, 1-7. A similar definition was made by Rita Atkinson et al. They claim that learning «is a relatively permanent change in behavior (sic; it's American of course) that results from practice». See RITA L. ATKINSON – al., *Introduction to Psychology*.

[100] Changes in behavior caused by the advancement in age certainly do not qualify as learning changes. See J. HOUSTON, *Fundamentals of Learning*, 6.

[101] See M. ULJENS, *School Didactics and Learning*, 29-34 and R. GAGNÉ, *The Conditions of Learning*, 1-2.

[102] H. LEHMAN, «Conditioning and Learning», 162.

[103] When it is used as a *product,* the emphasis is on the outcome of the experience. When it is used to describe a *process,* an attempt is made to account for what happens

as an individual and lifelong process. By learning, we are able to extract meaning from a wide range of experiences in order to create meaning and shape future experiences. Learning is a very personalized, complex, and, to some degree, indescribable and virtually self-enclosed process.

3.2 *Theories of Learning*

Due to the complexity of the nature of learning, theorists do not all agree about what learning is and how it happens. Psychologists, anthropologists, neurologists, philosophers, linguists and others are still trying to understand how the mind works and how people come to learn. Evidently, this disagreement accounts for the diversity of theories about learning.

In education and psychology, learning theories help us understand the process of learning by specifying both what is changing through the process of learning and how this change should be described. They have been put forward since the earliest Greek philosophers (Plato and Aristotle). Plato, in the «allegory of the cave» [*Republic*, Bk. 7] portrays an early conception of the learning process. His theory of anamnesis (recollection) also gives us his view on how learning occurs. Aristotle, in particular, in using empirical observations about biological and physical phenomena, theorized that all knowledge was based on sensory experiences that had been processed by the mind. With this emphasis, he had a profound influence on the further development of both educational and psychological theory of learning.

From contemporary literature, major classifications of learning theories have been identified. The scope of this section, however, does not allow for a detailed discussion of all the theories about learning. Thus, we will limit our discussion by outlining two major perspectives in learning theories, viz., the cognitive and the behaviorist.[104]

The behaviorist theory of learning, on the one hand, understands the environment as generative of what can be learned. In this sense, we learn when we are involved in the activities of a community and subse-

---

when a learning experience takes place. When learning is used to describe a *function*, the emphasis is on aspects (such as motivation) which are believed to help "produce" learning. See R. SMITH, *Learning How to Learn*. Regarding learning as a process see R. LINSKIE, *The Learning Process: Theory and Practice*.

[104] For the principles of learning emphasized in cognitive and behavioral psychology cf. J. HARTLEY, *Learning and Studying*, 17-19.

quently develop an identity in the specific community.[105] This theory of learning is grounded on ideas of J.B Watson,[106] E.L. Thorndike[107] and the seminal research of B.F. Skinner[108] and Ivan Pavlov;[109] these last two scientists are well known for their studies in animal behavior. Behaviorists consider learning as a matter of links between stimulus and response (S-R), i.e., they view learning as the result of the stimuli of the environment on the learner. This behaviorist theory of learning is the most commonly practiced because the behaviors of the learners can be easily viewed and therefore measured, a basic premise in the scientific method.

The cognitivist theory of learning, in sharp contrast, construes the learning process as a personal endeavor, where one internalizes concepts, rules and general principles. After one has internalized a specific knowledge, one will be able to apply it in different contexts. This is not to say that environment will not lend shape to concepts previously learned, but its basic content of will not change. Cognitive theorists,

---

[105] In this case, John Dewey's «problem-solving» theory could be placed under this perspective. The basic premise of the «problem-solving» theory is that learning happens because of our «doing» and «experiencing» things in the world as we successfully solve real problems that are genuinely meaningful to us.

[106] Cf. B.R. HERGENHAHN – M. OLSON, *An Introduction to Theories of Learning*, 48-51, 191-194.

[107] Thorndike also thought that people *stamp in* effective S-R connections and *stamp out* those responses, which are useless. He stressed the importance of satisfying and gratifying outcomes from a response so that S-R connections are reinforced whenever satisfying results are apparent. The statement that satisfaction serves to strengthen the S-R bonds is known as the Thorndike's *Law of Effect*. Cf. B.R. HERGENHAHN – M. OLSON, *An Introduction to Theories of Learning*, 57-75; E. THORNDIKE, *Human Learning*.

[108] B.F Skinners theory of operant conditioning is based on the fact that one's behavior will change due to the result of a stimulus in their environment. Reinforcement or rewards are the key thing in this theory however, the reward need to be a physical object it can be praise or a number of things. B.R. HERGENHAHN – M. OLSON, *An Introduction to Theories of Learning*, 80-119.

[109] Pavlov viewed behavior as responses initiated by stimuli. Pavlov's interests, however, were strictly focused on the physiological reflex actions of animals and less relevant in the study of human learning, albeit his studies introduced the process known as *classical conditioning*. Cf. B.R. HERGENHAHN – M. OLSON, *An Introduction to Theories of Learning*, 160-201.

such as J. Piaget[110] and A. Bandura,[111] place greater emphasis on the functioning of the brain, internal mental thinking and the role of experience, which modifies present behavior. We can classify the Gestalt theory of learning under this group since it considers learning as a cognitive phenomenon.[112] While the behaviorists consider learning as continuous, the Gestalt theorists believed learning as discontinuous because a solution is either reached or not.

The above-indicated theories have produced the ongoing dichotomy concerning the nature of the learning process. We must admit that instead of helping us to clarify our conception of it, we are literally torn between two lovers. We need to find out another perspective (but not a theory) to aid us in dissolving this evident dichotomy however maintaining the essential principles presented. The most acceptable candidate would be to consider the learning process in the perspective of fol-

---

[110] Piaget's theory of cognitive development in learning is still considered relevant in today's study of the learning process. He found four major developmental stages (with many subdivisions). For the first year and a half or two years of life, an infant learns by trial and error. The stage from 18-24 months to 7 years Piaget called preoperational, where children can think about things in symbolic terms. From 7 to 12 years, children gain new competence in thinking and are aware of events outside of their lives. From 12 years old and up, people are able to think about abstract relationships (as in algebra), understand methodology, formulate hypotheses, and think about possibilities and abstractions like justice. B.R. HERGENHAHN – M. OLSON, *An Introduction to Theories of Learning,* 274-291.

[111] Bandura considers the claim that one's environment causes one's behavior as too simplistic for the phenomena he was observing (aggression in adolescents) and so decided to modify the formula. He suggested that environment causes behavior, true; but behavior causes environment as well. He labeled this concept *reciprocal determinism.* Later, he went a step further. He began to look at personality as an interaction among three things: the environment, behavior, and the person's psychological processes. These psychological processes consist of our ability to entertain images in our minds, and language. At the point where he introduces *imagery,* in particular, he ceases to be a strict behaviorist, and begins to join the ranks of the cognitivists. Adding imagery and language to the mix allows Bandura to theorize much more effectively than someone like, say, B. F. Skinner, about two things that many people would consider the *strong suit* of the human species observational learning (modeling) and self-regulation.

[112] The Gestalt theory views learning as a process involving the attempt to think things out and then having 'it all come together' suddenly in the mind. Among the proponents of the Gestalt psychology were Wertheimer, Köhler and Koffka. Their most important contribution was their study of *insight.* B.R. HERGENHAHN – M. OLSON, *An Introduction to Theories of Learning,* 246-73.

lowing a particular rule. The value of this claim will become clearer in Chapter IV of this work.

Our discussion about the nature of the learning process and the diverse learning theories outlined above show that learning is relevant not only to the educational enterprise but also to human existence, to that fundamental aspect of humanity, that separates us from other species. According to Frank Smith, «learning is what happens as a consequence of rich and varied experience, and the worst way to learn is to isolate yourself from the world and other people»[113]. Not only a communal dimension critical to teaching and learning, it adds sociability to the educational progress. We shall examine the importance of community and its role in the educational process in the next section.

4. Community

4.1 *General View of a Community*

The word community has acquired certain connotations, some of which are idealistic and evocative, some critical and intransigent. However, since we intend to deal with the basics, we shall confine our discussion to the most fundamental meanings of the word *community*.

The first step in considering the meaning of community is to understand that, fundamentally, it is a fluid concept.[114] What one person calls a *community* may not match another person's definition.[115] From this perspective, it must be recognized that, while communities involve groups of beings, not all groups of beings are communities. What then transforms a group into a community? In one basic sense, according to Nisbet, the concept community means «all forms of relationship that are characterized by a high degree of personal intimacy, emotional depth, moral commitment, social cohesion, and continuity in time...It

---

[113] F. SMITH, *The Book of Learning and Forgetting*, 74.

[114] In this case, Lynda Stone proposes a new term *heteromity*. See L. STONE, «Disavowing Community», 93-101. «"Heteromity", is a concept that relies on the post-structural or postmodern notion of "difference" and the de-centered subject for its formulation. Under this new conceptualization, association is seen as the temporary and shifting relationships within and between different social groupings. Group/community boundaries are fluid, and their very identities difficult to isolate because they constitute the interactions of numerous subjectivities; thus, "heteromity" defines the group as a dynamic coalition of individuals». M. STOUT, «Response to "Disavowing Community"», 102.

[115] F.M. SCHULTZ, *Social-philosophical Foundations of Education*, 96.

may be found in...locality, religion, nation, race, occupation, or common cause. Its archetype [...] is the family»[116]. In another basic sense, it is a comprehensive group with two chief characteristics: (1) it is a group within which the individual can have most of the activities and experiences that are important to him. (2) The group is bound together by a shared sense of belonging and a feeling of identity.[117] Thus, from this perspective, community refers to a group of people united by at least one common characteristic. Such characteristics could include geography,[118] shared interests,[119] values, experiences, or traditions.[120] Its constitutive features, Raywid indicates, include the «interaction and mutual dependence, the intention of longevity and permanence, expressive ties, communication, common and mutual sentiments, shared belief, and an ethic of individual concern and sympathy. The impacts of these conditions on members are said to include: the shaping of individual identity, and acceptance of group standards and a desire to abide by them, commitment, a sense of place, and identification with the group, along with a sense of consciousness of kind»[121].

However, we need to indicate here the quite familiar ideal-typical dichotomy we have inherited from classical social theory: that between

---

[116] R. A. NISBET, *The Sociological Tradition*, 47-48. Nisbet's emphasizes three features: the type of relationships between persons, their quality; the idea of persistence; and the idea of shared ends, commitments, purposes, morality or identity.

[117] Cf. L. BROOM – P. SELZNICK, *Sociology: A Test with Adapted Readings,* 31.

[118] All members of a community share a common physical space. Talcott Parsons defines a community as «that collectivity the members of which share a common territorial area as their base of operations for daily activities». T. PARSONS, *The Social System*, 91. Roland Warren also emphasizes that a community is «that combination of social units and systems which perform the major social functions having locality relevance». R.L. WARREN, *Community in America*, p. 9.

[119] A fundamental reason for a group of people joining into a community is the shared interest or a common purpose. Something that provides the community with some form of shared meaning or reason for their co-existence. This can range from a common interest or passion to the need to make the best use of a shared space.

[120] Culture, in the context of a community, is a form of a collective identity. Inwardly, our identity includes our values, beliefs, attitudes, behavioral norms, and our accumulated experiences that shape these. Outwardly, culture then becomes the means of expression of our inward identity, including our language, behavior, appearance, rituals, traditions, artifacts, and events. See F. M. SCHULTZ, *Social philosophical Foundations of Education*, 96.

[121] M.A. RAYWID, «Community and schools: a prolegomenon», 3.

community (*Gemeinschaft*) and society (*Gesellschaft*).[122] The former is characterized by a *mechanical solidarity* arising from similarity among members, and the latter is characterized by an *organic solidarity* among individuals who are different but also share a common consciousness of the different roles they play as interdependent components of a larger system.[123] A society contains many differing groupings whose membership may overlap one another. If this were the case, then a community can be considered as a unit of a society as affirmed by Arensberg and Kimball: «one of the defining characteristics of "community" is that "community" is the basic culture organizing (creating) and culture transmitting social unit within a "society"»[124]. Hence, while members of a society are essentially separated in spite of all connecting factors, the members of a community remain essentially connected in spite of all separating factors because of the mutuality of relationships.[125]

We also need to point out that, as Schultz noted, «"Community" in its qualitative or normative uses, as opposed to purely descriptive use of "community", shares many of the defining characteristics relative to the qualities of human association which are part of the definition of "culture", yet the concept of "community" is subordinate to, although integrally linked with, the concept of "culture"»[126].

No community exists without some sort of organization. The community has its own function for the conditions and processes of its continuity and perpetuation in time.[127] It refers to the structure of relationships through which a localized population provides its daily necessities.[128] One of the main requirements of a community is the educational

---

[122] See Tönnies' distinction of *Gemeinschaft* and *Gesellschaft*, in F. TÖNNIES, *Community and Society*.

[123] The distinction between *mechanical* and *organic* forms of solidarity was developed by Durkheim partly to comment on the notion that a shift from *Gemeinschaft* to *Gesellschaft* entailed the inevitable loss of a sense of solidarity; see E. DURKHEIM, *Division of Labor in Society*, 31-87; 229-233.

[124] C. ARENSBERG – S.T. KIMBALL, *Culture and Community*, 15-17. Emphasis added.

[125] This mutuality is personal, interactive, and immediate. In community, persons cannot be distant or remain marginal. Individuals in community also are active, not passive. See J. MACMURRAY, *Person in Relation*.

[126] F.M. SCHULTZ, *Social-philosophical Foundations of Education*, 101.

[127] Cf. K.D. BENNE, *Education*, 29.

[128] Cf. A.H. HAWLEY, *Human ecology*, 180.

growth of its immature members. In fact, one of the functions[129] of the community is to guarantee the transmission of knowledge, values and behavioral patterns through education. This is the basis of Benne's (as for Dewey) affirmation that a community by its nature is a pedagogical enterprise.[130] Education, on the one hand, assures the continued existence of the community. The community, on the other hand, provides a means for developing good public relations by integrating human and physical resources in the community with the educational process. Its role influences the experiences within the school. Extramural activities generate a large part of background information about the student population. In this sense, the community provides an administrative framework within which organized groups can communicate with each other and establish identifiable boundaries for their activities. It not only maintains professional responsibilities but it also allows progress in education to accomplish the goals of education. Community involvement is an empowering mechanism that supports the mission of public education and the sustainability of change. Hence, one of the values very much embedded in our processes of change is the role of the community in education.

4. 2 *The School and the Community*

One clear indication of the reciprocal relationship between the community and the educational enterprise is the support and attention given to schools. However, while a school interacts with its local community, it can be considered in itself as community. It is the aim of this section to elaborate on the interaction between school and community and the nature of the school as community.

In a basic sense, a school is differentiated by society as that which takes care of the educational growth of its members. It consists of a location, an edifice, personnel and students. From this perspective, a school appears to be an institution that is distinguished both functionally and physically. According to Waller, schools have the following characteristics: (1) they have a definite population. (2) They have a clearly defined political structure, arising from the mode of social interaction characteristic of the school, and influenced by numerous minor

---

[129] These are the identified functions of a community: economic, socialization, social control, social participation and mutual support. See R.L. WARREN, *Community in America*, 208.

[130] K. D. BENNE, *A Conception of Authority*, 70-113.

processes of interaction. (3) They represent the nexus of a compact network of social relationships. (4) They are pervaded by a «we-feeling». (5) They have a culture that is definitely their own.[131] Well functioning schools foster learning and socially appropriate behaviors. They have a strong academic focus and support students in achieving high standards, foster positive relationships between school staff and students, and promote meaningful parental and community involvement. It is particularly the last theme that interests us here, i.e., the recurring educational thought – school/community interaction.

Schools do not exist in isolation from their communities. The school reflects the values of the community as a whole and incorporates many of the social and cultural characteristics of the neighborhood or other geographic area that it serves. To provide effective service, schools must be aware of community standards and must engage the community in constant discussion about educational goals and processes. The interaction between school and community takes place at numerous points and in a variety of ways, thus creating the need for a multidimensional administrative structure. In this context, the relationship between the school and community becomes the cornerstone of the efficient functioning of educational units.

The community has the responsibility of making certain that schools and other appropriate social institutions exist and are well supported. The community must also provide the family and the school with a supportive environment, which provides a wealth of opportunities for learning and development outside the confines of the classroom. Schools have the capacity to improve themselves, if the conditions are right. A major responsibility of the community is to help provide these conditions.

Concisely, the school, on the one hand, provides the community with the avenue for the educational growth of its members and allows the propagation of its values and behaviors, that is, they become the primary means by which society pursues the education of the people. The community, on the other hand, furnishes the school with adequate support and nourishment in order that the goals and purposes of such institution as well as education may be achieved. Hence, in education there is evidently a constant reciprocal channel of influence between the school and the community.

---

[131] W. WALLER, *The Sociology of Teaching*, 6-7.

John Dewey, who in different times visualized a somewhat different school and community relation, offered a modest proposal. Raywid confirms that «he advocated that schools constitute themselves as "miniature communities"»[132]. The idea that schools should be communities have become prevalent in today's educational thought.[133] The recognition of this idea is due to the impact of community influence upon education and the reality of disengagement of many students from schooling.[134]

A school as community differs significantly from the traditional view of school as a hierarchical organization. It has the following characteristics: shared values reflect democratic, not authoritarian principles, behavior results from widespread commitment to a shared vision and set of goals rather than from coercion, command, and control; individuals, respected for their unique talents and abilities, are free to make decisions consistent with the community's vision and goals; cooperation, collegiality, and a mutuality of interests replace competition and self-enhancement; individuals are connected because they care deeply about one another and about a shared set of ideas and ideals. In this perspective, a school community is a group of people - including teachers, school staff, students, and families of students - who are intimately attached to a specific school, share common educational values about the academic and social learning of its students, and communicate and associate with one another in furtherance of their shared educational values. Communities are defined by their centers of values, sentiments, and beliefs that provide the needed conditions for creating a sense of *we* from *I*.[135] Thus, the bonding together of people in special ways and the binding of them to shared values and ideas are the defining characteristics of schools as communities.

Let us now pull together what we have discussed in this chapter. In this segment we have examined the basic concepts of education, viz., teaching, learning and community. However, prior to the discussion proper of such concepts, we considered the character of philosophy of education through history with reference to the ideas of prominent phi-

---

[132] M.A. RAYWID, «Community and schools: a prolegomenon», 11.

[133] Cf. A.S. BRYK – V.E. LEE – P. B. HOLLAND, *Catholic Schools and the Common Good*, J. KAHNE, *Reforming Educational Policy*, C. MERZ – G. FURNAM, *Community and Schools*, and T. J. SERGIOVANNI, *Building Community in Schools*.

[134] Cf. L. STEINBERG, *Beyond the Classroom.*

[135] T. J. SERGIOVANNI, *Building Community in Schools*, 4.

losophers during the ancient, medieval, modern and contemporary periods.

The philosophy of education of each historical epoch manifests a particular characteristic representative of the current intellectual regime. The ancient world presented a fundamentally cosmocentric philosophy of education, i.e., educational discourses and ideas are merged with their views about the world. During the Middle Ages, we noted the shift from a cosmocentric to a theocentric or theistic character of philosophy of education. Thoughts on education were generally consonant with Christian doctrines, traditions and philosophy. This particular feature of philosophy of education soon disappeared during the modernistic discourse of the Enlightenment period. Here, the ideal of the individual person was divorced from the traditions of religious thinking. Educational philosophy became anthropocentric. It strived to achieve the improvement of the human condition by focusing on the significance of human development and environment. The twentieth century philosophy of education refined this focus on individual growth. Emphasis, however, was directed toward the merging of the individual with contemporary society and social progress. Thus, the individual's role within the socio-political context became a crucial factor in the development of educational ideas in the modern and post-modern philosophy of education. This historical perspective furnished the backdrop for our discussion regarding the basic concepts of education.

Teaching, learning and community, as we demonstrated, are fundamentally interrelated educational concepts. Although we found it difficult to distinguish the kind of relation that exists between these elements, they nonetheless form a network through which the goals of the educational process are achieved.

Teaching and learning occur simultaneously: teaching activity, although it does not necessarily result in learning, is aimed at achieving learning. The teacher employs different methods in order to obtain this goal. Learning, in contrast, becomes an active and continuous process manifested by growth and change in behavior.

Teaching and learning, albeit independent activities are seldom isolated from the rich and varied experiences within the world. This implies the importance of the community to the educational enterprise. The reciprocal channel of influence between the school and community fosters the development and growth in the educational activity.

After our study of the fundamental Wittgensteinian themes pertaining to education and its basic concepts, we shall now relate these themes to philosophy of education. We shall investigate how Wittgen-stein's ideas, specifically, meaning, rule-following, and philosophy as therapy furnish valuable insights into and different perspective in un-derstanding the dimensions of teaching, learning and community.

CHAPTER III

Meaning as Use and the Concept of Teaching

In the previous two chapters we have elaborated on select Wittgen-steinian themes and the basic concepts of philosophy of education re-spectively. Here and in the succeeding chapters, we shall engage in a confrontation and application of these concepts. We shall investigate whether or not these themes provide considerable influence and uniquely innovative understanding of *teaching*, *learning* and *commu-nity*.

In the first chapter we have seen Wittgenstein's two different views of *meaning*. Although we could still find in his early thoughts reference to educational concepts, it is in his later philosophy where such ideas are used recurrently. It is specifically in his analysis of *meaning as use* where affinity to teaching is made manifest. We need to remind our-selves here that we are not claiming that Wittgenstein explicitly enun-ciates that there is such a connection. We shall deal specifically with this issue on this segment. However, the principal aim of this chapter is to investigate whether the outcome of the philosopher's treatment of meaning offers a consistent adherence to the established understanding of the concept of teaching or provides an innovative outlook that would lead us to reconsider our present conception of it.

We shall approach this problem by first elaborating on the interest of Wittgenstein in teaching or the rationale behind utilizing the concept of teaching in his investigation. Second, we shall make an exposition of the character of *teaching* by extracting its features from his later works. In order to achieve this aim, emphasis will be made to his use of *train-ing* and *explanation* for the reason that both these ideas are directly connected to teaching. Third, after describing his use of teaching in his writings, we shall engage in an illustration of the *logical connection* between the concepts of *meaning* and *teaching*. We shall seek evidence for this claim by referring to the notions of intention, context and practice(s). Fourth, having thus examined the character of teaching in his works and established the logical relation we are now ready to demonstrate its impact, i.e., its indispensable role in Wittgenstein's analysis of meaning and then his comprehension of the concept of teaching taking into consideration the impact of his notions of language-games, family resemblance and form of life. Finally, based on our argumentation, we shall make an appraisal whether Wittgenstein's treatment of teaching in his analysis of meaning deviates or adheres from the accepted view of teaching as elaborated in the previous chapter.

1. Wittgenstein and Teaching

During the years when Wittgenstein felt like abandoning philosophical work, he chose to indulge himself in teaching. It was during these 'mystery years' that Wittgenstein enrolled in the *Lehrerbildungsanhalt* in the *Kundmanngasse* in September 1919. He trained at a teachers college for a year and then began a teaching career in the countryside towns of Austria. He even published during this period a dictionary entitled *Wörterbuch für Volksschulen* which was meant to aid the active learning of the schoolchildren in both spelling and grammar.[1] It is in this profession that according to Monk, «he would find something worth living for»[2].

Wittgenstein, in the course of his philosophical career often approaches philosophical problems by using educational situations. Distinct *pedagogical* themes run through much of his later works. [3] «Through the entire work of the later Wittgenstein pedagogical remarks on child language, thought, and action as well as didactic statements regarding the relationship between teacher and pupil are to be found»[4]. He frequently illustrates concrete activities of teaching, e.g., teaching of

---

[1] For a satisfactory account of Wittgenstein's teaching experiences, see W. W. BARTLEY III, *Wittgenstein*. Despite his notorious and insalubrious claims about Wittgenstein's sexuality, he is one of the few scholars to allocate any space to Wittgenstein's development during the 1920s; and R. MONK, *Ludwig Wittgenstein*, 192ff. Monk, devotes a chapter (*An Entirely Rural Affair*) to Wittgenstein's years as a school teacher in rural Austria.

[2] R. MONK, *Ludwig Wittgenstein*, 188.

[3] M. CHAPMAN – R. DIXON, *Meaning and the Growth of Understanding*, 1-2.

[4] K. BROSE, «Pedagogical Elements in Wittgenstein's late work», 11.

words for color and sensations, how to read, how to count numbers, and more. This manifests how significant it is in his philosophy in various ways. Wittgenstein himself makes queries or suggests us to ask «How does one teach a child?» [*PI* §208] or «How did we *learn* the meaning of this word?» [*PI* §77]. He was particularly interested in teaching for the reason that he considers it as a means to dispose of the misunderstanding of our language use.

This particular attention to teaching, although he obviously did not intend to establish a pedagogical theory at all, illustrates the point that his comments could be valuable for empirical study on teaching. According to Paul Smeyers, social sciences could gain from the rich consequences of his later philosophy.[5] However, if we consider his discussion to contribute to such type of research, then we are heading the wrong way. Wittgenstein's project was specifically *grammatical* in character. His discourse of teaching serves as a grammatical investigation – «Such an investigation sheds light on our problem by clearing misunderstanding away. Misunderstandings concerning the use of words, caused, among other things, by certain analogies between the forms of expression in different regions of language» [*PI* §90]. Such notice to teaching manifests the pedagogical purpose of his investigation.[6]

It is true that Wittgenstein wrote no particular philosophical work devoted to the topic of education in general and teaching in particular. This is because his philosophical insights are not intended to advocate a pedagogical theory. However, we will notice that throughout most of his later writings he cites educational contexts as basic elements in the elaboration of his philosophical thoughts.

According to Baker and Hacker, Wittgenstein is interested in teaching because the perspectives of teaching serve to highlight the presuppositions of linguistic competence. Furthermore, primitive models of teaching are useful in destroying misconceptions. It makes clear the standard of adequacy of explanations.

---

[5] For further discussion regarding this issue see P. SMEYERS, «Assembling Reminders», 287-308.

[6] Michael Peters, James Marshall and Nicholas Burbules recognize the pedagogical element of Wittgenstein's philosophy. See M. PETERS – J. MARSHALL, *Wittgenstein: Philosophy, Postmodernism, Pedagogy*. Nicholas Burbules co-authored chapter nine of the book *Wittgenstein, Styles, and Pedagogy*, 152-173. See also B. SAVICKEY, «Philosophical and Pedagogical Beginnings».

Most Wittgensteinian scholars consider Wittgenstein's allusion to educational concepts, specifically teaching and learning, as mere examples for concept-clarification, i.e., in order to elucidate his position regarding certain philosophical problems. They considerably undervalue how significant it is to his philosophy. Thus, it is the aim of the succeeding section to achieve a clearer understanding of the concept of teaching contained in Wittgenstein's works and consequently demonstrate its importance.

2. *Teaching* in the later works of Wittgenstein

Basic pedagogical terms such as, pupil (*Schüler*), teacher (*Lehrer*), teaching (*Lehren*), learning (*Lernen*), training (*Abrichtung*), explanation (*Erklärung*), instruction (*Unterricht*), understanding (*Verstehen*) and others are found in Wittgenstein's later writings. His reference to such a vocabulary obviously springs from his experiences as a teacher in rural areas near Vienna and as a university professor in Cambridge. It would be interesting to elaborate on his teaching style and the remarks he gave regarding teaching. However, we will here focus only on what he wrote regarding the phenomenon of teaching.

If we look at his claims regarding teaching thoroughly, we will find that Wittgenstein makes several different approaches towards it. His use of *teaching* is broad. According to Yasushi Maruyama, Wittgenstein discusses it in different yet interconnected advances: a) illustrating teaching as a concrete, particular activity in his examples; b) treating teaching as a general, primary function related to meaning; c) questioning the way of teaching words as a method of concept-clarification; d) expressing his purpose of dealing with teaching; and e) making comments on his teaching of philosophy.[7]

In the *Investigations*, language games of instruction and learning illustrate his views about the fact of teaching. At first glance, these do not yield attention on the pedagogical dimension. However, the problems being tackled by him are effectively evaluated by means of didactic contexts. For Wittgenstein, it is the question regarding how we were taught words that gives the underlying principle behind the illustration of language-games of teaching.[8] The philosophical significance lies in the fact that language-games must be taught and learned (mastered) in

---

[7] Y. MARUYAMA, *Wittgenstein on Teaching and Otherness*, 47-48.

[8] See L. WITTGENSTEIN, *Lectures and Conversations* §5. Hereafter considered as *LCA*.

order for an individual to make sense of the world – to obtain *normality* in a form of life.

In *PI* §5, Wittgenstein focuses his interest on the issue of when a child learns to talk or when he learns the meaning of words. In discussing this process of learning, he in turn highlights how this knowledge is attained, i.e., how we were taught. This is made manifest when he asks, «How did we learn the meaning of this word?» [*PI* §77] or «How does one teach a child…?» [*PI* §208] This leads to the idea that the general and primary function of teaching is to make sense of expressions or we might say concept-clarification. In *Zettel* §432 he states, «For I describe the language-game "Bring something red" to someone who can himself already play it. Others I might at most *teach* it»[9]. Elsewhere in the *Investigations* he claims that the meaning of a word is what its explanation explains.[10] In the *Blue Book*, Wittgenstein claims: «If we are taught the meaning of the word "yellow" by being given some sort of ostensive definition (a rule of the usage of the word) this teaching can be looked at in two different ways» [*BB* 12].

On one occasion, Wittgenstein explicitly makes a distinction between two kinds of language-games, i) the language-game in which we utter the word and ii) the language-game which gives a certain word its meaning (by means of which we learn this meaning) – «The word "lying" was taught to us in a particular way in which it was fastened to a certain behavior, to the use of certain expressions under certain circumstances. Then we use it, saying that we have been lying, when our behavior was not like the one which first constituted the meaning»[11]. Here, he underlines two modes of teaching which enables a child to understand the meaning of words; they are through *training* and *explanation*. He sometimes refers teaching as training for the use of words and at times as that which explains meanings. Although *teaching* is considered by Wittgenstein in both senses, he differentiates them clearly. He considers *training* to be the first type of teaching and *explanation* or *teaching which may supply rules* as the second one. Nevertheless, he considers training as the foundation of explanation[12]. We will elaborate on this assertion later on this section.

---

[9] L. WITTGENSTEIN, *Zettel*. Emphasis supplied. Hereafter considered as *Z*. See also *Remarks on the Philosophy of Psychology* §313. Hereafter considered as *RPP II*.

[10] See *PI* §560, *BB* 1 and *PG* §23.

[11] See L. WITTGENSTEIN, «Notes for Lectures», 275-320.

[12] See *Z* §419 and *RPP II* §327.

The difference between training and explanation is important since it clarifies Wittgenstein's position regarding the levels of teaching a student needs to undergo in order to grasp the meaning of a particular word or expression, i.e., how we come to learn and understand. If we aim to have a clear picture of Wittgenstein's concept of teaching we must then indicate the difference between these two modes of teaching.

2.1 *Training (Abrichtung)*

In this section, key passages in Wittgenstein's later works which emphasize the concept of training will be delineated and examined. Our aim here is to have a lucid comprehension of Wittgenstein's use of the idea of *training* or *exercise* (*abrichten, Abrichtung*)[13] and how his presentation of such a method demonstrates a uniquely Wittgensteinian approach to the concept of teaching.

Wittgenstein emphatically argues that when a child uses primitive forms of language when it learns to talk, «the teaching of language is not explanation, but training» [*PI* §5]. Wittgenstein's understanding of the term *training* is basically this: it is similar to that of giving drills to animals – «The child learns this language from the grown-ups by being trained to its use. I am using the word "trained" in a way strictly analogous to that in which we talk of an animal being trained to do certain things. It is done by means of example, reward, punishment, and suchlike» [*BB* 77]. He supplies no further description or sense of the word. If this were the case, then training can be considered as teaching without supplying reasons. «Macmillan holds that training or *abrichten* occurs primarily at a preliminary or early (perhaps even childhood) state in our acquaintance with language. This is the sort of training apposite for someone who is "prerational", someone as yet unable to appreciate the reasons one might give for certain claims»[14].

This mode of teaching consisted in a number of partial exercises. Wittgenstein presents the following: 1) the teacher says a word aloud

---

[13] Ryle makes a distinction between *drill* and *training*. «Drill (or conditioning) consists in the imposition of repetitions [...] Training, on the other hand, though it embodies plenty of sheer drill, does not consist of drill. It involves the stimulation by criticism and example of the pupil's own judgment». Cf. G. RYLE, *The Concept of Mind*, 42. This distinction somehow justifies the importance Wittgenstein gives to the pupil's reactions. For a discussion regarding Wittgenstein's usage of the word *Abrichtung*, see E. KONRAD SPECHT, *The Foundations of Wittgenstein's late philosophy*, 66.

[14] L.P. MCCARTY – D.C. MCCARTY, «Semantic Physiology: Wittgenstein on Pedagogy», 242. See also C.J.B. MACMILLAN, «Rational Teaching», 411-422.

and the pupil repeats it after him; 2) the teacher points to objects, and while attracting the child's attention to them, says the word e.g., *slab* aloud, while pointing out the particular object; 3) the learner *names* objects, i.e., he says the word when the teacher pints at a definite object.[15] He considers *ostensive teaching* as capable of establishing a connection between the word and the object.[16] In this kind of teaching *nothing is* explained. However, it results in understanding when accompanied by a particular training and significant state of affairs. Here, training definitely indicates an exercise to *do* something – «And now I train him to follow the rule – • – •• – ••• – etc» [*RFM* VI:19]. It denotes something *mechanical* or instrumental which aims at the acquisition of capacity and ability. «"Mechanical" – that means: without thinking. But entirely without *thinking*? Without *reflecting*» [*RFM* VII: 60]. However, Wittgenstein's use of the term goes beyond mere mechanical activity. When he says, «the learner *names* the objects; that is, he utters the word when the teacher points to the stone. – And there will be this still simpler exercise: the pupil repeats the words after the teacher...» [*PI* §7], he actually highlights the cultural aspect of training, i.e., one's initiation into a *form of life* - as a preparation for one's further application of language and participation within that particular *Lebensform*.[17] It is a sort of tuning of the human organism, i.e., the pupil, until it performs well linguistically. It is by means of these linguistic drills that one is able to make use of words –

> How do words *refer* to sensations? – There doesn't seem to be any problem here; don't we talk about sensations every day, and give them names? But how is the connexion between the name and the thing named set up? This question is the same as: how does a human being learn the meaning of the names of sensations? – of the word "pain" for example. Here is one possibility: words are connected wit the primitive, the natural, expressions of the sensation and used in their place. A child has hurt himself and he

---

[15] Cf. *PI* §§6 and 7.

[16] See C-P. BECKE, «Ostensive Teaching», 22-28. This paper compares Wittgenstein's analysis of ostensive definition and ostensive teaching with Tugendhat's and Loren's analysis of the structure of the predicative sentence. Wittgenstein's discussion of ostensive teaching reveals the fact that it is closely related to nonverbal behavior. Wittgenstein's remarks that linguistic acts are embedded in the *Lebensform* are considered in order to establish how ostensive teaching should be analyzed from the phenomenological point of view.

[17] M. WILLIAMS, *Wittgenstein, Mind and Meaning*, 50. Allen Pearson would call this type of teaching as a «tentative act», i.e., it steps towards the community see PEARSON, «Teaching, Reason and Risk», 110.

cries; and then adults talk to him and *teach* him exclamations and, later, sentences. They *teach* the child new pain-behavior [*PI* §244, *emphasis added*].

Wittgenstein's idea of language-games presupposes the need for training. It is through a formative action in language-games, usually by pointing and repetition, that one is able to obtain a certain degree of mastery. «To understand a sentence means to understand a language. To understand a language means to be a master of a technique» [*PI* §199]. It is important to note that we need training in order to engage ourselves in practice [*PI* p.185e][18]. This underlines the importance of training if we are to master the rudiments of an activity.[19] «The justification of the proposition 25 x 25 = 625 is, naturally, that if anyone has been trained is such-and-such a way, then under normal circumstances he gets 625 as the result of multiplying 25 by 25» [*RFM* VI: 23]. «Many rule-governed activities are learned by training»[20].

In the training process the trainer (teacher) is presumed to have already been sufficiently trained and have acquired the necessary mastery and familiarity with the linguistic terrain. He applies methods of pointing and repetition [*PI* §6] which are designed to instill an associative habit the intention of which is to enable one to recognize its use and consequently the original meaning of that particular word. If this were the case, then we can say that this demonstrative teaching may cause learning and it is a prelude to understanding. Wittgenstein considers it as preceding explanation «since no doubts, perplexities, or requests for clarification concerning word-meanings can as yet arise»[21]. One cannot yet raise questions about meaning. Training accompanies the proto-language as part of the teaching process [*BB* 77]. It is during training wherein one establishes the fundamental *tools* to be able to continue engaging in complex language-games. Wittgenstein points out in *PI* §143 that the ability to understand the formation rule rests upon a reaction to training.

«In discussing what is involved in teaching someone (a language), Wittgenstein emphasizes that we depend on the pupil's reacting in certain ways to our encouragement, and without such responses, teaching

---

[18] See J. SCHULTE, *Wittgenstein: An Introduction*, p. 106ff.
[19] Cf. R. FOGELIN, *Wittgenstein: the arguments of the philosophers*, 112.
[20] G.P. BAKER – P.M.S. HACKER, *An Analytical Commentary*, II, 43.
[21] G.P. BAKER – P.M.S. HACKER, *An Analytical Commentary*, I, 30.

would not take place»[22]. He is underscoring here the role of encouragement or motivation.[23] This enables the pupil to correlate words and pictures by using a table or other means. It also allows him to use new tables or yet build them for himself. However, these acts of encouragement are only possible, «only have a role, given certain responses»[24]. It is through the child's reaction(s) that we can ascertain whether or not the *mastery of a technique* is achieved. Without mastering the techniques one would not be able to know what to do – «We may perhaps refer to the fact that people are brought by their education [training] so to use the formula $y = x^2$, that they all work out the same value for y when they substitute the same number for x. Or we may say: "These people are so trained that they all take the same step at the same point when they receive the order 'add 3'"» [*PI* §189]. Thus, success in this type of teaching depends upon the reaction(s) manifested by the pupil – «the effect of any further *explanation* depends on this *reaction*» [*PI* §145]. It is upon generally shared human reactions which allows the possibility of training (teaching) – «The origin and the primitive form of the language game is a reaction; only from this can more complicated forms develop» [*CV* §31].

It is important to note here that Wittgenstein's assertions about training are not manifestations of a kind of Stimulus-Response (S-R) conception of accord.[25] It is a question of training in a normative activity. The pupil develops the ability to know what to do and what to be done with what is learned. [26] That is, knowledge of the «role of the word» is attained by being taught (trained) the typical modes of application of the individual words in certain very primitive language-games. Gradually, an understanding of the typical characteristics of individual words within a particular form of life will be acquired.[27] Although this process may be useful against non-understanding, and is a recurrent and essential moment in the pedagogical progress, it is not enough to clarify

---

[22] D. STERN, *Wittgenstein on Mind and Language*, 119. Parenthesis added.

[23] Cf. *PI* §223b and *BB* 89 ff.

[24] G.P. BAKER – P.M.S. HACKER, *An Analytical Commentary*, I, 278.

[25] The stimulus-response model describes a statistical unit as making a quantitative response to a quantitative stimulus administered by the researcher. The object of this kind of research is to establish a mathematical function that describes the relation f between the stimulus x and the response y: $y = f(x)$. This study is commonly associated with Watson, Thorndike, Pavlov as well as the behaviorists.

[26] Cf. *PI* §198.

[27] Cf. *PI* §29.

the acquisition of meaningful language.[28] If we expect others to be able to understand our use of words or our forms of life, then we should teach them with reasons, i.e., through explanation. Thus, we shall now elaborate on this second mode of teaching in the succeeding section.

2.2 Explanation (Erklärung)

After building on the concept of training, Wittgenstein introduces another mode of teaching, namely, explanation (*Erklärung*). Macmillan considers this approach as pertaining to a higher level since it is where rationality enters in to teaching.[29] Wittgenstein, in his discussion regarding the initial learning of language-games and the acquisition of world pictures plainly contrasts this with training.[30] However, there is a need to make a clarification here regarding the apparently negative view of explanation in his later writings – «We must do away with explanation and allow only description in its place» [*PI* §109][31]. This pessimistic view is not directed to *explanation* in the pedagogical sense of clarification of meaning but to the scientific method of explanation, i.e., concerning the introduction of methods and goals of our science when assessing the value of religious language.[32] Unfortunately, the scope of this section does not allow us to elaborate on this issue.

The idea of explanation (*Erklärung*) comes with other related concepts, viz., *Erklären, Klärung, Klarlegung, Klarwerden, Klarmachen, Erläuterungen*, etc. They all refer the same sense of *making clear* or of *clarification*. It is interesting to investigate into the implications of this thought to the other areas of Wittgenstein's philosophy. However, it is not possible to deal with this problem within the scope of this section. We are here concerned with the didactic aspect of explanation.

As we have stated earlier, explanation comes after training. Teaching, in this sense, enters into a new echelon in view of the fact that the learner has already acquired the mastery of a technique – «In giving explanations I already have to use language full-blown (not some sort

---

[28] Cf. G.P. BAKER – P.M.S. HACKER, *An Analytical Commentary*, I, 276.

[29] Macmillan, focusing on the rationality aspect of teaching, offers another mode superior to that of explanation, namely, *persuasion*. For further discussion regarding this issue see Macmillan's distinction between different modes of teaching. Cf. C.J.B. MACMILLAN, «Rational Teaching», 411- 422.

[30] Cf. *PI* §5.

[31] Cf. *PI* §§126 and 654-655.

[32] Cf. L. WITTGENSTEIN, *Remarks on Frazer's the Golden Bough*.

of preparatory, provisional one)» [*PI* §120] – meaning, the elements of our explanation are already known otherwise we won't be able to understand the explanation at all. Pedagogically, imitation, repetition, pointing and other methods used (preparatory methods of language-use) in training are no longer considered expedient given that explanation now requires the supply of reasons and the recognition of rules which offer grounds of justification. If this is the case, then *persuasion*, i.e., instruction by creating new reasons or changing a world-picture, belongs to this type of teaching. For example, Wittgenstein says that if we meet a man who, due to his distinctive cultural background, was «taught that the earth came into being 50 years ago, and therefore believed this», then «we might instruct him» in various ways. But in doing so «we should be trying to give him our picture of the world [*Weltbild*]. This would happen through a kind of *persuasion*» [*OC* §262][33]. Or if a king was «brought up in the belief that the world began with him», Wittgenstein does not think that the right view could be *proven* to the king. Rather, he would have to be *converted* to the right view in a special way. In being «brought to look at the world in a different way», his world-picture would consequently have shifted [*OC* §92]. Although Wittgenstein insinuates that persuasion only takes place when giving rational proofs and arguments doesn't work, he does not necessarily rule out its affinity to explanation in the sense that the giving of *our* world-pictures to others involves showing our reasons.

According to Malcolm, «the terms "explanation", "reason", [and] "justification", have a use *exclusively within* the various language-games»[34]. *Explanation* or the teaching together with reasons enables the pupil to learn our system of judgment to be able to enter into a particular (linguistic) community of practice.

There are two uses of the verb *to explain*. It can be used as a *task verb* meaning trying to get someone to understand, e.g., «I explained X to Peter a thousand times but he still doesn't get it»; or it can be used as an *achievement verb* meaning to succeed in getting someone to understand something, e.g., «I explained to Peter why I left home». Wittgenstein does not discriminate between these two uses since both cases require the occurrence of a reason.

Explanation, in the sense of Wittgenstein's use, denotes an intention to achieve understanding in a logical and consistent manner. This

---

[33] L. WITTGENSTEIN, *On Certainty*. Hereafter considered as *OC*.
[34] N. MALCOLM, *Wittgenstein: A Religious Point of View?*, 77.

standpoint implies grounding, i.e., justification of the use of words in the standard contexts. Teaching in this perspective now involves the understanding of rules – at this level teachers are expected to provide reasons and underlying principles about what is being taught. It is a different thing to teach a child that one added to one yields two, two plus two equals four, and so on and *why* «1 + 1 = 2», «2 + 2 = 4», and so forth. The latter case involves explanation since one is supposed to present rules for understanding. Explanations of meaning that this type of teaching presents are normative. They are rules or standards of correctness that enter as the criteria for understanding.

The pedagogical significance of teaching by explanation lies in the fact that it allows one to provide and to identify the fundamental rules upon which correct and incorrect understanding of the subject matter is evaluated. In case of misapplication or misunderstanding, further explanation, i.e., auxiliary rule(s) for the use must be given – «Whereas an explanation may indeed rest of another one that has been given, but none stands in need of another – unless *we* require it to prevent a misunderstanding. One might say: an explanation serves to remove or to avert a misunderstanding – one, that is, that would occur but for the explanation; not every one that I can imagine» [*PI* §87][35]. This implies that we give explanations in order to evade misapprehension. «We can never reach a self-evident stopping point: every explanation, even a simple colour chart, can be given a deviant interpretation»[36]. If such thing happens, then we can say that Wittgenstein admits grades of explanation, i.e., different levels of understanding imply diverse stages of explanations.[37] For instance, an explanation to a secondary school student concerning the *rain* phenomena would be different from that of a geophysical student. This would account, in some sense, for his affirmation that «explanations come to an end somewhere» [*PI* §1], i.e., to demarcate the boundary for another *grade* of explanation to take place or to indicate the attainment of understanding.

«Our acceptance of explanations by examples as legitimate explanations does not presuppose that they are known to bring about a mental state causally necessary for understanding the explained expression»[38]. In this context, the learner has to go beyond the given examples or be

35 Cf. *PG* I, §4.
36 D. STERN, *Wittgenstein on Mind and Language*, 119.
37 Cf. *PI* §§71-72.
38 G.P. BAKER – P.M.S. HACKER, *An Analytical Commentary*, I, 153.

deemed capable to go on before he can be said to have learned what the teacher is conveying.[39] Nonetheless, successful teaching by explanation is achieved upon the correct understanding and application of the rules, i.e., the standard of satisfactoriness of explanations is made clear by teaching.

Wittgenstein distinguishes it from a *definition*.[40] In the *Tractatus*, he considers *definition* to be that which is capable of introducing the logically complex but not the logically simple, in the way a chemist can decompose complex substances yet cannot analyze primitive elements to any further extent. However, in his later philosophy this sense of the Tractarian definition shifted. He says,

> If I explain the meaning of a word "A" to someone by pointing to something and saying "This is A", then this expression may be meant in two different ways. Either it is itself a proposition already, in which case it can only be understood once the meaning of "A" is known, i.e., I must now leave it to chance whether he takes it as I meant it or not. Or the sentence is a definition. Suppose I have said to someone "A is ill", but he doesn't know who I mean by "A", and I now point at a man, saying "This is A". Here the expression is a definition, but this can only be understood if he has already gathered what kind of object it is through his understanding of the grammar of the proposition "A is ill" [*PR* §6][41].

The later Wittgenstein describes this kind of definition an *ostensive definition*. It basically functions as a replacement of one sign for another. «"'Red' means the colour that occurs to me when I hear the word 'red'" – would be a *definition*. Not an explanation of *what it is* to use a word as a name» [*PI* §239]. No matter how useful ostensive definition might be in ordinary communication, according to Wittgenstein, it can-

---

[39] «Examples» are evidently considered by Wittgenstein as forms of *Erklärung*. For further discussion regarding his use of examples see L.A. MARCUSCHI, *Die Methode des Beispiels*.

[40] There is apparently a shift of meaning of the German term *Erklärung* as presented in the *PI*. For instance, while it is considered as *definition* in *PI* §§3, 6, and 29, it is translated *explanation* in §§1, 30, 209, 239. See T. FUJIMOTO, «The Notion of Erklärung». See also J.J. ACERO, «Wittgenstein, la Definicion ostensiva», 5-17. This article examines Wittgenstein's remarks on ostensive definition and concludes that attributing that view to him is a mistake. It offers a more balanced interpretation and suggests that he did nothing to convince his readers that the relation between language and reality are illusory. On the contrary, his main aim was to undermine a naïve understanding of how those relations are set up.

[41] L. WITTGENSTEIN, *Philosophical Remarks*. Hereafter considered as *PR*.

not by itself account for meaning of a word. While explanation is directly associated with the use of a word, definition isn't.

Baker and Hacker claim that «"definition" is a species belonging to the genus explanations»[42]. In the *Blue Book* Wittgenstein said, «What one calls "explanations of the meaning of a word" can, *very roughly*, be divided into verbal and ostensive definitions» [*BB* 1]. This implies that definitions are part of an explanation (of meaning). This is due to the fact that «it is explanation, not definition which is the "correlate" to understanding (*BT* 11). Being able to *explain* what it means [...] is a criterion of understanding a word, but being unable to *define* it is not a criterion for not understanding it»[43]. Nonetheless, this claim does not entirely render the teaching act superfluous. With these statements, Wittgenstein does not intend to impugn the idea of a definition. He wants to differentiate explanation from definition because the latter concept primarily has the absence of a sharp boundary as a fundamental feature and that no aspect of a rule is present in it, i.e., a definition is nothing other than the substitution of one sign for another. In this case, we know that no definition will match exactly to what we understand by a word.[44] Subsequently, what we understand cannot in this case correspond to a definition. Wittgenstein's arguments reflect his confidence that teaching by explanation in fact arrives at understanding. «"The meaning of a word is what is explained by the explanation of meaning." I.e.: if you want to understand the use of the word "meaning", look for what are called "explanations of meaning"» [*PI* §560].

What we have delineated so far in this section is a picture of teaching contained in the later works of Wittgenstein. All that is left for us to do is to stress that the accent he places on training and explanation is congruent to his affirmation in *PI* §109 which is of crucial importance, «The problems are solved, not by giving new information, but by arranging what we have always known». This affirmation directs us, in a sense, to another view of the teaching process. The relevance of this point will be discussed in the concluding section of this chapter.

---

[42] G.P. BAKER – P.M.S. HACKER, *An Analytical Commentary*, I, 140.
[43] G.P. BAKER – P.M.S. HACKER, *An Analytical Commentary*, I, 141.
[44] Cf. *PI* §§75-76.

3. «Meaning» and «Teaching»: A Logical Connection

Current educational philosophy, resulting from the present interest in the philosophy of language, has recognized the importance of the concept of "meaning" in education. Investigations are now being made to establish a correlation between *meaning* and *teaching*. We shall now investigate in this segment into the philosophically important concepts of *meaning as use* which, as we endeavor to achieve, would enable us to assert whether or not there is a logical connection between the concepts of *meaning* and *teaching*.

3.1 *A Premise for the Logical Connection Argument*

We have stated at the outset of this chapter that there is no *explicit* claim of a connection between *meaning* and *teaching* in the later works of Wittgenstein. However, on one occasion, Wittgenstein said, «Am I doing child psychology? I am making a connection between the concept of teaching and the concept of meaning» [*RPP II* §337][45]. What is he implying with this statement? Wittgenstein originally directs the passages of *RPP II* §336-§343 to what the McCartys call the *hypotheticalists* - «those philosophers whose business it was to purvey the idea that every physical object statement is a "probably" statement and to encourage hyperbolical doubts about chairs»[46]. With these arguments, he straightforwardly impugns their position regarding the arbitrary will (*Willkür*). He maintains that «the mechanisms which underpin the workings of language are not transparent to the intellect and not subject to volition. We do not, according to Wittgenstein, express our meanings and communicate our thoughts thanks solely to intellectual or intellectual/emotional processes»[47]. This evidently alludes that our activities of thinking and speaking are embedded within a factual system. Education functions within this system.

Macmillan points out that the remark §337 of *RPP II* adverts to a logical connection rather than a psychological one. Wittgenstein is keen on not putting teaching itself in correlation with meaning itself but rather an association between the concepts of these two things. Indeed,

---

[45] See also *Z* §412. The McCarty's translation runs, «Am I engaged in child psychology? I am bringing the concept of teaching into association with that of meaning». See L.P. MCCARTY – D.C. MCCARTY, «Wittgenstein», 74.

[46] L.P. MCCARTY – D.C. MCCARTY, «Wittgenstein», 65.

[47] L.P. MCCARTY – D.C. MCCARTY, «Wittgenstein», 73.

to contend for a logical connection is not far-fetched given that in order for A to know the meaning of p, he should have been taught the use of p.[48] We are not concerned here in evaluating the validity of the afore-mentioned statement but rather underline that in every instance of S (i.e., A knowing the meaning of p) it is presumed that teaching should have taken place otherwise it would be difficult to assess S.[49] Although the McCartys acknowledged that this assertion does give rise to questions concerning the logical truth, they did not negate the fact that there is such a relationship.[50] We are not going to elaborate, in this section, on Macmillan's stance nor criticize the approach of the McCartys regarding this issue. We shall maintain, however, the idea that there is a logical connection between teaching and meaning.

In order for us to ascertain the connection between both concepts, we shall look into three concepts contained in Wittgenstein's analysis of meaning that manifestly give good grounds for an avowal of this logical connection. We shall elaborate on these concepts respectively in the succeeding sections.

3.2 The "Logical Connectors"[51]

There are three concepts which indicate the particular relation between meaning and teaching that we are alluding in this section. We are not claiming, however, that these, by themselves, explicitly demonstrate such a connection. We need to engage ourselves in a conceptual analysis in order to validate our contention. The concepts we are referring to are *intention, context* and *practice(s)*. They are here considered as *logical connectors* for the reason that they imply a kind of logical relationship between *meaning* and *teaching*.

---

[48] My version of McCartys formulation: «(A) In order to grasp the concept X, one has already to have undergone a process of teaching/learning via p». See L.P. McCARTY – D.C. McCARTY, «Wittgenstein», 64.

[49] In special cases of a child prodigy, grasping by installation, and spontaneous adults, this assertion may seem to collapse. However, these are exceptional situations which can only be claimed as «possibilities» against the backdrop of this affirmation. Cf. L.P. McCARTY – D.C. McCARTY, «Wittgenstein», 64.

[50] L.P. McCARTY – D.C. McCARTY, «Wittgenstein », 64.

[51] The expression *logical connectors* is used here to refer to the concepts that join or connect two ideas that have a particular relationship. The specific relationship we are dealing with is *reason and purpose*, and not sequential (time) or adversative (opposition and/or unexpected result) condition.

3.2.1 Intention

The issue that we shall deal with in this part will not be on how Wittgenstein develops his views about *intention*. We are rather concerned here about how the idea of intention becomes an important element in our inquiry into the correlation between teaching and meaning. We shall proceed in our investigation by first discussing the function of intention in his analysis of meaning, especially regarding *use* and then indicate the key point(s) wherein we can determine that the concept of *intention* is a plausible basis for the logical connection.

Wittgenstein's analysis of «meaning as use» can properly be understood only when looked at as involving intention-embedded practices, which characterize all (or about all) human actions. If this were the case, then Wittgenstein would agree that there is no such thing as an unintentional meaning. What we have in mind about intention, however, needs to be qualified. Here, intention is not to be viewed as a private mental act or something inner that precedes human action – a Cartesian one, but should be understood as an emergent property of social interactions and thus is not necessarily located in individual minds.[52] «Those actions and responses can help identify the meaning only if they are seen and understood as intentional»[53].

Wittgenstein considers meaning within a certain nexus of human activity.[54] The significant thing about «meaning as use» is that it emphasizes that there are no facts that determine what the meaning of a sign is. This is rather done by practices, customs, and institutions [*PI* §199]. The point of Wittgenstein's critiques, which is contrary to the Cartesian and Augustinian (we can even include the Kripkean)[55] position is that no accompanying fact can account for the life of any sign. There is no objective meaning for a word that is present every time it is uttered. He

---

[52] «Intention is neither emotion, a mood, nor yet a sensation or image. It is not a state of consciousness. It does not have genuine duration» [*Z* §45].

[53] B. STROUD, «Mind, Meaning and Practice», 310.

[54] The important connection between the *TLP* and the *PI* that Stroud tries to indicate is that in both works meaning is described as some sort of location within a nexus («logic» in the *TLP* and «form of life» in the *PI*). Cf. B. STROUD, «Mind, Meaning and Practice».

[55] Cf. S. KRIPKE, *Wittgenstein on Rules and Private Language*. Kripke, as far as his influence is concerned, must now be rated among the top three of living Anglo-American philosophers. He revolutionized important areas of logic and wrote two major works on meaning: *Naming and Necessity* (1972) and *Wittgenstein on Rules and Private Language* (1982).

insists that the life is bestowed to these things by the signs humans use
and not the contrary.

The tone of Wittgenstein's application of *use* (as «usage» as well as
«practice») entails that something particular need to be fulfilled. One
does not use words or make statements for personal idiosyncrasy. Descriptions, commands, inquiries and most other modes of speech are
used with a certain expectation in view. In Wittgenstein's builders [*PI*
§2], intention becomes evident by the association of the individual's
use of words to the network of human activity.[56] The builder's utterance of *slab* is made with certain anticipation that the assistant would
bring a particular slab to him when it is expressed. In as much as words
are significantly used, certain effects are clearly projected. Wittgenstein's consideration of meaning can certainly be viewed in terms of intentions and effects. This means that when one is engaged in using a
word, there is an accompanying intention that a certain effect should
take place after its employment. This particular intended effect is for
someone to *understand* or *grasp* of the meaning of that specific word or
an utterance used. Now, this precise aim is achieved through the *teaching* of such use. Thus, the completion of the intention in the use of a
word is rendered attainable by the process of teaching. Wittgenstein's
elaboration of *training* and *explanation* gives very good grounds supporting this claim. In this sense we can conclude that the idea of intention underscores the logical connection between *meaning* and *teaching*.

3.2.2 Context

Another feature significant to the concepts of meaning and teaching
is the notion of *context*. We shall be investigating into its functions with
the aim of demonstrating its relevance as a positive element that demonstrates the logical connection.

In the later part of his philosophical development, Wittgenstein began to broaden the concept of context from *words* to *propositions* –
«Here we might say – though this easily leads to all kinds of philosophical superstition – the sign "R" or "B", etc. may be sometimes a word
and sometimes a proposition. But whether it "is a word or a proposition" depends on the situation in which it is uttered or written» [*PI* §49].

---

56 Cf. *PI* §337 and §581. For a discussion regarding Wittgenstein's builders see J.
PERRY, «Davidson's Sentences and Wittgenstein's Builders», 23-37 and M. RING,
«"Bring me a slab!"», 12-34.

The statement shows the gradual widening of the confines of context. He no longer considered language as a calculus.

His reference to use implies a dependency upon context. Wittgenstein was convinced that the meaning of a word is understood by considering how the word is utilized in a particular context (linguistic community). His later view of language admits that meaning is not fixed by a formal structure of language but by its use within the context – «To understand a sentence means to understand a language. To understand a language means to be a master of a technique» [*PI* §199][57]. Here the shift from the concept of language as a calculus to a careful attention of the philosophical significance of activities, of which the use of language is an integral part, is evident.

The role of *context* in meaning is strengthened by Wittgenstein's appeal to the concept of a language-game. It is intended to distinguish the fact that the speaking of a language is part of a form of life [*PI* §23]. This implies that the meaning of what we say may change depending on varying contexts. Without a context words would become lifeless, i.e., without meaning [*BB* 5]. Hence, in Wittgenstein's later philosophy, *context* serves as a matrix upon which language works and thus is of fundamental significance to his analysis of meaning.[58]

Wittgenstein, in claiming that a use of a word depends on a context, whether linguistic or non-linguistic, implies that the existence of varying contexts (verbal, historical, cultural, physical, etc.) account for the diverse uses of words. However, the context itself does not determine the correctness or incorrectness of use. There has got to be some process or procedure that establishes whether a word is used correctly in a particular context. And this is done through the teaching of use. Although the context may dictate what words will be used it is by the manner in which we were taught the use in that context which makes meaning most clear. It is clear from this aspect that *context* indeed provides the basis to affirm the logical connection between *meaning* and *teaching*.

---

[57] This passage is referred to when dealing with the issue of holism in Wittgenstein. For further discussion regarding this matter cf. M. DUMMETT, *Frege, Philosophy of Language*; J. FODOR – E. LEPORE, *Holism*; C. PEACOCKE, «Holism» and C. PENCO, «Local Holism», 290-303.

[58] Cf. *AWL*, 34-36.

3.2.3 Practice(s)

The third aspect that evidences a logical relation between meaning and teaching is the idea of *practice*. Our inquest will primarily involve an examination of the significant characteristics of such concept which may render such connection between meaning and teaching viable.

Philosophy is certainly not famous for its understanding of *practice*. Philosophers have tended to regard practice as merely a theme defined by theory. They have a propensity, when attending to such a phenomenon, to capture it through a systematic or formal account, e.g. providing models, offering exemplary studies of particular cases, developing conceptual frameworks or categories, etc. However, despite this seemingly clear attitude, recent years have seen philosophy show an increasing interest in the notion of *practice*. Nowadays, it is a philosophic commonplace that *practice* be attributed a more important role than it previously received. Wittgenstein figures as one of the contemporary philosophers who value the significance of *practice* in philosophy.

Wittgenstein considers the term «practice» in two senses: (i) that it is equivalent to a certain type of action, i.e., we do not speak of practice *that m*, but of practice *to n*, where «*n*» is replaced by a description of a kind of action - «To understand a sentence means to understand a language. To understand a language means to be a master of a technique» [*PI* §199]; «Where is the connexion effected between the sense of the expression "Let's play a game of chess" and all the rules of the game? – Well, in the list of the rules of the game, in the teaching of it, in the day-to-day practice of playing» [*PI* §197], and (ii) that it is an interweaving of human life (nexus of human actions) and language - « a person goes by a sign-post only in so far as there exists a regular use of sign-posts, a custom» [*PI* §198].

The first sense of practice underlines the relevance of the idea of training. It is important to note that we need *training* in order to engage ourselves in practice [*PI* p.185e][59]. So as to achieve mastery of *a* technique in understanding language, we must have been taught it through praxis - «But if a person has not yet got the *concepts*, I shall teach him to use the words by means of *examples* and *practice*» [*PI* §208]. With practice, we can see not only how we use signs but also what we actually do with these signs. To consider it as a method in teaching is not difficult to observe. Teachers will often employ a repetition of an ac-

---

[59] See J. SCHULTE, *Wittgenstein: An Introduction*, 106ff.

tion so as to make its performance habitual or routine – for instance, training airline pilots by using electronic simulators. This is a common approach in teaching. It aims towards mastering something – primarily a skill. Nonetheless, this kind of practice is found in formal as well as in informal instructional situation. In both cases, teaching by practice fosters, in a way, the achievement of learning.

The second sense demonstrates a wider perspective of the term practice. Here, practice is not considered as an isolated phenomenon. It is rooted within a situation, in human customs and institutions. A particular use of an expression is its distinct role in human activities in which it is or might be utilized. A certain nexus of human activity serves as the *locus* whereby meaning is manifested – it is considered as that place where signs have life. Imagine uttering a word without human practices. In what sense does the term «helix» there have meaning? It would only be empty and void of sense without the practice of genetics (or a community of geneticists). We learn how to use or apply rules when we learn the relevant practices. The intelligibility of the world and knowledge of objects is made possible by a shared language and practices. Unless we shared a language, where language is understood to include background practices, we could not say anything, true or false [*PI* §241].

Wittgenstein's appeal to practice is drawn from his effort to dislodge the *mentalistic* answers to philosophical questions which claim that philosophical problems can be solved by alluding to mental objects or an inner state. «He denies that one expression is linguistically dependent upon another because of what a speaker who uses those expressions thinks or intends»[60]. Meaning, according to him, can only be determined by our use of a word or an utterance, learned by training within the context of our shared practices and not some occult, essentially inner (mental processes, images, experiences or feelings) faculty.[61] The dynamism of actual practice(s) influences our comprehension of *use* and *meaning*. Wittgenstein saw the notion of practice as serving to highlight an aspect of the meaningful use of language. The importance he gives to the idea of practice is summed up in the following passage:

---

[60] M. RING, «"Bring me a slab!"», 29.

[61] Allegations of behaviorism have been attributed to this assertion. However, Wittgenstein saw this interpretation of his views likely to appear soon and denied it antecedently in *PI* §§307 – 308. Although Wittgenstein considers *practice* as *regularity in behavior* or *reproducibility of human action*, this comparison should not, however, be treated as indicating deep affinities with behaviorism.

We judge an action according to its background within human life, and this background is not monochrome, but we might picture it as a very complicated filigree pattern, which, to be sure, we can't copy, but which we can recognize from the general impression it makes. The background is the bustle of life. [...] How could human behavior be described? Surely only by showing the actions of a variety of humans, as they are all mixed together. Not what *one* man is doing *now*, but the whole hurly-burly, is the background against with we see an action, and it determines our judgment, our concepts, and our reactions [*RPP II* §624-625, 629].

Both these senses of practice as treated by Wittgenstein include the explicit and the tacit dimensions of the rules, precepts, codes, principles, guides, commitments, affects, and behaviors that one observes or advocates within a domain of teaching action. Although practice may have an intangible dimension, it must include the connotation of something observable, transferable, and teachable. It is a seemingly ordinary phenomena yet rich in content. It is the multifarious elements contained in practice(s) which influence effectiveness, competency and performance of the teaching of use. Whether we consider the concept of practice *per se* or its relation in the determination of meaning, teaching is of paramount importance. Thus, we can confirm through practice the logical connection between meaning and teaching.

What we endeavored in this section was to demonstrate how a *logical* connection between the concepts of *meaning* and *teaching* can be attested. We have discovered that the relation between both concepts emerges based on three fundamentally relevant philosophical concepts, viz., *intention, context* and *practice(s)*. Through a conceptual investigation of such notions (inasmuch as they all come about concurrently in our conception of both phenomena) we found out that «meaning» and «teaching» are logically connected concepts.

3.3 *The Teaching Process: An Indispensable Role*

We have affirmed in the prior section the existence of a logical connection between *meaning* and *teaching*. The relation of both concepts involves a certain degree of significance one has on the other. Given this kind of connection, we can affirm that there is a crucial role of teaching in Wittgenstein's analysis of meaning, i.e., his philosophical position about «meaning» is weakened if teaching were not posited.

The phenomenon of teaching figures significantly in Wittgenstein's analysis of meaning. According to him, when we talk about words we always ask how we were taught it, i.e., how to talk sensibly using words or how these words are taught to us.[62] In either case, *teaching* appears to be vital. It is through the process of instruction where linguistic competence is emphasized and its general and primary function of making sense of expressions is rendered as useful in destroying misconceptions. Let us now discuss in detail how teaching becomes essential in his analysis of meaning.

Wittgenstein's principal argument regarding meaning consists of negating the name-object relation and appealing to *use* as determining the meaning of a word. The fundamental import of Wittgenstein's view about the «meaning of the word is its use in the language» [*PI* §43] is that to understand the meaning of a term it is necessary for us to consider how that particular word or expression is used in a language. For instance, to be able to engage in a *correct use*, e.g., of the words *wrench* and *spanner*, *vacuum* and *hoover* and *trash* and *rubbish*, or expressions «acquired in dubious circumstances» and «fallen off the back of a lorry», presupposes that one has already been taught their uses in American and British English – «We know that the people who used the language *were taught the use* of the signs in such-and-such a way» [*PI* §53]; «What is the criterion for the way the formula is meant? It is, for example, the kind of way we always use it, *the way we are taught* to use it» [*PI* §190, *emphasis added*]. These passages point to the fact that we are not taught (directly) the meaning of the word or an utterance but instead we are taught their use and from there establish their meaning. Now *use* can be taught either by demonstration/showing or by giving reasons. These modes of teaching use are underscored in Wittgenstein's exposition of *training* and *explanation*.[63] Both types of instruction assure the teaching of «use» to the other (the learner) which, in turn, enables the determination of meaning. Wittgenstein implies that in every instance of *S* (i.e., *A* knowing the meaning of *p*) it is presumed that teaching (of use) should have taken place otherwise it would be difficult (if not ludicrous) to assess *S*. Thus, *teaching* results essential in Wittgenstein's analysis for the reason that in order to achieve any understanding of meaning there has got to be prior instruction.[64] This ob-

---

[62] Cf. *LCA* §5.

[63] See Chapter 3 sections 2.1 and 2.2 above. It is within these teaching modes where Wittgenstein's distinction between *ostensive definition* and *ostensive teaching* is clarified.

[64] This assertion might open the door to misinterpretations which I wish to avoid. The claim does not, however, allude to any *causal connection* between teaching and

viously undermines Allmaker's assertion that «teaching [and learning] may occur when an overview of all known facts is taken»[65] since to identify such data we need to be taught their meaning beforehand. Bede Rundle states, «The use is something we can master, something that can be shared by the members of a community, and the meaning determined is accordingly not something occult, something forever hidden from us»[66]. According to Hartnack, «the meaning of word is learned by discovering its use» for «if its use has been learned (through teaching), its meaning has been learned too»[67]. This undoubtedly supports the indispensable role of teaching in Wittgenstein's analysis of meaning as use.

The relevance of an emphasis on a logical connection between meaning and teaching is that it allows us to assert, albeit with minor difficulties, the indispensable role that education plays, particularly teaching, in Wittgenstein's philosophy. This view is intensified by his conviction that in actuality words have no true meaning given to them by some independent power. They have meanings people give them through *teaching*.

4. A Wittgensteinian Conception of Teaching

We have stated earlier that Wittgenstein neither intended to offer by his later writings any pedagogical theory nor wrote specific treatises on philosophy of education. However, this did not restrain us from investigating on the pedagogical insights that are contained in his opus. His use of educational situations, specifically instructional contexts, provided us with sufficient grounds to examine on its repercussions to the idea of teaching.

Wittgenstein claims that language-games must to be taught and learned (mastered). Here, he introduces the pedagogical significance of *training* and *explanation*. He points out that it is "teaching" which provides the rudiments and reasons in order to understand the meaning of a particular word. Although both types have their particular functions in different language-games, it is through their general pedagogical con-

---

understanding of meaning since we only intend to emphasize the fact that whenever meaning is determined there has already been an occurrence of teaching (of use). This indicates the logical connection between both concepts.

[65] A. ALLMAKER, «*Wholeness*», 187.

[66] B. RUNDLE, «Meaning and Understanding», p. 103.

[67] J. HARTNACK, *Wittgenstein and Modern Philosophy*, 69. Text added.

text that clarification regarding meaning is obtained. Wittgenstein's conception of teaching can be viewed in the following perspectives: i) it does not merely involve a rational/intellectual activity but it also involves a consideration of practice(s), ii) it is not a single activity but an array of interrelated activities, iii) it is progressive, iv) it is an activity done by someone with proficient qualification – *mastery of a technique*, and finally, v) it is a normative activity, i.e., the undeniable presence of authority in teaching.

4.1 *Not merely a rational activity*

Teaching when taken in its ordinary sense is dominantly an intellectual activity. It is mostly identified with the rational activity of an individual called *the teacher*. It commonly involves, as what *hardcore* analysts claim, a *rational persuasion*, i.e., behind the gestures, procedures, pronouncements, and questions, that individual determines when teaching occurs by the conscious intention to teach. When we encounter the problem with *teaching* we often resort to the intentional aspect as an indispensable note for teaching. Wittgenstein, based on his analysis of meaning, does not view teaching in this manner. He is more concerned in seeking equilibrium between the rational and the practical aspects of teaching. We should have, as what Wittgenstein calls a perspicuous representation (*übersichtliche Darstellung*)[68], of teaching. He considers the active and not merely a passive involvement of the student in the educational enterprise and instigates an intuitive examination within the student. Hence, for him teaching involves both the formal and the informal aspect, i.e., it is not exclusively and primarily a rational engagement but in it one is also fundamentally occupied in a *practice* in a form of life – «it is not a specialized technical term that refers exclusively to sophisticated intellectual acts performed only by professionally-trained teachers; it is one of the most widely spread polymorphous activities and permeates all human societies and institutions – from the simple life of the cavemen to the modern technological world, from the nuclear modern family to the graduate school in a university»[69] .

---

[68] This is the goal of Wittgenstein's philosophical project. This is reflected in Allmaker's claim that, teaching is «bringing the student to "see" for himself» See A. ALLMAKER, «*Wholeness*», 175.

[69] T. KAZEPIDES, «Wittgenstein and the rationalists», 330.

4.2 *Not a single distinct activity*

Based on the aforementioned argument, teaching then is viewed by Wittgenstein not as a *single* definite activity but a conglomeration of interrelated activities. This particular insight relates to his idea of *family resemblance*. [70] This assertion insists that the concept of teaching has no clear boundaries, i.e., there are only what can be called patches and parts of teaching, for instance *training, instruction, explanation, etc.* As an activity, teaching can be best understood as a family of activities within which some members appear to be of more central significance than others. According to T.W. Moore, «For one thing, the word "teaching" is not the name of *any one* activity. Teaching may involve many different kinds of activities: talking, asking questions, writing on blackboard, setting up situations in which pupils can learn, and many others»[71] - it is one of the most generally extended *polymorphous activities* that pervades all human societies and institutions. This view is affirmed by Thomas Green with his claim of the molecular concept of teaching. «In order to more clearly understand the concept it may suffice to simply describe in schematic form what are the logical properties most central to this family of activities and to display in what respects other less central activities do or do not bear the marks of teaching»[72]. If this were the case, then Philip Jackson's assertion that «there is no such thing as "genuine" teaching. There is only an activity that people call teaching, which can be viewed from a variety of critical perspectives»[73] agrees with this Wittgensteinian view of teaching.

4.3 *It is progressive*

The notion of "progress" here does not suggest adherence to the ideals of *progressivism*. What is rather underlined here is the development of the teaching process. Wittgenstein's treatment of training and explanation basically insinuates a continuous progression from a *mechanical/practical* type of teaching to a *rational* one.[74] For instance, before I can teach (by explanation) someone why there is rain, how rain is formed, I should have taught him/her (by training) how to use the word

---

[70] In such case, Wittgenstein considers teaching as a family resemblance concept of related activities. Cf. A. PEARSON, *The Teacher: theory and practice*, 65.

[71] T.W. MOORE, *Philosophy of education: an introduction*, 67.

[72] T. GREEN, «A Topology of the Teaching Concept», 37.

[73] P. W. JACKSON, *The Practice of Teaching*, 95.

[74] L.P. MCCARTY – D.C. MCCARTY, «Reading in the darkness», 390.

rain. The contrary would be implausible for it renders explanation superfluous at the first instance. This entails that mastery of the use of a word (by training) is supposed to take place before meaningful understanding (by explanation) could occur. In this case, Wittgenstein would disagree with Komisar's assertion that only in the act level of teaching is learning expected.[75] Training, on the one hand, may be considered to cause learning (of the use of a word).[76] Indeed «certain concepts seem to be implanted by training and, importantly, this is as true of games we learn as adults as it is of those we learnt as children»[77]. Explanation, on the other hand, would be given in terms of words common to both the teacher and the student and thus offers reasons and justifications for the learner's correct understanding. Evidently, the recognition of intention is rendered patent at this level – the learner will realize that the teacher wants him to learn something whether or not realizing that the teacher intends him to realize this fact. Both modes indicate a specific growth of knowledge on the part of the learner. This means that for Wittgenstein appropriate *Abrichten/Abrichtung* and *Erklärung* can occur – or may even need to take place – at all sorts of stages in one's educational career. This is evidently manifested in the principles that he developed during his teaching career in Vienna, viz., self-activity (*Selbsttätigkeit*) and integrated instruction.

4.4 *It is done by someone with proficient qualification*

Even if teaching may be congeries of activities, «anybody can teach» would be a statement that Wittgenstein would not immediately agree with. We have indicated in the previous chapter that teaching is not restricted to professional teachers. However, this does not mean that those outside the community of professional teachers may be qualified as «teaching» in Wittgenstein's sense. In order to competently teach one needs to be *adequately* educated. His insistence on the acquisition of *mastery of playing the game* gives us a hint on the character of teaching Wittgenstein has in mind, i.e., that it be an activity done with competence. Now, proficiency here would mean that one who teaches must have sufficient qualifications which in Wittgensteinian jargon

---

[75] Cf. P. KOMISAR, «Teaching: Act and Enterprise», 168-193 and M.I. BERGER, «Philosophizing about Teaching», 282-292.

[76] M. BIGGE, *Educational Philosophies for Teachers* 114.

[77] L.P. MCCARTY – D.C. MCCARTY, «Semantic Physiology: Wittgenstein on Pedagogy», 234.

would refer to the concept of *mastery of a technique* [*PI* §§150, 199]. This would correspond to what Michael Oakeshott calls the "learned" – teaching is an activity «in which a "learned" person (to use an archaism) "learns" his pupils»[78].

Statements such as "my child has taught me to treasure life" or "being trapped in that burning house taught me..." do not imply that the use of the term "teaching" is invalid but that it would not carry the sense of Wittgenstein's view since aside from the lack of an agent proficiently qualified to teach, emphasis is given more on the aspect of learning than in teaching. «To understand a language means to be a master of a technique» [*PI* §199] presumes that in order to teach the use of a word one must have mastered that particular use. This mastery does not only confirm the validity of content but of teaching as well. For Wittgenstein, "anybody can teach" would be true provided that it would contain the qualification mentioned. When it deals with the concept of teaching, he would undoubtedly vouch for the legitimacy of professional teachers.

4.5 *It is a normative activity*

The previous outlook leads to a contention that teaching should be normative. This usually refers to *authority* which is seldom mentioned in discussion of teaching. In training, the teacher normatively sets those standards in which the pupil is prompted to comply. When the teacher says, for example, «Repeat after me...» or «Look! This is a...» and so on, the acceptance of the rule by the pupil is basically required. The normativity of this type of teaching hinges upon the channeling of behavior – the legitimate influence of the teacher over the pupil. Although the prescriptive character is evident, being normative does not mean being coercive. Authority in training presents an unusual quality of being reciprocal, and thus dependent upon others for its fulfillment.

In an explanation, on the other hand, the determination of the rule, its understanding and its consequent conformity are not established by the teacher but by the explanation itself. In this sense, normativity connotes the recognition on the part of the students of the rule contained within the explanation and based on that acts and re-acts according to what they have understood. Suppose that X teaches (explains) the subject matter P to A. If we knew X to be playing some language-game S then

---

[78] M. OAKESHOTT, «Teaching», 13.

we know something about the standards of correctness which govern *P* thus taught. Here, teaching may not seem to be concerned directly with behaviors and thus turns up to be descriptive. However, it becomes normative by virtue of the necessity to recognize those rules which constitute the basis for the correctness and incorrectness of understanding. Teaching would also be prescriptive even if it is not focused on influencing behavior(s).

It would be very interesting to see how Wittgenstein demonstrated these aspects in the course of his teaching career in Vienna and Cambridge. However, this is not part of the purview of our study. It is nonetheless a suitable area for further research.

5. Conclusion

Wittgenstein's analysis of *meaning as use*, in recent literature, has received notable attention because of its principal impact upon *philosophy of language* but very few have recognized its significance on *philosophy of education*. In this chapter we endeavored to place Wittgenstein's investigation within the ambit of educational philosophy. Our aim was to find out whether an overall appraisal of the philosopher's analysis of meaning offers a consistent adherence to the accepted understanding of the concept of teaching or provides a new perspective which allows a reconsideration of our comprehension of such concept.

Based on the discussions developed in this chapter we conclude that 0057ittgenstein's analysis of meaning, when generally assessed, does not present a radical shift or an evident divergence from the acknowledged conception of teaching. Fundamental points, such as the teaching-learning relation, presence of authority, the intentional aspect of teaching, and others, are not by any means repudiated by his investigation. We do not need to discuss this matter in great detail since we have sufficiently drawn attention to it in the previous sections. However, this claim does not make our study futile in view of the fact that, although Wittgenstein did not intend to advocate a pedagogical theory, his analysis of meaning provides us with a novel viewpoint regarding the function of teaching in the educational enterprise.

Based on a general consideration of Wittgenstein's analysis we observe that teaching functions as a means of *normalization* in education. His allusion to the concepts of *use, language-games, family resemblance, pratice(s)*, and *form(s) of life*, underlines the fact that teaching aims at enabling the learner to take over and go on by himself – to bring the student to see for himself and to paraphrase Wittgenstein's assertion, be able to arrange what he has always known [*PI* §109]. This implies that teaching is directed towards *normality*. Being normal here is not used in the psychological context but it refers to the way one behaves, acts or participates (regularity) within particular practices, i.e., we expect the students, in teaching them certain skills and knowledge, to do what we would do by maturely making use of what they have learned in the context of a form of life. We should not, however, construe that whenever teaching occurs, as anticipated by Wittgenstein's investigation, it would necessarily achieve the intended normality. This is due to the fact that teaching is often accompanied by abnormal reactions of learners because of the «asymmetry between teaching and learning»[79]. Nonetheless, the stress placed on training and explanation as well as persuasion (progressive character of teaching) implies that although there may be deviant reactions of students, we should not renounce teaching altogether. Instead, we should reinforce it so as to arrive at the intended purpose. Even so, we should not presume that the rationale of teaching, as used in this context, is merely making the same person or recreating our *Lebensform* but rather as enabling the students to see similarities as well as dissimilarities (family resemblance and language-games) [*PI* §130].

This particular conception of teaching appears uncomplicated when dealing with the teaching of practical skills but may have some problems when confronted with the form of teaching in the more speculative field of study, e.g., physics, theology, philosophy, and the like. However, such predicament would not hold ground if we consider each of these specific areas of study, in a Wittgensteinian optic, as individual communities of practice playing their own «language-games» (a *form of life*). This indicates that teaching endeavors to make possible that the learner does what others (*normal* members) in the particular community of practice would do. The sense of teaching that aims for normality is still maintained.

This innovative point of view regarding the teaching process as an upshot of Wittgenstein's analysis of meaning, however, is not immune to attacks. We recognize the fact that it is arduous to completely comprehend his ideas. Nevertheless, we are certain that the understanding of meaning (through use) [*PI* §43] and his allusion to an agreement in a form of life [*PI* §241] is made possible by the teaching process which

---

[79] S. CAVELL, *The Claim of Reason*, 111-112.

besides learning intends to achieve *normality* – that the learner would become an independent individual (one who understands the grammar of words and the rules used of their application) within a particular community (of practice), i.e., in a certain form of life.

CHAPTER IV

Rule-following and the Process of Learning

We have elaborated in the preceding chapter the significance and implication of Wittgenstein's concept of *meaning as use* in our understanding of the concept of teaching. Here we shall focus on another paramount concept in the educational enterprise which is a complement to the teaching practice, i.e. *learning*. As we have pointed out in chapter two of this work, psychologists have presented motley of conflicting learning theories. However, according to Richard Peters, «Of all branches of psychology one would have thought that learning theory would be most relevant. Yet the fact is that very little of learning theory is of much interest or relevance to the educator»[1]. We take Peters' statement not to blame educators for taking *learning theories* for granted but to highlight the fact that, although some may take interest in developing a consistent account of the concept of learning, much of the studies regarding this phenomenon are taken over by the field of psychology. However, based on Peters' observation, educators should see the fact that it is precisely the results of these studies undertaken by psychologists that should be examined and not jettisoned if we are to fully understand the process of learning.

One of the results of these varying theories is the prevailing dichotomy (cognitivist vs. behaviorist) in our conception of learning. Although each camp may have plausible data and arguments that would support their contention, confusion as to what learning is all about still remains. We are often forced by their assertions to take sides whenever we try to explain it. In this chapter we shall attempt to develop a con-

---

[1] R. PETERS, *Authority, Responsibility and Education*, 119.

ceptual investigation of the *process of learning* in the light of Wittgenstein's idea of rule-following. We are not here concerned with providing another learning theory and further obfuscate our understanding of it but rather endeavor to demonstrate that Wittgenstein's idea of rule-following provides a unique view of the process of learning. The contention that we shall defend here can be described in two points. First, the dynamism of rule-following provides an understanding *sui generis* of the process of learning, i.e., the fundamental features of rule-following, such as practice and training (teaching), provide a considerable contribution to the emerging paradigm of learning. Wittgenstein's notion of rule-following is of major importance in our investigation to provide backing for our contention and thus will be highlighted here. Second, based on our arguments we will discover that Wittgenstein was neither a cognitivist nor a behaviorist in the strict sense of the word but one who incorporates both camps in his philosophical analysis. Thus, our main claim bridges, in a way, the gap between the cognitivist and behaviorist theories of learning and consequently dissolves the dichotomy.[2]

We shall proceed with our discussion by first providing an account of the character of the *process of learning* in the later works of Wittgenstein. Specific attention will be given to his account of language learning in order to determine the significance of rules and rule-following in such process. We shall also include in this section a differentiation of his views regarding the concepts often confused and interchanged with learning, namely, *understanding* and *knowing*. Since Wittgenstein's argument on rule-following is not immune to attacks, we shall then elaborate on the skeptical point contained in his idea. We shall here include an examination of the Kripkean position and determine how his reading (although some of it is relevant to Wittgenstein's philosophy) deviates from that of Wittgenstein's idea. After this has been done, we shall then discuss the fundamental features that consti-

---

[2] Unfortunately, I have not encountered any specific investigation regarding this issue presented in the level of studies in philosophy of education. However, one such attempt is implied in the works of the social theorists like Albert Bandura. Social learning theory explains human behavior in terms of continuous reciprocal interaction between cognitive, behavioral, an environmental influences. Bandura's work is related to the theories of Vygotsky and Lave, which also emphasize the central role of the cognitive theory and behaviorism. For further details see A. BANDURA, *Social Learning Theory*. See also L.S. VYGOTSKY, *Mind in Society* and J. LAVE, *Cognition in Practice*.

tute, according to Wittgenstein, *rule-following*. This will be followed by an exposition of the rule-following like character of the learning process. To conclude, we shall discuss the impact of our claim to the psychological learning theories and its pedagogical implication.

1. The Process of Learning in the Later works of Wittgenstein

Our inquiry would seem to be, from the outset, a task of looking for a needle in a haystack given the fact that Wittgenstein's later writings were not intended to offer a pedagogical theory and that he at no point explicitly defined or explained what *learning* is. However, this is not entirely the case. Aside from the sporadic uses of the term *learning* (*Lernen*) in the *PI*, if we pay close attention to its early part we notice that Wittgenstein draws attention to the fact that language must be learned and actually begins his philosophical inquiry with a particular case of learning, i.e., language learning.[3] Although an elaboration of the concept may not have been included in the *leitmotiv* of his work, nonetheless it is from this particular context where the development of his philosophical ideas is set in motion. Hence, if we endeavor to advance and build up a picture of *learning* contained in his later works, then it is fitting that we should first examine his conception of the process of learning a particular language. However, the details of what transpires during the course of action is not, as we shall see later on, a very important issue in itself, but we are rather concerned in extracting from his treatment of language learning the peculiar features of the process of learning *per se*.

Wittgenstein cites a passage from Augustine's *Confessions* to illustrate an instance of language learning. We shall not expound on the details of Augustine's theory but it will suffice to say that the ideas contained in the *Confessions* as well as in the *De Magistro* regarding language learning are concerned mainly of how meaning is attached to words and their relation to reality and whether or not we can teach and learn from words. Vital to his discussion is the idea about *memory* which, considered generally, would lead us to the view of learning as

---

[3] Other writers prefer to use «acquisition of language» rather than «learning of a language» obviously to avoid the polemical nature of the concept of learning. Nonetheless, I prefer the latter rendition of the case since it serves the purpose of underlining the significance of his notion of rule-following in the process.

an internal process more or less depicted in Donald Norman's learning theory.[4]

Wittgenstein's criticisms do not indicate that Augustine's idea is totally wrong. He is rather concerned with the lack of account concerning *use* in such a theory. As a result, he classifies it as an explanation for how words gain meaning, i.e., as one-to-one correlation between words and meanings [*PI* §1] rather than the real understanding of how meaning is negotiated through language [*PI* §32]. His insistence on the aspect of *use* and his allusion to *language-games* in learning a language demonstrates that such a process underscores the significance of *rules* (be it implicit or explicit). His discussion regarding *practice* and *form of life* which are obviously rule-governed further evidence this fact. Although he puts more emphasis on the relation of learning with training, he nonetheless shows that since explanation is founded upon training we can always connect it to learning as well. This aspect gives us the idea that although learning may *involve* an internal process at *some point*, Wittgenstein does not consider it as a straightjacket conception.[5] He maintains equilibrium in his views regarding the phenomenon by his emphasis on *use* and *practice*, i.e., learning within the accepted usages in a linguistic community. This gives us a hint how such a process is akin to rule-following.

It may seem that he walks a line that borders a cognitivist theory on one side and empiricist on the other. It is exactly this bridging of gap that gives Wittgenstein's view its uniqueness. He is careful not to fall on either one of these extremes. This distinct Wittgensteinian outlook regarding *learning* will appear clearer as we go along our examination of its character implied in his later writings.

In order for us to determine the fundamental features of the learning process in Wittgenstein we need to discuss two concepts which are oftentimes interchanged or mistaken with the phenomenon of learning. We are here referring to the concepts of *understanding* and *knowing*. They are found in his later works and are given considerable attention by Wittgenstein especially in the *Investigations* and *On Certainty*. We shall be discussing them respectively in the succeeding sections.

---

[4] Cf. R. HERGENHAHN – M. OLSON, *An Introduction to Theories of Learning*, 361ff.

[5] I want to emphasize here that although Wittgenstein tried to heal us from reifying internal (mental) processes, he nevertheless did not totally reject the idea of using the terms.

1.1 *The Concept of Understanding*

In common discourse we often use the concepts of *understanding* and *learning* interchangeably. However, as we shall see later on, there is a notable difference between both of them. The main points that we are going to discuss in this section are: (a) in Wittgenstein's later writings *understanding* is not taken as equal with *learning* and (b) in order of precedence learning goes before understanding.

Before we discuss their diversity, let us first of all consider two evident characteristics that manifest their resemblance. Firstly, understanding like learning is commonly determined to have taken place by an evidence of a certain observable manifestation either by a gesture – pointing at an apple at the sight of one [*PG* §52] or as indicated by Stanley Cavell «a gesture of the eyes in a particular circumstance of obscurity»[6], or an utterance – «Ohh!», «Aha!» or «Now I understand!». According to Alberto Voltolini such manifestation of comprehension is for Wittgenstein a necessary condition for understanding.[7] Indeed, there is no sense in contesting this assertion since Wittgenstein draws attention to this fact by affirming that understanding involves a certain type of reaction – «And if a child does not react to our encouragement, like a cat that one wishes to teach to retrieve, then one does not succeed in getting it to understand one's explanation; or rather, understanding begins here with reacting in a determinate way»[8]. These manifestations are however varied depending on the different situations (language-games).[9] Warren Goldfarb accentuates this aspect in his claim that we find no physical or physiological regularity in things that we call manifestations of understanding. Hence, we should not expect to find mere physical systematicity in understanding.[10] Nonetheless, the presence of a particular manifestation of understanding is expected and is not negated otherwise it would be arduous for us to say that one has understood or not. Secondly, the problem that beset learning, i.e., whether or not it should be considered as entirely an inner (mental) state or process

---

[6] S. CAVELL, «Notes and Afterthoughts», 284.

[7] A. VOLTOLINI, *Guida alla Lettura*, 66.

[8] L. WITTGENSTEIN, *Eine Philosophische Betrachtung*, 131.

[9] Any relation between understanding and its manifestation does not possess the invariability that a direct causal relation entails, i.e., one does not produce manifestations of one's understanding at all times. This may be due to the fact that one does not want to or he makes a mistake or is bored or has simply misheard what was said. Cf. W. GOLDFARB, «Wittgenstein on Understanding», 116.

[10] W. GOLDFARB, «Wittgenstein on Understanding», 118.

is somehow also applicable to understanding. This argument is considered by Wittgenstein as problematic. The subsequent discussion will articulate this particular aspect.

We can observe that Wittgenstein's main argument regarding the phenomenon of understanding claims that we should not consider it as a subject of an *inner* (mental or psychical) state or process.[11] Two obvious references to the term *inner* are implied in his works. One refers to the *conscious* or *experiential* state or process (mentalistic) and the other denotes one's subconscious mechanism. Wittgenstein's rejection gives more attention to the *mentalistic* rather than the *mechanistic* account.

> Try not to think of understanding as a "mental process" at all. – For *that* is the expression which confuses you. But ask yourself: in what sort of case, in what kind of circumstances, do we say, "Now I know how to go on", when, that is, the formula *has* occurred to me?- In the sense in which there are processes (including mental processes) which are characteristic of understanding, understanding is not a mental process [*PI* §154].

There are two aspects which support his contention. First, there is a *grammatical* difference between a state e.g., pain, depression and excitement and understanding [*PI* p. 59e]. Particular types of states or processes have certain temporal duration, i.e., temporal concepts are applicable to states but not to understanding. We can speak of pain to have started in a specific point in time and ends in another or experiencing an interruption for a few minutes. We can not apply this to understanding. Furthermore, concepts of intensity also highlight the difference – we can say that a particular pain is described as intense or an emotion strong but it makes no sense speaking of understanding in this manner.

Second, it seems that having an image is what understanding (a word) amounts to.[12] However, to have some particular thing to come before one's mind, as in understanding a word in a flash, is not a necessary condition of understanding.[13] Stern warns us that the subjective side of understanding (grasping the meaning in a flash) is a dangerously lim-

---

[11] Cf. *PI* §§138-242, 318-325. See also B. RUNDLE, «Meaning and Understanding», 108.

[12] Bertrand Russell, at one stage, argued that describing a past event involved picturing it in the mind and choosing our words so as to describe the picture. This is actually one of the targets of Wittgenstein's criticisms.

[13] For example understanding the word *cube* cf. *PI* §§139-141.

ited basis for any insight into the nature of understanding.[14] Although motley of images or mental representations may accompany under- standing a particular thing or a word, no *one* of these seems essential for understanding it in a particular way.[15] Introspection cannot be relied upon since we sometimes understand without any item coming before our mind. It is no more essential to understanding that one considers an inner mental picture than it is that one possesses an external physical picture.[16] We can thus agree with what Baker and Hacker said that nei- ther mental nor explicit presentation of such a picture is what under- standing a word in a flash consists in; rather it is how one uses and ex- plains the word that manifests whether one understands.[17]

With the aforementioned fundamental arguments Wittgenstein has dislodged the mentalistic stance of understanding. However, we still need to elaborate on his point of view regarding the mechanistic posi- tion.

There are very scant passages in his later writings which tackle this particular problem. The claim he wishes to reject here is that the differ- ence between one who understands and one who does not consists in their being different unconscious or physical states [*PI* § 158].[18] Witt- genstein would deny that understanding requires any basis in a person's physical states, i.e., there is no need for such a basis and if one would exist it would be extraneous to the concept of understanding. He strongly objects to the idea that understanding is an inner or internal state since to claim that it is *mental* would be to assimilate it to pain, depression and excitement, hence inviting and erroneous *inner state* conception. In this regard, Hacker's contention that understanding is «a process that takes place *in the mind* and mediates between, e.g., hearing the words of an order and acting on it»,[19] is evidently misguided since it is, according to Wittgenstein, «more than any of those more or less characteristic *accompaniments* or manifestations of understanding» [*PI* §152]. He admonishes us not to absolutely think of understanding as

---

[14] See D. STERN, *Wittgenstein on Mind and Language*, 123.

[15] Cf. G.P. BAKER – P.M.S. HACKER, *An Analytical Commentary*, I, 259-260.

[16] In the *Blue Book* Wittgenstein advises us always to substitute the supposed men- tal picture with a physical one in order to demonstrate the weakness of the mental pic- ture. See *BB* pp. 4-5.

[17] G.P. BAKER – P.M.S. HACKER, *An Analytical Commentary*, I, 260.

[18] See *Z* §§ 608-610. Here Wittgenstein's gives a fuller statement of the relation between the psychological and the physical.

[19] P.M.S. HACKER, *Wittgenstein, Mind and Will*, 45. Italics supplied.

something *mental* – not something that *goes on* in you upon hearing an utterance – neither conscious, unconscious, nor physical.[20] Voltolini's claim that understanding does not reside in any mental or cerebral event nor does it have to do anything with determinate neurophysiological experiences or processes supports this point.[21]

Wittgenstein thus considers *understanding* as related to the concept of *use* (application). In his *Lectures on the Foundations of Mathematics*, he expresses that one only understands an expression when one knows how to use it, i.e., i) «he understands it [a word] if he always uses it right in ordinary life, millions of times and ii) if he does this…we take his doing this as a criterion of his having understood».[22] Hence, he is justified in saying that understanding involves a mastery of a technique [*PI* §199]. Bede Rundle explains this clearly when he says, «It is by solving and explaining it [the calculus solution] to others that we show our understanding of the calculus, what matters being what we *can do*, and not what thoughts or image should accompany or proceed the exercise of the ability»[23]. Richard McDermott suggests that «to know a topic or a discipline is not just to possess information about it. It is the ability to use information»[24]. The conclusion, we believe, is that both the mental state and the use of a term are criteria for whether a person understands an expression or not. However, while the person's application of an expression determines (or comes close to constituting) their understanding of it, the mental event is considered as an occurrence which accompanies understanding insofar as it is a signal that they will apply the expression in a certain way. For even if there is no logical connection between mental state and application, there may still be a contingent connection that supports the inference from one to the other. Let us now proceed in elaborating our main contention.

---

[20] Cf. *PI* §693; *Z* §26; *BB* pp. 3, 78. See also D. STERN, *Wittgenstein on Mind and Language*, p. 106.

[21] «Il punto (di vista) è che la tesi della connessione interna tra significato e comprensione non comporta affatto l'assunto mentalista che il significato risiede in un evento mentale o cerebrale. Per avere una tale implicazione, anche il comprendere dovrebbe essere un evento del genere; ma per Wittgenstein comprendere un significato non ha a sua volta nulla a che fare coll'avere determinate esperienze vissute o processi neurofisiologici». A. VOLTOLINI, *Guida alla Lettura*, 52 ff. See also B. RUNDLE, «Meaning and Understanding», 19.

[22] C. DIAMOND, ed., *Wittgenstein's Lectures*, 20-21. Hereafter considered as *LFM*.

[23] B. RUNDLE, «Meaning and Understanding », 109. Text added.

[24] R. MCDERMOTT, «How Information Technology Inspired», 106.

Wittgenstein's discussion about training (*Abrichtung*) and explanation (*Erklärung*) manifests the diversity between understanding and learning. There are two aspects that underline their difference. First, learning on the one hand, implies or alludes to the establishment of what is fundamental or rudimentary in a specific subject matter, i.e., to grasp what is taught without focusing attention to reasons. This is due to the fact that learning, as we shall see later on, is precisely comparable to the process of *following a rule*. Understanding, on the other hand, presupposes that the individual already possesses these rudiments and is more concerned with reasons which explanation provides. If this were the case, then Wittgenstein would agree that it is nonsensical to say that one understands something he has not learned. Second, in learning one *seeks to achieve* a mastery of a technique while in understanding one is already equipped with such mastery. In this case then it implies that training is important in understanding.[25]

The aforementioned arguments direct us to affirm that learning precedes understanding. This is so because understanding requires that we already possess the basics of what we want to comprehend. This means that whenever there is an occurrence of understanding this is certainly due to the fact that learning has already taken place.

Wittgenstein's exposition of the concept of understanding demonstrates that since it is not a mental state or process, it obviously has recourse to action (practice and use). To adhere to this idea would imply that understanding does involve rules which are now *internalized*. We do not need to digress on this point but it will suffice to say that while in learning there is a case of basic rule-following, there is an *internalization* of these (followed) rules within understanding. This would account for the fact that to understand *A* or *B* we need to have followed the particular rule(s) of *A* and *B* respectively. A concrete example for this would be the game of chess. To say that we understand the game we ought to have followed its rules correctly otherwise such comprehension would not be possible.

Having thus delineated the basic points underpinning Wittgenstein's arguments regarding understanding, we have discovered that learning and understanding are different concepts and thus should not be interchanged. We also found out that since learning is concerned with the

---

[25] Cf. D. STERN, *Wittgenstein on Mind and Language*, 127.

basics, it evidently precedes understanding. Let us now proceed with our investigation of the other concept often confused with learning, i.e. *knowing*.

1.2 *Knowing and Learning*

It is important to stress at the onset of this section that although we are concerned with developing a basic picture of the concept of knowing, we are not going to deal with a thorough epistemological analysis of Wittgenstein's later writings. The fundamental problem that we are dealing with here is to differentiate the knowing and learning processes. This inquiry concerns the questions whether Wittgenstein's arguments treat knowing as process of mere acquisition of concepts/ facts/information, whether knowing precedes learning due to the fact that it seems to imply knowledge, and whether it is, in any particular case, equal to understanding.

A major setback of an attempt to develop a detailed account of Wittgenstein's ideas about the act of knowing is the lacuna of specific claims regarding the process. Much of what can be mustered concerning the phenomenon of knowing comes from his grammatical analysis in the *Investigations* of how the word «to know» is used (or misused)[26] and his investigation of knowledge-claims in *On Certainty*. However, this should not render our investigations futile since there are plausible evidences that we can gather from his major arguments that could support our study.

Generally, when we talk about the act of knowing we refer to that process wherein the knower grows in knowledge by apprehending something (conceptual or practical). In this case we have a picture of *knowing* as a course of accumulation to further enhance the repertoire of knowledge. This position entails a kind of passive receptivity on the part of the knower. It is as if it is made up of discrete and transferable granules of perception of reality which can be added to an extant heap of knowledge. Is this particular view of the process of knowing congenial to Wittgenstein's treatment of the problem of knowledge?

Let us begin our inquiry by stating synthetically his conception of knowledge. Wittgenstein's ideas primarily consist in an effort to eradicate the representationalist view which claims that knowledge is a representation lodged in an individual's mind. It obviously carries with it a

---

[26] See *PI* §§ 30, 78, 187, 148, 187, 303, 363-364, pp. 220-221e.

Platonic sense of something *innate*.[27] Although Wittgenstein does not deny that there are psychological states and processes, he nevertheless objects to the idea of equating them with knowledge.

The later Wittgenstein has a strong repugnance to mentalistic explanations of concepts. This accounts for his insistence on the aspect of use and practice.[28] In this case, according to J.C. Spender, «knowledge is tied up with the context of its development and use»[29]. It is comprised of theoretical statements whose meaning and practical implications depend on their use and on the framework in which they are deployed. This assertion evidences that knowledge should not be viewed as a representation but rather as internal to a *framework*, e.g., language-game(s) and practice(s). If this were the case, then the process of knowing is not limited to the acquisition of representations or models from the wide rage of phenomena (as proposed by Descartes or Chomsky), but it involves an application of arbitrary structures on the basis of conventions that belong to ordinary practice. It consists in a dynamic interaction with the outside world and not a static relationship. Wittgenstein's arguments allow us to conclude that the process of knowing is not purely mental (psychological process)[30] but an *active construction* of models found in the framework of practice. For instance, John Heaton suggests that «We have to be able to employ words before we can point to things and know them».[31] In this vein, knowing involves a *conscious reflection* – «One has to know (or be able to do) something in order to be capable of asking a thing's name » [*PI* §30].

If we are to admit that knowing entails a conscious reflection then this means that it is differentiated from the process in which the giving of justifications is out of place, i.e., that which is presented in training –

---

[27] Others attribute the same characteristics to *tacit knowledge*. However, I see the need to differentiate both concepts since the Platonic sense of innateness is different from a non-linguistic non-numerical character of tacit knowledge that is highly personal yet context specific and deeply rooted in experiences, ideas, values and emotions. Cf. M. POLANYI, *The Tacit Dimension*.

[28] See *PI* §381, *OC* §§114, 306, 472, 560.

[29] J.C. SPENDER, «Organizational Knowledge», 75.

[30] This is so because psychological states are merely accompanying aspects of what we call *knowledge* since the criterion of whether or not one is actually knowing something must be shown in one's actions, for instance, in answering questions correctly or being able to justify one's assertions. Cf. *PI* § 150; *OC* § 535; *Z* §71- 72, 75-83; L. WITTGENSTEIN, *Last Writings on the Philosophy of Psychology*, II. Hereafter considered as *LWII*.

[31] J. M. HEATON, *Wittgenstein and Psychoanalysis*, 37.

«For how can a child immediately doubt what is taught? That could mean only that he was incapable of learning certain language-games» [*OC* §283]. This demonstrates that Wittgenstein considers the process of learning as a foundation that enables us to proceed in engaging in a more advanced and complicated language-games which, in our case, includes the process of knowing.

The above discussion resolves our second query, i.e. whether learning precedes knowing. Following Wittgenstein's line of argument, it is implausible to suppose that knowing comes before learning since the latter excludes the concept of doubt that is most important to the former. According to Wittgenstein «And the game which includes doubt is simply a more complicated one than a game which does not» [*PO* p. 381; cf. *OC* §317].[32] In learning we are still incapable of doubting or asking for justifications – «A child learns there are reliable and unreliable informants much later than it learns facts which are told it» [*OC* §143]. Further evidence of this position is found in *OC* §538 where Wittgenstein states, «The child, I should like to say, *learns* to react in such-and-such a way; and in so reacting it doesn't so far *know* anything. *Knowing* only begins at a later level»[33]. The next problem that we need to confront now concerns the distinction between knowing and understanding. We shall investigate whether or not knowing is equal to understanding.

In general cases understanding is analogous to knowledge in the sense that, when I have understood something, when I have solved the task of understanding, I am usually able to put my understanding in words: «I understand that the enemy is ready to surrender», «… that she is trying to make amends for what she did to us», etc. Wittgenstein seems to have this idea when he says, «The grammar of the word "knows" is evidently closely related to that of "can", "is able to". But also closely related to that of "understands". ("Master" of a technique)» [*PI* §150]. In the main, understanding has a knowledge-like character in the sense that someone who has understood a matter has thereby come to be in a position to make correct judgments or correct predictions or to act wisely or expediently in relation to the object of understanding. Connected with this is the fact that understanding, roughly speaking, refers to a concept of *competence*. Although both concepts imply an ability, the thin line that distinguishes them lies in the aim of such

---

[32] L. WITTGENSTEIN, *Philosophical Occasions*. Hereafter considered as *PO*.
[33] Emphasis added.

manifested ability. While knowing is primarily concerned with *justifications* and *reasons* on the one hand, understanding involves the *application* and *use* on the other – it is dependent on your skills, insights and knowledge, and on your ability to turn these resources to good use. It is basically engaged in making connections.

To sum it all up, due to Wittgenstein's distinctly anti-mentalistic attitude he views knowing not as an mental process, i.e. an accumulation of representations but as a conscious and active construction (an ability) of models based on ordinary practice(s). Having knowledge (knowledge-claims), according to Wittgenstein, does not exclude doubt. Since the process of learning, being akin to rule-following, obviously leaves out the possibility of doubt and reasons, it implies that knowing comes after the process of learning has occurred. However, we should not take knowing and understanding on equal grounds. Although both notions are referred to the concept of competence, it is the distinctive characteristic purposes of these abilities that constitute the fragile line that distinguishes them.

We can now pull together the things that are purported in Wittgenstein's later writings regarding the concept of learning. The most evident characteristic that we have seen about learning is that it is a *process* which does not involve reflection, reasons, and justifications. It is an activity that underscores the significance of training (teaching) and ordinary practices. Because of this peculiar aspect, learning exhibits a character similar to rule-following. Details of this issue shall be discussed in section three of this chapter. Furthermore, we need to distinguish learning from the concepts of knowing and understanding. Based on our discussion, Wittgenstein's later works evidence the fact that they are family-resemblance concepts. However, we need to recognize the order of their occurrence. Since there is no preoccupation about doubt or justifications (reasons) in learning, it is evident that both knowing and understanding comes after learning has occurred. This viewpoint along with the importance of practice and training direct us to consider learning as akin to rule-following. However, before we elaborate on this claim let us first investigate the problem of the paradox implied in following a rule.

2. Rule Skepticism: The Rule-following Paradox

Wittgenstein's discussion regarding rule-following has been considered to manifest a sort of rule-skepticism. This doctrine claims that since any step, on some interpretation of the rule, can be seen to accord with it, we cannot know what a rule requires. This particular contention bases its arguments from Wittgenstein's affirmation contained in this passage: «But how can a rule shew me what I have to do at this point? Whatever I do is, one some interpretation, in accord with the rule» [*PI* §198]. From this section, Wittgenstein investigates how a rule is able to determine an application since any exercise could be in accordance with the rule, i.e., how does a grasp of a rule for applying a term determine how to apply it. The second paragraph states, «Then can whatever I do be brought into accord with the rule?» [*PI* §198]. We seem to be able to draw a positive answer to this question, however, if whatever action one does can be said to accord with a rule, then it would be nonsense to say that one is following a rule correctly or incorrectly. Here we are now presented with a paradox. Hence, Wittgenstein says, «This was our paradox: no course of action could be determined by a rule, because every course of action can be made out to accord with the rule. The answer was: if everything can be made out to accord with the rule, then it can also be made out to conflict with it. And so there would be neither accord nor conflict here» [*PI* §201]. This specific segment in the *Investigations* has become the basis for a skeptical argument about rules in general and rule-following in particular.

2.1 *Kripke and the Skeptical Solution*

Wittgenstein's views on the above quoted passage are somewhat confusing and are therefore open to various interpretations. One of the famous interpretations of is presented by Saul Kripke in his book *Wittgenstein on Rules and Private Language*.[34] In this section, we shall summarize Kripke's discussion, which has been prominent in debates concerning Wittgenstein's rule-following considerations and evaluate how his views vary from Wittgenstein's. By this means we shall be able to come up with a reading of the text close to Wittgenstein's general philosophical thoughts.

In his book, Kripke proposes an interpretation of Wittgenstein's text and advocates for what he takes to be its correct interpretation. In his reading of the *Investigations* and Wittgenstein's rule-following consid-

---

[34] Kripke, as far as his influence is concerned, must now be rated among the top three of living Anglo-American philosophers. He revolutionized important areas of logic and wrote two major works on meaning: *Naming and Necessity* (1972) and *Wittgenstein on Rules and Private Language* (1982).

erations, Kripke posits a skeptical paradox, which claims to demonstrate «all language, all concept formation, to be impossible, indeed unintelligible»[35]. He suggests that this impossibility is manifested in the statement Wittgenstein makes in *PI* §201. He introduces a radical skeptic who, referring to the rule of addition, claims that there is nothing in the past usage of «+» that can be employed to give good reason for the answer that one should give in any present or future circumstances. The point here is that there is nothing in any past usage that determines how one should apply the rule in future cases.

In the alleged skeptical paradox, Kripke considers the comparison of two mathematical operators, plus «+» (addition) and what he calls *quus* «⊕» (quaddition). [36] Even as we might believe that we understand how we go about addition, he points out that we can never know that the rule we have been using all along has been *plus* and not *quus*. Absurd as such a suggestion might at first instance appear, there does not seem to be anything in our previous usage of our mathematical practices that could mean that we were using plus and not *quus* all along. The challenge Kripke shows is to provide a fact about previous mental, behavioral, or physical history, which can be considered as constituting meaning plus rather than quus. The claim points that no one can give reason for such an assertion since there is no such fact that proves the intention of using one rather than the other. In order to be able to arrive at an end of the process, one must posit a last rule, which is not interpreted, and hence, not determined. In other words, the skeptic searches for a fact that is both constitutive and normative.[37] This gives the skeptic grounds in claiming that there are no facts-of-the-matter concerning meaning. Kripke offers three responses to the skeptic.

One response is the *dispositionalist* account.[38] When we are talking of the meaning of *plus* we are not simply talking about our previous uses of the function but it amounts to a disposition (I have a disposition

---

[35] S. KRIPKE, *Wittgenstein on Rules*, 62.

[36] Aside from applying the skeptical paradox to mathematical rules, Kripke also claims that the paradox applies to all words and to support this contention briefly generalizes it to common nouns and sensations see S. KRIPKE, *Wittgenstein on Rules*, 19; an adaptation of Nelson Goodman's *grue paradox* (p. 20) is also presented to bring color words under the paradox.

[37] S. KRIPKE, *Wittgenstein on Rules*, 11.

[38] A disposition is a tendency to act in a certain way under certain conditions. Persistent mental states such as belief should be seen as dispositions as held by behaviorist and functionalist theories of mind. For the dispositionalist response to the paradox, see S. KRIPKE, *Wittgenstein on Rules*, 22-37.

to add, not to quad). This account claims that it is the disposition to make certain utterances that indicates that we are using *plus* and not *quus*, and that we can say, if we were to perform 58 + 67 we would answer 125. Kripke considers at great length the dispositionalist solution in his own paradox. However, he criticizes this position primarily because of the following reasons. First, dispositions are finite while rules are infinite. Kripke calls this the finitude objection. It states, «the analysis cannot account for the fact that our dispositions are finite, and will give out before the application of the term does»[39]. Secondly, dispositions are not normative. This «maintains that even if my dispositions did correspond perfectly to the addition function, that would not be enough to show that I meant addition by «+». The mere fact that I am now, and have been in the past, disposed to answer a question in a certain way does not show that I should answer it in that way»[40]. Thirdly, the dispositionalist argument would also exclude the chances of mistakes, i.e., it makes no room for the notion of a mistaken application of the rule. This is the error objection discussed by Kripke. This objection states that the analysis does not make room for dispositions to misapply the expression. Obviously, it is a possibility that one could come up with 115 adding 58 to 67 but we do not want to say that this means 58 + 67 is 115. The only way to justify our answer (125) is to say that «we have a disposition to correctly appraise 58 + 67 as 125», and this apparently will not do at all.[41]

Another important case that Kripke treats in detail (41-53) is the argument from *introspection*, i.e., we know that we mean addition by 'plus' because we possess a private access to our inner experience. We are sure what we intend by a word just as we are certain with our intentions, beliefs, etc. no matter what method lies behind this access. However, just like the dispositionalist view, Kripke rejects this response because it is greatly uncertain to consider that such mental states always accompany the act of meaning [*PI* §§165-184]. Furthermore, notwithstanding that they exist, they are not normative, i.e., they cannot determine the correct manner to confinue a finite sequence of examples in

[39] S. SOAMES, «Skepticism about Meaning», 218. Soames allots a good space (212 - 232) for a discussion regarding Kripke's analysis of the skeptical argument and the dispositionalist analysis. However, his article is aimed at proving that both Quine and Kripke committed the error of equivocation.

[40] S. SOAMES, «Skepticism about Meaning», 219. Emphasis added.

[41] See Soames' ideas concerning this matter in SOAMES, «Skepticism about Meaning», 217-218.

such a way that a person can follow a rule. «No internal impression, with a quale, could possibly tell me in itself how it is to be applied in future cases. Nor can any pile up of such impressions, thought of as rules for interpreting rules, do the job. The answer to the skeptic's problem, "what tells me how I am to apply a given rule in a new case?", must come from something outside any images or "qualitative" mental states»[42]. A feeling has no ability to instruct one on how to apply the accompanying rule.

After having seen the weakness of both the dispositionalist analysis and the argument from introspection Kripke offers the so-called skeptical solution to the skeptic's challenge. He closely follows the ideas of Wittgenstein in the presentation of this solution but applying a Humean tinge[43] to it, i.e., one that grants the «skeptic's negative assertions are unanswerable. Nevertheless our ordinary practice or belief is justified because [...] it need not require the justification the skeptic has shown to be untenable»[44]. It is called skeptical because Kripke denies that there is essentially a problem. The solution consists of replacing truth-conditions with assertibility (justification) conditions. Particular assertions make sense only in the context of a community of speakers, i.e., one cannot say of an individual 'this particular behavior is an example of following a rule', except it can be seen under a larger practice of behaving that way in the community, and the community asserts it to be a case of rule-following. Kripke actually does not answer the skeptic's challenge directly but modifies the question from«what fact makes my saying "add" mean addition rather than quaddition?» to discovering what conditions actually license such assertions and what role this license actually plays.[45]

2. 2 *An Examination of the Kripkean Position*

Kripke's proposed skeptical solution to the rule-following paradox certainly did not escape scrutiny and great deal of critical attention from other Wittgensteinian scholars. The limit of this work does not permit a detailed evaluation into these various criticisms. Nevertheless, it would not be futile in this section to make an examination of

---

[42] S. KRIPKE, *Wittgenstein on Rules*, p. 43.
[43] See A.C. GRAYLING – B. WEISS, «Frege, Russell and Wittgenstein», 779. See also KRIPKE, *Wittgenstein on Rules*, 67 ff.
[44] S. KRIPKE, *Wittgenstein on Rules*, 66.
[45] S. KRIPKE, *Wittgenstein on Rules*, 86-87.

Kripke's solution, its faithfulness to Wittgenstein's ideas and some of its arguments that commit him to an apparently incoherent position.

The first part of Kripke's solution eradicates the truth-conditional approach in favor of the assertibility conditions[46], in which one is warranted in asserting a sentence just in case one can secure communal agreement with one's statement. Thus, one is not compelled to draw any assertion as long as he gets the community's agreement. This purports that independent meaning of words is denied and instead meaning is ascribed as a comparison to how someone uses them. In this case, Kripke would admit that to say that «John is counting correctly» would be the same as saying that he counts in the way that we do. To have understood a rule of counting is, basically, to propose that one will continue to count in just the same way as we would count. If we accept this then it would mean that in order to explain the meaning of a statement we must be able to obtain *justification conditions* of that statement. However, as Wittgenstein indicated, we all reach bedrock: are sooner or later exhausted. «If I have exhausted the justifications I have reached bedrock, and my spade is turned. Then I am inclined to say: "This is simply what we do"» [*PI* §217].

This would indicate at first sight that the skeptical solution has not stepped on firm ground and destined to fail since justifications fail to determine meaning. However, Kripke insists that this would be the case if only isolated individuals are considered rather than his interaction to the wider community[47]. This brings us to the second element of the solution.

The second part introduces the community. Assertibility conditions function only by reference to interaction with a community. Here, the particular community is considered to have defined practices concerning rules – a «form of life» (to use Wittgenstein's term)[48]. Kripke, however, makes it clear that Wittgenstein does not claim that to apply a rule in the same way as other fellow speakers means to apply it *as* the community does since this claim seems to attribute Wittgenstein with a certain (logical) conventionalism[49] about meaning. Community in-

---

[46] J. Koethe maintains that Kripke's claim that Wittgenstein, in response to the paradox abandoned the truth-conditional account of meaning in the *Tractatus* positing the assertibility conditions is mistaken. Cf. J. KOETHE, *The continuity of Wittgenstein's Thought*, 10-11.

[47] S. KRIPKE, *Wittgenstein on Rules*, 89.

[48] S. KRIPKE, *Wittgenstein on Rules*, 90; 96-97.

[49] P.A. BOGHOSSIAN, «Analyticity», 349-351.

volvement is, as Kripke claims, essential to provide for the normativity of meaning. The point of the skeptical solution is that a rule can only be determined, not by a final interpretation, but by an agreement of judgment that a community shares. If this solution indeed was provided by Wittgenstein, then this would mean that it would not be possible for one to follow a rule in isolation from the community – thus, the affirmation: private language is impossible. Based on this argument, the whole of Kripke's solution relies on the nature of *agreement*. Agreement is necessary to be able to affirm the existence of rules (concepts). It will depend on particular practices, not on its conformity to the factual character of the concepts. Wittgenstein makes the following statement regarding this: «"So you are saying that human agreement decides what is true and what is false?" –It is what human beings *say* that is true and false; and they agree in the language they use. That is not agreement in opinions but in form of life» [*PI* §241].

What is central to this passage is the *concept of agreement*. Here, Wittgenstein distinguishes between matters of *opinion* and matters of *language*. For Wittgenstein, agreement is conclusive only in the sense of the latter and not of the former. Although both Kripke and Wittgenstein admit the significance of agreement and the social formation of concepts in understanding rule-following, there is still an obvious disagreement with regards to their understanding of *agreement*. Kripke fails to deal with the ambiguity of the term.

Kripke seems to have overlooked this distinction. For Wittgenstein, agreement is operative not at the level of *opinion* but at the *form of life*. It is not crucial whether people agree about matters of fact but that they share the same uses of words. Kripke fails to indicate this distinction in his affirmation of the «brute fact that we generally agree»[50], which presupposes that agreement about matters of fact determines agreement in usage. If it seems facile for Kripke to shift his account of agreement then this is due to his equivocation of the term *responses*[51]. For Kripke this term refers to both particular cases and to those that contribute to the form of life, which Wittgenstein is excluding in his statement [*PI* §§241, 242]. On this account, Kripke's insistence on the *agreement with a community* falls short of the full import of the *use in language*. «Kripke's reading effectively empties the idea of form of life of any specific content –it is simply a different way of saying that we agree

---

[50] S. KRIPKE, *Wittgenstein on Rules*, 97.
[51] S. KRIPKE, *Wittgenstein on Rules*, 96.

about particular cases»[52]. He is here making the claim that what we agree on to be the meaning of any given word determines the rules for using and employing that word. This assertion is obviously opposite to Wittgenstein's idea that what is fundamental in determining meaning is *practice* and *action*. If major attention would be given to this equivocation then we have reason to throw doubt on the success of Kripke's skeptical solution. Nevertheless, if Kripke's puts emphasis on the role of the community then this would serve to highlight Wittgenstein's argument throughout the *PI*, i.e., to shift our attention from mental processes, and individual psychological events to language-games, practices, customs and institutions.

3. Following a Rule and the Character of the Learning Process

We have evaluated in the preceding section Kripke's reading of Wittgenstein's rule-following consideration. Although he endeavored to clarify the intricacies of such a phenomenon, which is interesting in its own right, he nevertheless fails to address satisfactorily the nucleus of Wittgenstein's original thoughts. It is for this reason that we consider it too risky to adopt Kripke's interpretation of rule-following if we attempt to justify our claim that the learning process exhibits the character of following a rule. If this were the case, then we still have to delineate exactly those aspects that would demonstrate and support our contention. In this case, we need to specify the rudiments of the actual rule-following process, i.e., what really constitutes when we say we follow rules.

We shall proceed in our discussion by first confronting with the problem of rule recognition, i.e., whether or not such a recognition (detection) is a *necessary* condition for following a rule. We shall maintain the claim that following a rule, although it posits a particular recognition of a rule, is *not necessarily* impelled by such. After this has been established, we shall then advance to the dynamics involved in the actual rule-following. We shall be indicating on this part of the section the fundamental factors that comprise such a phenomenon. It is by this means that we shall be able to affirm that indeed learning possesses a rule-following like characteristics.

---

[52] D. BARRY, *Forms of Life and Following Rules*, 21-22.

3.1 *Rule Recognition*

In the ordinary sense of *following a rule*, it is generally presumed that before a rule follower applies (follows or obeys) any rule he already must have recognized it in advance.[53] This could most likely be applied to rules of games, for instance chess. But is this always the case?[54] Before we present any reply to this query let us first clarify what we mean by *recognition*.

Recognition here does not have any other connotation beyond that which is purported by the terms *detection* or *identification*. It straightforwardly involves an emphasis on the aspect of perception of rules (whether explicitly or implicitly expressed). If we are to examine whether the recognition of the symbolic formulization conditions in any way our application, i.e., following, of rules, then we should consider the concepts of *categorization* and *interpretation* as crucial here. To clarify our point let us take Friedrich Hayek's idea regarding perception formation.[55]

Hayek's theory of mind insinuates that perception formation through the categorizing disposition of the mind is a plausible basis for *every* type of action including rule-following. This idea implies that before an individual performs any type of action he has to undergo a process of classification of recurring elements. This apparently includes the aspect of *rational choice*. The choice process begins with the recognition of available alternatives. In this case following a certain rule would then appear to be a result of an individual's conscious choice process that requires rules to be identified before he sets out to follow them. David Stern seems to favor this idea in the subsequent statement, «No rule can unambiguously determine its application: one can *always* raise a ques-

---

[53] Note that «recognition of the rule» here is different from the «recognition of the rule requirements». We are here in fact concerned with the perception of the rule formulation (explicit or implicit). For instance, «when the cake rises, turn off the oven», «add 2», «red can be predicated to *x*», and similar cases, and not the steps/moves in its application implied by these particular rules.

[54] The primacy of rule-recognition in following a rule is presupposed by the normative-mentalist claim. It maintains that the formulation of the rule will determine its application upon the presence of a *mental act*. This is expressed clearly by Voltolini: «la formulazione in termini generali della regola determinerà le sue applicazioni nella misura in cui vi è un *atto mentale* che coglie al volo tutte queste applicazioni prima ancora che siano concretamente eseguite: una sorta di intuizione, oppure di intendimento anticipatore». Cf. A. VOLTOLINI, *Guida alla Lettura*, 79.

[55] See F. A. HAYEK, *The Sensory Order*.

tion as to how it is to be applied in any particular case»[56]. This entails that upon the recognition of a particular rule, we begin to categorize certain elements that might comprise the requirements of its application.[57] These accumulated categories are then (re)interpreted before the actual following of the rule can commence. Again Stern makes a statement that appears to endorse this point, «any formulation of a rule is always, in principle, open to a further, [...] interpretation»[58]. This idea makes it easy to affirm the primacy of rule-recognition, i.e. before any rule can be followed we have to identify (detect/recognize) them otherwise we are, strictly speaking, not following any rule. This seems to be a very nice way to understand the value of recognition. However, if we take a closer look at Wittgenstein's statement regarding basic cases of rule-following we will notice that the aforementioned argument is misleading. This is due to the fact that Wittgenstein's rule-following consideration finds the concepts of *choice* and *interpretation* wobbly.

In the *Investigations* it is indicated that in following a rule we primarily act without reasons.[59] According to McGinn «it is an important element in Wittgenstein's conception of rule-following that it be represented as unreflective and automatic, not as forming of a hypothesis upon the basis of evidence – rule-following does not involve *taking thought*»[60]. We find this assertion convincing for the fact that we are not baffled with tracking independently constituted requirement in following a rule. If this were the case then the claim that rule-following is a robustly cognitive accomplishment is ungrounded. If we are to admit that choice is fundamental in following a particular rule then this implies that it is considered as «something fixed in the mind, as a kind of "quale", as an image or formula»[61] and calls for a *conceptual repertoire* anterior to the understanding of a rule. [62] This is a great mistake as Wittgenstein in the *Investigations* emphatically maintains because fol-

---

[56] D. STERN, *Wittgenstein on Mind and Language*, 119. Emphasis added.

[57] B. LOWENKRON, *Joint Control and Rule Following*, http://www.calstatela.edu/faculty/zlowenk/abal1999/rule-following. html.

[58] D. STERN, *Wittgenstein on Mind and Language*, 120.

[59] Our moves in following a rule are *uninformed* by an appreciation of facts about what the rules require, i.e., one's judgments about the input condition for correct application of the rule are not informed by the exercise of concepts other than that which the rule concerns - the concepts whose expression the rule regulates.

[60] C. MCGINN, *Wittgenstein on Meaning*, 16, 20 and 23.

[61] L. CARUANA, *Holism and the Understanding of Science*, 47- 48.

[62] This repertoire is needed to grasp the input conditions, and the association of them with a certain mandated or permissible form of response which the rule effects.

lowing a rule *blindly* suggests that it is uninformed by an anterior rea-son-giving judgment, i.e., we don't have paradigmatically several hy-potheses before our minds – choosing the one that best fits the rule. We lack puzzlement in following a rule. It is not or does not happen inter-nally which is subsequently translated into action. As Malcolm asserts that in a new case we carry on, all in accord – without guidance.[63] Based on this assertion, the position which holds that there is an inter-nalized *normative content* in the individual's mind/brain which con-strains a unique pattern of exercising a rule becomes extremely ques-tionable. Thus, our arguments lead us to affirm that although choice may come about at *some point*,[64] it is not a crucial aspect when it comes to dealing with following a rule.

Next, we have the problem regarding *interpretation*. Wittgenstein emphatically asserts [*PI* §§ 201, 506] that although a rule may be inter-preted in many ways, following a rule does not have to be an interpreta-tion - «...any interpretation still *hangs in the air* along with what it in-terprets, and cannot give it any support. Interpretations by themselves do not determine meanings» [*PI* §198, emphasis added]. We don't need to go into details regarding Wittgenstein's rebuttal against the idea of interpretation. However, we need to stress the fact that it could not in any way fix the application of the rule. Just by imagining that you are following the *plus* interpretation in your mind does not mean that you are really following a rule. The phrase «to follow a rule», for the later Wittgenstein, implies that there is only one possibility open to follow. What is to grasp a given rule cannot be divorced from actually obeying it or some other rule. If we want to convince people that every rule is open to various possible interpretations (for instance, → could mean «go left» or «go right»), then that's obviously wrong since every rule will require a deeper level of justification — another rule — to fix which is the correct interpretation. But then, that further rule is also open to various interpretations. If any given rule is open to various pos-sible interpretations, there is no ultimate ground of justification upon which the correct interpretation can be fixed. If we maintain this we would be lead right into the trap of an interpretation-regress which gives rise to the paradox in *PI* § 201. According to Donald Barry,

---

[63] N. MALCOLM, *Nothing is Hidden*, 170-180.

[64] I do not negate the possibility of the existence of choice during the process rule-following. But I do not agree that it be a constitutive element. See Caruana's assertion about our dependence upon our *extrapolative inclination* in following a rule. Cf. L. CARUANA, *Holism and the Understanding of Science*, 49.

«every attempt to determine an interpretation of a rule by means of an-other, more basic, rule, it is always possible to repeat the skeptical move at the level of the more basic rule»[65]. Indeed, we take Barry's ac-count as affirming that interpretation does not serve as an intermediary between a rule and its applications. Wittgenstein does not conclude that there is no ultimate justification or correct interpretation. Rather, he suggests that we are looking for the wrong thing when we look for ul-timate grounds of correctness. The mistake we make is in accepting that every rule is open to various possible interpretations. The sign, →is not open to various interpretations: we never stop to wonder if it means «go left» or «go right». Interpretation and justification are not applica-ble to everything, nor do they serve to determine correctness. They are only called upon in genuine cases of ambiguity where we do not know how to go on without a justified interpretation. They may occur in rule-following but they *need not*.

Based on our foregoing discussion, we are now ready to answer the main question posed in this section, i.e., whether rule-recognition *nec-essarily* conditions our following a rule. Our response is no. We have pointed out that essential to the primacy of rule-recognition argument are the concepts of choice and interpretation. Both are considered by Wittgenstein as misleading and unnecessary foundations of rule-following, it therefore ensues that rule-recognition does not need to oc-cur prior to our following a particular rule and it does not guide my be-havior in following it.

To sum up, there is more to rule-following that is just mere recogni-tion of a particular rule formulation. Rules as not there to be recognized prior to being followed but they are recognized once there arise uncer-tainties regarding how that rule is to be followed [*RFM* VI:24]. Witt-genstein clearly meant this assertion when he said in the *Blue Book* that in principle and in typical cases, any explicit formulation of the rule cannot be relied upon. Although Wittgenstein does not deny the exis-tence of a determinate *mental content* in following a rule, it is not de-termined by such. David Bloor says the following, «our saying "he is following a rule" has to be analyzed in terms of the actor's *participation* in the activity that is called "following a rule"»[66]. This statement cer-tainly drives home that point that we intended to show, i.e., to grasp a given rule cannot be divorced from actually following it or some other

---

[65] D. BARRY, *Forms of Life and Following Rules*, 9.
[66] D. BLOOR, *Wittgenstein, Rules and Institutions*, 67. Emphasis added.

rule. However, to fully elaborate and support our position we still need to establish some columns. We shall thus elaborate on the succeeding section the core of the actual following of a rule which is relevant to our central claim.

3.2 Fundamental Aspects of Following a Rule Relevant to the Process of Learning

In this section I do not want to get into the particular debates regarding rule-following, for instance, the interpersonal accessibility or the epistemological dimensions of following a rule. There is appropriate literature regarding this matter.[67] What we are concerned here is to establish the focal points in Wittgensteinian rule-following consideration that fit within the margins of our contention, i.e., to delineate the concepts that manifest the correlation between the process of *following a rule* and the *process of learning*.

There are two features of rule-following which play a major role in justifying our claim. They are the concepts of *practice* and *teaching*. We shall discuss them respectively in the succeeding paragraphs.

Central to Wittgenstein's elucidation of rule-following is the idea of agreement or social formation - typified by his use of the terms customs, traditions, and specially *practice*.[68] Emphasis on communal accord indicates the critical role of the social component which explains the integrity of rule-following.[69] Wittgenstein points out that we do not agree because we follow the same rules but it's the other way around – we follow rules because we have such an agreement in our judgment. Crispin Wright sustains that it is the basic agreement which sustains all rules and rule-governed institutions. The requirements which our rules impose upon us would not be violated if there were not this basic agreement – a shared uptake.[70] Without this neither rules nor rule-following would so much as exist. The existence of the rule itself de-

---

[67] See for instance G. EBBS, *Rule-following and Realism*; C. WRIGHT, «Rule-Following, Objectivity and the Theory of Meaning»; P. PETTIT, «The Reality of Rule-Following», 1-21.

[68] According to Norman Malcolm, Baker and Hacker have assigned this aspect with less importance. Cf. N. MALCOLM, *Wittgensteinian Themes*, 145-146.

[69] Norman Malcolm emphatically attests to this contention. See, N. MALCOLM, *Nothing is Hidden*, 175, 178.

[70] Wittgenstein insists that there can be rules only within a framework of overwhelming agreement. For examples see Malcolm's quotations from Wittgenstein's MS 165. N. MALCOLM, *Wittgensteinian Themes*, 148-149.

pends upon the existence of its paradigmatic application. David Stern further attests that «for the later Wittgenstein even formal rules must be understood in terms of their practical background – a change of view that emphasizes practice over theory»[71]. We reckon that for Wittgenstein the right way to follow a rule is determined by the customs embedded in a particular shared form of life. [72] In this line of thought we can say that for Wittgenstein following a rule must be understood as a *practice*, a *use*, a *habit* - «And hence "obeying a rule" is a practice» [*PI* §202]. Consequently, to follow a rule is intelligible only from the background of «the common behavior of mankind» [*PI* § 206]. This aspect allows us to view rule-following as eventually governed without reasons. We plainly do it. This does not indicate however that we act unreasonably or irrationally, for that would imply that we could offer a reason for our patterns of use, whereas we cannot. In Wittgenstein's view the question of choice simply does not occur when we follow a rule.

The next indispensable (we believe the most important) feature is *teaching*. It is inevitable that if we take the *practice/community view* argument as a valuable element in understanding the dynamics of following a rule, then we need to posit the crucial role of training and instruction in the said phenomenon. Practice is something one can be instructed in or trained to engage in. This is evident in Wittgenstein's statement that «following a rule is analogous to obeying a rule. We are trained to do so; we react to an order in a particular way» [*PI* §206].[73] This actual procedure can be seen to be instantiated by training, i.e., the connection between the rule and the steps (actions) that are required in following it are provided by training[74] which we have categorized as teaching: a person is *trained* to take *these* steps. It is through the process of teaching (training in Wittgenstein's terminology) that a *standard* procedure, i.e., the *correct* one, for following a particular rule is inculcated.

Consequently, this aspect in rule-following establishes the legitimacy of correction. If someone does not share these natural responses used in teaching others to participate in our practices, and does things differently then we may say that she does them in a way that is to be incor-

---

[71] D. STERN, *Wittgenstein on Mind and Language*, 120. Cf. *OC* §139.

[72] «Le règles sont des règles à l'intérieur des nos pratiques, et de même la signification des mots». S. LAUGIER, «Où se trouvent les règles?», 508.

[73] See also *PI* §198.

[74] Cf. C. MCGINN, *Wittgenstein on Meaning*, 35.

rect. This presupposes the possibility of getting things right, i.e. following a rule in a manner we would judge as correct. It is obviously the normative but not constraining character of teaching that assures us to continue the series «+2» in a particular way (the correct way), i.e. we do it unquestioningly and without hesitation. Invoking the correct way of following a rule in teaching entails that it is in the course of enjoining others to follow it, and in the course of telling them they have abided by it or not followed it correctly that ensures the grounds for the decisiveness of our actions in following a rule – for *trained* rule-followers there seems to be only *one way* to act in accordance with a rule.

It should be evident to us by now that for Wittgenstein the integration of these elements is vital in understanding what *following a rule* really consists in. We are guided by a rule when we do what the rule requires us to do, and what the rule demands us to do is revealed in *practice*, i.e. a regular sequence of steps that has become standardized as the correct application of the rule. We are *trained* to engage in this practice, i.e. *teaching* allows us to achieve a mastery of a technique – and as a result of our training we follow the rule in a matter-of-course fashion, without hesitation or doubt and without necessarily engaging in any interpretation of it.[75]

With the aforementioned discussion we are now ready to deal with its relevance to the learning process. We shall elaborate in the subsequent section the main argument of this segment.

3.3 *The Rule-following Character of the Learning Process*

In the previous sections we have been dealing with an analysis of the dynamics of rule-following according to the later Wittgenstein with the intention of establishing grounds to support our main contention, i.e. the process of learning exhibits the character of rule-following. We need to be reminded that our claim is not *exclusively* applied to learning within the formal instructional setting (classroom/school) but to the learning process in general – to actual learning activities in its varied appearances (methods and styles). The *process of learning* generally

---

[75] Much of this contention is summed up in *PI* §190.

understood here can be illustrated as {[**P**] →learner →([**P**] learned)} as opposed to {[*Experience/Information/Stimuli*] →storage as knowledge and skill →(*Peformance/behavior*)} and other similar formulations.

We want to demonstrate that learning is an activity which could be appositely considered as intimating the attribute(s) of following a rule. Our line of argument does not indicate learning to be a mere conformity and naïve acting in accordance with a precise and given rule. Maintaining otherwise would be too ingenuous to support our claim. What we mean when we say that it shows a rule-following like character can be described in two points. First, it is a process which indicates the cogency of practice and training (teaching). Second, these elements consequently point out that learning is not *ultimately* based upon reasons, i.e. it can be considered as a process that is automatic and unreflective.

A facet of the consideration of learning as a *process* is focused on the circumstances that favor the achievement of learning objectives. This entails that learning is not simply an event that happens naturally; it is also a process that occurs under certain observable conditions. These conditions are identified by reference to the situations of ordinary life – within practice, i.e., the «common behavior of mankind» [*PI* §206]. When we talk about practice(s), we are referring to social practice(s).[76]

Much of our basic understanding of the process of learning has the picture of the individual human mind steadily being stocked with ideas. With this view we are neglecting the fact that the learner belongs to a particular environment along with other learners and not a spectator aloof from the world. This perspective highlights the significance of practice. According to Wittgenstein it is considered as a certain nexus of human activity which serves as a *locus* whereby meaning is manifested. From this standpoint the learning process occurs against the backdrop of the achievement of shared meaning where the experience of the process becomes part of the meaning. This entails that learning is a matter of engagement, typified by the terms *interaction* and *participation*, in socially defined practices. These practices impact significantly on the process by providing the valuable framework of structures and

---

[76] The notion of practice has a long intellectual history. The work of Bourdieu on the nature of practice has helped to establish its importance as an influential sociological framework. Cf. P. BOURDIEU, *Outline of a Theory of Practice*.

proper context for learning to take place.[77] Looking at the learning process through the lens of practice shifts our attention from the accumulation of context-independent abstract ideas to the perspective of participation. If we are to maintain this point of view then learning as a community-dependent *process* can in this respect be described as a formed activity, i.e. it is intrinsically a social and contextual phenomenon. Segregated from it the process, with all its complexities, becomes indefinable. To paraphrase David Bloor's statement – our saying that «he is learning» has to be analyzed in terms of the learner's participation in the activity (practice) that is called *learning*.[78]

It is a basic fact about us that ordinary forms of explanation and training do succeed in perpetuating practices of various kinds. Since we have argued that practices affect the learning process then we can in this regard claim that *training* occupies an equally important role in developing the learning process.

One of the major problems inherent in any attempt to deal satisfactorily with the concept of training is its confusion with *conditioning*. Traditional philosophy of education has undervalued and maintained the inadequacy of training precisely because no distinction has been made between both ideas. Training is a concept quite different from that of conditioning and leads to the development of abilities that are more flexible than the responses evoked by conditioning. Educationists who regard it as solely tending towards the vocational or practical are misguided. In training the learning process does not involve a mere response to positive and negative reinforcers or rests on force which leads to an unthinking response (passivity) in a limited set of situations; but engages in an exercise of perception and judgment. In other words, mental capacities are utilized to the greatest extent. If employed effectively, then training leads to the confident deployment of skill and technique in a wide variety of situations and hence can promote learner independence and autonomy. These are the aspects, we reckon, which demonstrate the importance of training in the learning process. We believe that this is the element David A. Kolb took no notice of in developing is four-stage learning process which is often referred to in describing experiential learning.[79]

---

[77] Cf. J. LAVE – E. WENGER, *Situated Learning*.

[78] D. BLOOR, *Wittgenstein, Rules and Institutions*, 67.

[79] David A. Kolb (with Roger Fry) created his famous model out of four elements: concrete experience, observation and reflection, the formation of abstract concepts and testing in new situations. He represented these in the famous experiential learning

What we have underlined in the previous discussion is the fact how the fundamental aspects of practice and training (teaching) influence and foster the learning process. These bring about a view that in participating with the established practice(s) and enduring suitable training we are able to undergo the process of learning without the guidance of reason, i.e. it becomes immediate, automatic and unreflective activity similar to Wittgenstein's idea of rule-following.

The claim that the learning process does not rest upon a foundation of justifying reasons primarily involves a reaction to the overly rationalistic cognitivist view. Although we admit that there are diverse learning methods and styles, the idea of an *essential* inner process in learning is mythical. According to McMahon learning is not a *purely* internal process[80] nor can we reduce it to mere synapses of neurons. To express the matter more precariously, we need to have nothing *in mind* when we are engaged in the course of learning.[81] This underscores the point that *during* the process there is no prevailing preoccupation to supply reasons to rationalize how we are engaged in the learning activity. We simply move on to achieve that which should be learned. This is evidenced by the fact that our action in every learning situation (conceptual or practical), whether or not we learn, is *immediate*, i.e. it does not involve the formulation of proofs and we are never worried in producing conceptual schemes for it.[82] This does not mean that we cannot articulate reasons but the very having of reasons would demand the superimposition of what Crispin Wright calls the *modus ponens model* in rule-following.[83] We are simply not concerned in the condition of con-

---

circle. Kolb and Fry argue that the learning cycle can begin at any one of the four points - and that it should really be approached as a continuous spiral. Cf. D. A. KOLB, *Experiential Learning*.

[80] M. McMAHON, «Social Constructivism», http://www.ascilite.org.au/conferences /perth97/papers/Mcmahon/Mcmahon.html.

[81] I am not negating the existence of *mental content* in learning. What I am emphasizing here is that *during* the process we should not expect the learner to have something in his mind which would *basically* be regarded as working out or justifying the necessary course of action.

[82] Perhaps this process is ultimately dependent upon our gregarious instinct, i.e. to form part of a group participating actively in the shared practices of that particular form of life.

[83] Wright introduces this particular model to show the possibility of following a rule syllogistically. He provides two examples, namely, the case of castling in chess and the predication of *red*. Cf. C. WRIGHT, «What is Wittgenstein's point in the

sciousness when we undertake the course of learning in the precise case that one's judgments about the input conditions are not informed by the exercise of concepts.

The presence of a natural capability to engage oneself in the process of learning is beyond dispute. In this sense, therefore, we can say that learning as a process, like following a rule, is characterized as an unreflective and natural activity of an individual based on his participation in practice(s), training and the inherent ability for comprehension. It is something we engage in without exerting much effort.

It seems to be that our argument is stepping within the threshold of behaviorism in the sense that our claim tends to make obvious reference to external manifestations rather than the internal. However, we are not advocating here a crude behavioristic view as proposed by the *conditioning theories* of learning. We nonetheless would acknowledge the fact that we are assuming a *quasi*-behaviorist position due to the stress we give on the habitual character of learning, i.e. we are establishing a criterion of the learning process in behavioral terms. But this does not imply that we are fully hinging our arguments on the Stimulus-Response (S-R) theory. We are simply trying to demonstrate how the process of learning per se based on this aspect of automaticity and unreflectiveness manifests an attribute akin to rule-following as presented by Wittgenstein.

4. Conclusion

Our main aim in this chapter was to discover the aspects of Wittgenstein's rule-following consideration that contribute to a unique (novel) approach to our understanding of the ever elusive concept of learning. Due to its seemingly ambiguous nature (as a product, a function, or a process), we have chosen to focus on learning as a process *sui generis*. It is by attention to this aspect of learning that the fundamental characteristics of Wittgenstein's ideas regarding rule-following emerged and became relevant.

We opened our investigation with a description of the picture of learning from the later works of Wittgenstein. Although he never made explicit his ideas about the concept of learning, his treatment about language learning supplied us with sufficient views from where we gathered key arguments that demonstrate, in one way or another, his stand-

---

rule-following discussion?», http://www.nyu.edu/gsas/dept/philo/courses/rules/papers/Wright.pdf.

point regarding the phenomenon. It was crucial in our discussion to make a distinction between learning and the concepts which we normally confuse with it – oftentimes regarding them as interchangeable or even synonymous, namely, *knowing* and *understanding*. It appeared that Wittgenstein considered the process of learning as anterior to both of them due to the fact that it does not involve a preoccupation with reflection, reasons, and justifications. Thus, it can be regarded as a foundation of our competence for knowing and understanding. This peculiarity of the learning process is attributed to the cogency of practice and training (teaching) which, as we have demonstrated, is vital in Wittgenstein's treatment of following a rule. It is through them that rule-following becomes usual, automatic, and unreflective.

Our consideration of the learning process under the perspective of rule-following yields two noticeable consequences. First, it dissolves the prevalent dichotomy between the two major psychological theories of learning, namely, the cognitive and the behaviorist standpoints. Second, the significance it gives to training provides an impetus to establish better teaching designs that facilitate the learning process.

We have indicated in the outset of this chapter that in the fields of psychology and philosophy of education there is a prevailing dichotomy – two extreme views as to the nature of the process of learning. The cognitive approach, on the one hand, tends to view learning merely as acquiring and using conceptual and cognitive structures. The behaviorists, on the other hand, exalt the force of reinforcement of stimulus-response which manifests an approach that is rigid and overly mechanical. Both views are evidently one-sided. It is in this aspect where we can see the relevance of Wittgenstein's idea of rule-following in eliminating this bifurcation. It seeks to develop a new understanding of learning based on the idea that the basic form of learning is being trained into pattern-governed behaviors, i.e. a process which is engaged in activities licensed by practice or custom. The learning process, under this perspective, is considered as a normative social practice avoiding the mentalistic presuppositions, on the one hand, and the crude behaviorism on the other, that have shaped most philosophical thoughts on this matter. The learning process viewed as rule-following clearly goes beyond this abovementioned traditional dichotomy.[84]

Our treatment of learning as comparable to rule-following equally highlights the role of teaching. It is indubitable that when employed ef-

---

[84] Cf. M. WILLIAMS, «The Significance of Learning», 173-203.

fectively, teaching influences to a great extent the process as well as the outcome of learning. Thus, teaching should be designed to aid the learners in achieving the contents of learning and it should also be conceived in such a way as to enhance the learners' abilities to engage in ordinary practice(s) in order to make the course of learning a normal activity, i.e. spontaneous, effortless and undertaken without the restrain of reason. Teaching should be planned accordingly to make the process merge with our practices to reach the threshold of learner independency – enabling him to take over and simply go on learning. This position exactly concords with the Wittgensteinian view of teaching that aims for normalization.

With the arguments presented in this chapter we therefore conclude that Wittgenstein's ideas concerning rule-following, particularly his emphasis on practice and training, provides a novel perspective in our approach to the phenomenon of learning. A view that dissolves traditional dichotomies and motivates an enhancement in teaching design(s) intended for progress in learning.

CHAPTER V

Philosophy as Therapy, Education and the Community

After our application of Wittgenstein's ideas about meaning as use and rule-following to teaching and the learning process respectively in the previous chapters, we will now proceed in our investigation of the relevance of his thought regarding the nature of *philosophy as therapy* in the field of education.

The question of whether Wittgenstein's later philosophical project, i.e. philosophy viewed as a form of therapy, is effective has been debated and criticized many times. On the other hand, most of the defenders of Wittgenstein's view of philosophy indicate that these issues arise because of an inadequate understanding and unsuccessful evaluation of the therapeutic aspects of his later writings.[1] However, we are not concerned with the problem whether Wittgenstein's use of this method is legitimate or not. We shall maintain nonetheless that such point of view is valuable in assessing the linguistic competence of children in classroom (instructional) situations and the function of the community within the educational enterprise. This is the main inquiry that we are going to consider in this chapter.

We shall proceed in our discussion by first elaborating on the import of Wittgenstein's idea about philosophy as therapy. We shall include here an elucidation on philosophical problems as specific forms of intellectual illnesses, the suggested method(s) for restoring health, and the image of the philosopher as therapist. After this we shall advance into an application of the therapeutic approach to education focusing our attention on a particular classroom situation indicating the signifi-

---

[1] Cf. J. PETERMAN, *Philosophy as therapy*, 2.

cance of the picture of an educator as therapist. We shall reinforce our discussion concerning the classroom environment by considering the role and function of the community in the educational growth of students. We are here concerned with indicating the benefits and the negative impact that communal practices bring which evidently affect the disposition of learners. Finally, we shall deal with the significance of the therapeutic method in the educational activity, i.e. its impact on the teaching practice and as a way to finding cure for the negative practices incurred from the community.

We shall demonstrate in this chapter that Wittgenstein's idea of philosophy as therapy highlights the prevailing interaction between communal practices and the educational system. It is through an investigation of the elements of his thoughts on the therapeutic nature of philosophy that we make evident the particular function and contribution of the community in the sphere of education which directly affects the instructional approach of educators and downgrades the idea that learners come to be educated as *tabula rasa*.

1. The Import of Wittgenstein's Idea of *Philosophy as Therapy*

We have indicated in the first chapter of this work that from harboring a view of philosophy as a logical clarification of our thoughts in the *Tractatus* the later Wittgenstein renewed his point of view. Rather than upholding to the conviction of traditional philosophy, i.e. as a cognitive discipline that aims at uncovering new truths, and strives to add to human knowledge he does not anymore consider doing philosophy as explaining the nature of things, or searching for the essence(s), or discovering new truths.[2] We certainly do not intend, according to Wittgenstein, to dig out what is hidden from view when we philosophize.[3] We

---

[2] This is a rather delicate point. Not all Wittgensteinian scholars agree on this position. I prefer to avoid claiming directly that he did not want to arrive at the truth. To maintain this contention would probably amount to a logical contradiction in the sense that by proposing the *Investigations* as a correction to the *Tractatus* then he is actually claiming that the former is more trustworthy, closer to the truth than the latter. The viewpoint that I am trying to accentuate here is the misguided comparison between philosophy and natural science. For further discussion see D. PEARS, *Wittgenstein*, 105ff.

[3] The term *philosophize* is used here rather than the gaudy *to do philosophy* current in semantic-positivist writing due to the fact that Wittgenstein himself uses *philosophieren* exclusively and not *Philosophie betreiben*. Furthermore, his use of the term

should see clearly what is before our eyes. He is referring to our ordinary use of language. It is the misunderstandings and the confusions in our use of language that lead us to deep disturbances which are sometimes referred to, according to James Peterman, as «mental cramps»[4]. Here we have a new sense of philosophizing, i.e. a process which Wittgenstein calls therapeutic. This method employed in order to untie the knots in our thinking is purely descriptive. It doesn't concern itself anymore with metaphysical theories and deep explanations that cut to the core of the concepts that govern human life and reality, which, Wittgenstein asserts, lead us astray. The kinds of puzzlements that he identifies do not only crop up when we sit down to study philosophy; they are general characteristics of abstract thinking. Thus, there is a need to eradicate these philosophical troubles by showing that such problems are nonsensical. This line of thought manifests the therapeutic character of philosophy.

In order for us to be able to make an assessment of the impact of Wittgenstein's idea of philosophy to the sphere of education we need to identify its significant contribution. To do this, we shall elucidate in this section the major elements of this idea and its relevance as a honed method by which we are able to avoid such conceptual errors. We shall proceed by indicating the prominent philosophical problems pointed out by Wittgenstein and then elaborating on the idea of a perspicuous representation (*Übersichtliche Darstellung*) as a cure and a way to intellectual well-being. By this means we shall be able to see the significance of his idea of philosophy.

1.1 *Philosophical Problems as Intellectual Illnesses*

It is particularly a natural attitude to consider philosophy as dealing with a search for solutions to specific philosophically pertinent problems, such as the mind-body problem, the problem of other minds, of skepticism, of the external reality, the problem of universals and the like. It is due to this fact that philosophers, according to Wittgenstein, lose sight of the source whence these problems usually arise. Instead of being aware of how the conflicts and contradictions created by confusions in the use of language create problems, they try to force them into a specific pattern to achieve a desired result. They are caught up in the

---

philosophize, whenever he wrote in English, is evident in the *Blue and Brown Books*. For examples see *BB* 25.

[4] J. PETERMAN, *Philosophy as therapy*, 17.

web of formulating and establishing solid and well-formed theories as if it is at par with the scientific enterprise and consequently they fail to grasp what philosophy really is all about.[5] In so doing, they discover more problems rather than solutions. This explains why similar philosophical tribulations that were already troubling the Greeks are still disturbing us today.

According to Wittgenstein, these philosophical problems arise basically out of the misleading features of our language, due to the fact that different concepts in similar appearances are presented in our language. Ronald Suter echoes this assertion in stating that in both his earlier and later views Wittgenstein considers philosophical problems as results of misunderstanding the language[6]. A. C. Grayling considers the aforementioned contention as implausible as a diagnosis of the causes of philosophical perplexity. He claims that it is an overstatement by Wittgenstein to generalize that *all* philosophical problems come from the same source, i.e. the misunderstandings of language. However, A.C. Grayling's argument fails to indicate (as most authors do) the vital element in Wittgenstein's position, i.e. the importance on the concept of *language use*. His critique seems to hinge upon a misleading emphasis on the intricacies of the concepts: *understanding* (or misunderstanding), *cause and effect, urge* in language users.[7] We should be careful not to equate «misunderstanding of language» with «misunderstanding of the *use* of language». Although misapprehending a language may indeed bring about confusion and puzzlement, stress on our misconception of the workings of language or our misapplication of the use justifies Wittgenstein's insistence of it being a source of philosophical problems.

In what sense is a philosophical problem an intellectual illness? The concept of illness, says James Peterman «indicates an impairment of the person's ability to do certain things a healthy person ought to be able to do or an impairment of a person's ability to be a certain way a healthy person ought to be able to be»[8]. For Wittgenstein, philosophical problems are always seen as symptomatic of some conceptual confusion, i.e. perplexities arising from the misapplication of language use. These confusions are always the bewilderment of the intellect and

---

[5] For a discussion regarding the distinction between the task of science and philosophy see P.M.S. HACKER, *Wittgenstein: On Human Nature*, 8-9.

[6] R. SUTER, *Interpreting Wittgenstein*, 7.

[7] For a thorough elaboration of his position see A.C. GRAYLING, «Wittgenstein's Influence», 63-64.

[8] J. PETERMAN, *Philosophy as therapy*, 3.

imagination. If these problems are indications of conceptual entanglement in the web of language then we can positively assert that such
problems point towards a certain limitation of one's ability to engage in
otherwise normal and unproblematic understanding of language use. It
is however a mistake to presuppose that philosophical problems are
problems *of* language, they are rather problems that originates *from* the
misuse of language. So it is evident, according to Wittgenstein, that it is
our failure to understand our language use or our misconceptions that
results in the bewitchment of our intelligence and misleading ways of
looking at things – a form of intellectual neurosis that is not often recognized by academic philosophy.

Philosophical problems according to Wittgenstein arise from the particular use of and our wrong way of looking at language. These are
manifested in cases like fixing the meaning of a proposition (or a word)
by reference to something that corresponds to it[9] or when we presuppose, says Wittgenstein, that there are certain definite mental processes
bound up with the workings of language [*BB* 5][10]. In this case, he admonishes that there is always a danger of wanting to find the meaning
of a proposition by looking at the frame of mind in which we form such
propositions - «And nothing is more wrong-headed than calling meaning a mental activity!» [*PI* §693] These tendencies to think that a
proposition points out to an object it represents or symbolizes thought,
mental processes, etc. produce a false grammatical attitude to how we
look at language [*PG* §85].

The subliming of language is an indication, says Wittgenstein, that
one has already been led astray in philosophy. He implies here that philosophical problems are the result of our tangled thinking. Wittgenstein
indicates three principal factors that give rise to our tendency to sublime the logic of our language: the craving for generality, the lure of
surface grammar, and the misleading analogies.

In the *Blue and Brown Books* Wittgenstein mentions that «our craving for generality» [*BB* 17] is a source of philosophical confusion. He
indicates three human tendencies where this particular attitude comes
from. (a) We are inclined to think that there is something common to
things subsumed under general terms – terms like *game* or *leaf* – which
justifies our calling them games or leaves. (b) We have a tendency to
think we understand a general term, say, the term *leaf*, if we possess a

---

9 Cf. *AWL*, p. 110.
10 See also *OC* §601, *PI* §329.

general picture of a leaf [*BB* 17-18]. (c) We are preoccupied with the methods of science. Following Wittgenstein's line of thought this craving for generality – the search for a common essence, whether in diverse instances of words or functions of individual words, would make us unfamiliar with the terrain of language. Consequently, we lose our way – «A philosophical problem has the form: I don't know my way about» [*PI* §123][11].

Another aspect that conceptually confuses us is when we are taken by the surface grammar.[12] Words are essentially embodied in grammar. Wittgenstein argues that grammar is also the source of illusions and misunderstanding, creating the puzzles and seemly insolvable problems of philosophy[13] given that not being able to describe the grammar of our language would mean that we are at a loss of ever understanding language. Fu-Ning Ting states that «to understand the meaning of word or the logic of language we have to see how grammar actually works in language»[14]. Consider, for instance, the terms *exists*, *is good*, and *is red*. They are all classified as predicates. So we assume they must work in much the same way. We integrate different uses of words. In philosophy, Wittgenstein notes, we are constantly misled by grammatical similarities which mask profound logical differences in our language. Based on these arguments he admonishes us that we must pay attention and try to understand the deeper grammar of our language, i.e. that grammar that ordinary grammarians fail to notice. Otherwise we would proceed on to find justifications, explanations, or foundations for our linguistic practices – we concede to the tendency to look for hidden essences and to sublime our language. If we overlook the grammatical differences of language in cases like: the difference in the use of the same terms or difference in the use of closely connected terms, then we are committing a misapplication of analogy.[15]

In the *Blue and Brown Books* Wittgenstein states that «when words in ordinary language have prima facie analogous grammars we are inclined to try to interpret them analogously; i.e. we try to make the analogy hold throughout» [*BB* 7]. Misleading analogies crop up because similarities in verbal form persistently bring about false notions of how

---

[11] This statement can be better understood upon reference to the comparison Wittgenstein made between language and an ancient city. See *PI* §18.

[12] See R.P. MOLLANEDA, *Concrete Approach and Therapeutic Activity*, 135ff.

[13] H.L.R. FINCH, *Wittgenstein – The Later Philosophy*, 149.

[14] F-N. TING, *Wittgenstein's Descriptive Method*, 38.

[15] Cf. *PI* §§90, 132; see also *MWL* 257.

the similar expressions work and therefore of the realities discussed by their means.[16] Wittgenstein is not suggesting here that we should discard analogies completely. He is rather cautioning us to be careful not to be misled by such analogies. The error in analogy is the overemphasis of the apparent similarities between cases which are actually different. We are able to avoid this mistake the moment we have clarity, according to Wittgenstein, over the differences in the use of language and the distinctiveness of each language-game.

How is the identification of this intellectual illness relevant to Wittgenstein's idea of philosophy? Basically he neither denies the existence of philosophical problems nor feels uncomfortable upon encountering them in philosophizing. He was rather concerned in showing us the source of these problems and how they affect our point of views and the way we behave in our form of life. Identifying philosophical perplexities as forms of illnesses highlights the fact that we are not immune to them either philosophically or in ordinary circumstances. Furthermore, through the awareness of these puzzlements Wittgenstein succeeded in stressing the proper function or task of philosophy – to describe and not to explain. Descriptive method is meant to be the conceptual and grammatical investigation of the use of language, i.e. to obtain a perspicuous representation or synoptic representation of the grammar of the use of language.

1.2 *A Perspicuous Representation: A Way to Health*

We have indicated in the previous discussions the sources that, according Wittgenstein, give rise to philosophical problems. Since these confusions are basically affected by the way we understand the use of language, he considered it as an illness in our theoretical attitudes – a sort of intellectual neurosis that results in complicating what is actually simple. It gives rise to our inability for normal apprehension of concepts. In order to dissolve these problems – to get us familiar with the terrain, Wittgenstein offers us therapeutic methods, viz. rearrangement of grammatical facts of the actual workings of language or the rules of grammar step-by-step in the right order [*WVC*, 183-184][17], exposing false analogies, searching for immediate cases.[18] These methods how-

---

[16] G. HALLETT, «The Theoretical Content of Language», 312.

[17] F. WAISMANN, *Wittgenstein and the Vienna Circle*. Hereafter cited as *WVC*.

[18] For a thorough discussion see F-N. TING, *Wittgenstein's Descriptive Method*, 65-88.

ever, we reckon, can be condensed under the concept of a perspicuous representation (*übersichtliche Darstellung*).[19]

Wittgenstein asserts that it is the business of philosophy to attain a clear view of the conceptual structure that troubles us. The following passage drives home the point:

> A main source of our failure to understand is that we do not *command a clear view* of the use of our words. – Our grammar is lacking in this sort of perspicuity. A perspicuous representation produces just that understanding which consists in "seeing connexions" [...] The concept of a perspicuous representation is of fundamental significance for us. It earmarks the form of account we give, the way we look at things [*PI* §122].[20]

Perspicuity is fundamental in obtaining clarity because it brings awareness of the way we breed problems in our misuse and misunderstanding of language. It brings about a sort of, according to John Heaton, a «Gestalt-switch by laying emphasis on a new aspect of our use of words»[21]. Once we arrive at this stage of lucidity, we already have, so to say, a map of the conceptual terrain that enables us to move without difficulty.

> The aim is a surveyable comparative representation of all the applications, illustrations, conceptions [of the relevant part of the grammar of a philosophically problematic array of expressions] ... The complete survey of everything that may produce unclarity. And this survey must extend over a wide domain, for the roots of our ideas reach a long way [*Z* §273].

The above-quoted segment indicates that the achievement of an overview of the use of language produces just the understanding which consists in seeing conceptual connections which is commonly ignored and once overlooked generates confusion. Having a perspicuous representation – the rearrangement of the rules for the use of words which, according to Wittgenstein, lie open to view, but which are not readily taken in as a whole enables us to perceive a clear vision of the logical

---

[19] The corresponding German term for perspicuity is *Übersichlichkeit*. It basically means the quality of something of being able to take all of it in at a glance. A teacher's representation of English grammar rules has *Übersichlichkeit* or *surveyability* if the student can comprehend the rules as an ordered whole through the representation. For further discussion regarding this issue see F-N. TING, *Wittgenstein's Descriptive Method*, 59-69.

[20] See also *BB* 125.

[21] J.M. HEATON, *Postmodern Encounters*, 26.

character of the words or propositions that baffle us in our philosophical reflection [*PI* §109].

Could such an idea of a perspicuous representation bring about intellectual health? Based on Wittgenstein's arguments we reckon a positive response to the question. How? Conceptual well-being, as indicated by Wittgenstein, connotes the normal ability to distinguish the correct use of language, i.e. to be able to see the proper way concepts actually functions. Now, we have indicated in the previous discussions that this nature of perspicuity helps us uncover the conflict between philosophical notions and the actual concepts, i.e. to make transparent the very foundation of construction, to render its non-constructive foundation evident. We become aware of the grammatical differences in how concepts in different regions of our language are used. Let us take for instance the problem regarding the notion of *time*. When we reflect on the philosophical subject about time itself (if there ever were one) our grip of the concept suddenly becomes unwieldy. This insecurity is an evident manifestation of our conceptual confusion. Our ordinary ways of characterizing time are enormously complex, i.e. they are embedded within a diverse variety of idioms in which the notion of time plays a role. It would be a mistake, according to Wittgenstein, to strive to dig deeper in order to find the essence or real meaning of "time". Rather he proposes that we should look more closely how these expressions are used in the whole language game. Avrum Stroll says,

> One who looks closely at how temporal expressions are employed in daily life will realize that this is what "time" means. By describing such uses, he will not impose a factitious conceptual model on actual practice, but will "leave everything as it is". He will eventually "see the world rightly".[22]

Thus, if we were to look for a cure of particular philosophical sickness we can do no less than to strive to find a perspicuous representation of otherwise philosophically troublesome phenomena. James Peterman attests to this by saying that «Wittgenstein is thinking of perspicuous representations [...] as the essential conditions of a healthy human understanding»[23]. The cure comes when one finds the right way to clarify what has become puzzling by highlighting language use and thereby bringing back one's intellectual health. Having a perspicuous representation that resolves the tension between the misleading similes embed-

---

[22] A. STROLL, *Wittgenstein*, 91.
[23] J. PETERMAN, *Philosophy as therapy*, 21.

ded in our speech and that actual practice evidently does this. In this case, it is the main challenge for a philosopher to arrive eventually at a sound human understanding and clarity and to achieve this by applying Wittgenstein's suggested therapeutic method. Thus we have a figure of a philosopher as therapist.

1.3 The Philosopher as Therapist

We have discussed in the previous sections the main elements of Wittgenstein's view of philosophy. In the development of his outlook, focus was given to philosophical problems. These were considered by Wittgenstein as intellectual illnesses brought about by our propensity to sublime language, i.e. falling into the trap of the misleading features of our language – to use nonsensical expressions. However, this is not a hopeless case for Wittgenstein shows us a cure for this kind of sickness through the concept of a *perspicuous representation*. We have to undertake this process in order to arrive at an *emendatio intellectus*. Wittgenstein describes this process as «therapy» [*PI* §133] for the diseases of the intellect or the «treatment of an illness» [*PI* §255]. Based on these arguments we can see the therapist image of a philosopher.

Before we go any further a clarification of our use of the term *therapist* is in order. Commonly our understanding of the word *therapy* runs around an image of a process by which a therapist endeavors (normally through individual sessions) to cure a patient's particular physical, mental or social disease or disorder. Thus, a *therapist* is one who is primarily concerned with a treatment of a specific form of illness. However, the sense of Wittgenstein's use of *therapy* does not connote a treatment of a physical, psychological or social sickness but of philosophical perplexities as a result of our misunderstanding of the fundamental functions of language. Hence, while maintaining the more general characteristics of a therapist, i.e. someone who aims at restoring health, a philosopher in Wittgenstein's sense performs distinctive tasks that are designed to specifically re-establish intellectual health.

How does a philosopher proceed in this undertaking? Wittgenstein states in *The Big Typescript* that «The philosopher strives to find the liberating word, that is, the word that finally lets us grasp that which, ungraspable, has continually weighed upon our consciousness» [*BT* §87][24]. He must find exactly the right enunciation of the philosophical

---

[24] The expression «liberating word» (*das erlösende Wort*) recurs often in his war diaries *Geheime Tagebücher*, Cf. L. WITTGENSTEIN, *Geheime Tagebücher 1914-1916*.

confusions. He does this, James Peterman indicates, «by means of the clarification of the similes, pictures, their influence, and their proper application as well as from the presentation of alternative similes capable of producing a deeply felt transformation in one's habits of thoughts and view of the world»[25]. The philosopher seeks to establish forms of descriptions which are transformative otherwise one will either continue to indicate how things are or construct reasonable theories about things but will not strive to achieve conceptual health. Furthermore, Wittgenstein stressed that a philosopher therapist should not strive to teach new facts, but rather tells us things which we all know already [*PI* §§109, 126]. He elaborates this task by referring to the following therapeutic approaches: re-arrangement, reminding, searching for immediate cases and the use of imagination.

A remarkable illustration of the method of re-arrangement is found in the *Blue Book* concerning the arrangement of books in the library.[26] The philosopher endeavors to find a specific kind of arrangement, a surveyable one, of things we already know. Success of such an approach lies in putting two hitherto separated concepts together, or putting two hitherto contrasted concepts upon separate locations. The picture is very clear. In dealing with philosophical problems what the philosophical therapist would have to do is to arrange grammatical facts according to the necessary state of affairs – to establish *an* order (not *the* order) in our knowledge of the use of language [*PI* §132]. The order of arrangement previously achieved will have to be rearranged if the grammatical facts and circumstances regarding the use of language were changed. There is no ultimate arrangement, but a gradual and provisional arrangement and rearrangement.

In *PI* §127 Wittgenstein states that «The work of a philosopher consists in assembling reminders for a particular purpose». This is congruent with his claim that nothing is hidden. Thus, a philosopher is never expected to discover anything for everything lies open to view. The specific object of these reminders would be the rules of our use of language which we ordinarily follow without thinking about them. We

---

It is also found in Typescript 213 which is here referred to as the *Big Typescript*. Hereafter cited as *BT*. Most of the notes made here are taken from sections 86-93 (pp. 405-435) of the *BT* which is entitled «Philosophy». For reference see «*Philosophie* §§86-93 (S. 405-435) aus dem sogenannten Big Typescript (Katalognummer 213)», 175-203; «Philosophy: Sections 86-93 (pp. 405-435)», 3-22.

[25] J. PETERMAN, *Philosophy as therapy*, 74.

[26] Cf. *BB* pp. 44-45.

need to be reminded of the differences in the use of the same term, of closely connected words, and between language-games. This particular approach is aimed at combating our urge to misunderstand our language, i.e. losing our way in the linguistic terrain.

It is undeniable that the actual use of language is in constant variation or gradual transition. The therapist must be aware that we do not possess a whole picture of the various cases of language use. We are only cognizant, according to Wittgenstein that they form a family of cases. In order to help us understand these gradual transitions and connections of diverse usage of language and how the entirely different language-games belong to a family, a therapist should be able to find intermediate cases that allow us to see connections and change within the differences. It is important that one should be able to see connections [*PI* §122] since the apparent collision will disappear if we see that no picture has to be applied in only one way.[27] We think the following passage regarding the picture of the use of a word, e.g. *cube* clarifies the issue:

> The picture of the cube did indeed suggest a certain use to us, but it was possible for me to use it differently [*PI* §139].
>
> What is essential is to see that the same thing can come before our minds when we hear the word and the application still be different. Has it the *same* meaning both times? I think we shall say not [*PI* §140].

The significance of searching for intermediate cases is tied up with the therapist's aim to obtain a perspicuous representation of the various ways of using language.

Another important therapeutic approach employed by Wittgenstein is the methodical use of imagination. What our concepts and the forms of our expressions are, are usually affected by all sorts of facts. However, to be able to imagine something evidently does not require facts. If this were the case, then no fact is needed for the formation of concepts. By imagining Wittgenstein aids us in seeing the diverse alternatives in using language. This method aims towards changing our ways of looking at language. A therapist in this sense should conduct his therapy by means of a host of highly imaginative examples so as to shake us free

---

[27] For a series of examples concerning the finding of intermediate cases see *PI* §§138-142. These passages deals with the apparent conflict between «meaning as practice extended in time» and «meaning as something grasped in a flash». By way of intermediate cases the therapist will help us see how two apparently different conceptions might both be called «understanding the meaning of a word».

from our conviction that the concepts we possess are absolutely correct, i.e. the presumption of a corresponding fact as the foundation of the concept formation. Let us take for instance the case of the use of the term *red*. We say: «There is a red patch» and «Here there isn't a red patch». The term appears in both sentences. It does not necessarily mean the presence of something red. Imagination helps us in making the second sentence meaningful [*PI* §443]. It is evidently beyond the question of truth and falsity. The therapeutic function of imagination lies in the fact that it enables us to see the arbitrariness of language hence it liberates us from certain ways of looking at things.

From the aforementioned approaches to philosophical therapy we can suppose that a therapist should have training and experience. He must be well and extensively trained in the use of language. He must also be at the level wherein he is not generally bothered from conceptual neurotic and psychotic difficulties. He must be keenly aware of the limits of language. Only at a high level of self-awareness can a philosopher-therapist be able to make it possible for us to get a clear view of the conceptual structure that troubles us; the state of affairs before the contradiction is resolved. A therapist should *show* us the way not to say what the way is.

We have laid out in this section the fundamental elements of Wittgenstein's therapeutic view of philosophy. We have stressed that for him it is important that we are aware of the source of philosophical problems (intellectual illnesses), i.e. the bewitchment of our intelligence because of our misuse (misunderstanding) of language. He proposed that we should obtain a *perspicuous representation* as a cure for such sickness – a kind of understanding which consists in seeing what is before our eyes, but which we had previously neglected. As a therapist the philosopher must help each person to work upon himself. He is up against the *will* not only the intellect.[28] His insistence on having a clear purview of the whole terrain of language directs us into his intention of helping us work ourselves out of the confusions we become entangled with in philosophizing. By attention to our everyday forms of expression and to the world whose forms of expression serve to reveal Wittgenstein emphasized his goal to the fly out of the bottle – to establish clarity about the essentially grammatical-linguistic confusions at the bottom of many of philosophy's traditional problems. P.M.S.

---

[28] Cf. *BT* §86.

Hacker sums up the import of Wittgenstein's view of philosophy as therapy in the following passage:

> In philosophizing, we may not *terminate* a disease of thought. It must run its natural course, and *slow* cure is all important [*Zettel* §382]. For philosophical error is rooted in a multitude of false analogies and can rarely be rectified by uprooting *one* confusion. One must slowly survey the structures of intellectual illusion from all sides, for they cannot be taken at a glance. In all cases, the therapeutic endeavour, like the psychotherapist's, is to make *latent* nonsense *patent* nonsense [*PI* §464].[29]

This particular aim of this method in philosophy, i.e. not to seek abstract definitions but to use illustrations that again and again seem to make the same philosophical point from various perspectives [*PI* §133] – arranging what we have always known [*PI* §109], as have been pointed out, is of educational significance specially concerning teaching and learning process. We shall then apply in succeeding segment this therapeutic approach to education.

2. The Therapeutic View of Philosophy Applied to Education

We have elaborated in the previous sections the fundamental implications of Wittgenstein's idea of philosophy. His arguments were aimed at demonstrating how the therapeutic approach determines the proper task of philosophy, i.e. not to seek to establish theories or explanations but to offer description(s) – a therapeutic removal of obstacles to understanding (intellectual illnesses) through an account of the actual use (of words or expressions) in the language. This view is reflected in his statement: «The problems are solved, not by giving new information, but by arranging what we have always known» [*PI* §109]. If we take a closer look at this method we will notice that it is also of educational significance particularly for the concepts of teaching and learning.

There are two important aspects contained in Wittgenstein's therapeutic view of philosophy which manifest its applicability in the field of education. They are: a) the recognition of various conceptual confusions or what is called in Wittgensteinian jargon, intellectual diseases and b) the employment of the *descriptive method*, i.e. as a cure for the conceptual illness. We are not insinuating here a creation of a Wittgensteinian philosophy of education since this would entirely contradict the spirit of his philosophy. What we do maintain is that there is a valuable

---

[29] P.M.S. HACKER, «Philosophy», 337.

impact of such method to the teaching and learning processes as it goes on inside the classroom. In this regard, we shall expound in the succeeding sections the consequences brought about by an application of such an approach in the context of a basic classroom instruction. We shall also include a discussion concerning the figure of educator as therapist.

2.1 Language-based Conceptual Confusion: A Basic Classroom Pathology

Before we begin our discussion proper a clarification of some terms used in this section is in order. *Conceptual confusions* are here considered in the sense of Wittgenstein's understanding of philosophical problems. In this case then they are viewed as that which students encounter and experience in ordinary learning situations – the difficulties that the child goes through in organizing thoughts and understanding the meaning of words. We are not implying them to be consequences of physical or psychological disorders. We qualify them as *language-based* in view of the fact that language is the preeminent venue through which formal education is conducted in schools. Thus, the corruption of one's comprehension of the workings of language or inattention and misunderstanding of its use within language-based activities, such as reading, writing, speaking and listening is a critical aspect in an investigation regarding the rise of these complexities. It is regarded as a *basic pathology* due to the fact that this kind of an illness is generally experienced within a typical classroom instructional situation.[30] Teachers should be aware of the occurrence of such a problem. Our aim in this section is to indicate the factors that give rise to conceptual confusions which are manifested in a normal teaching situation and their implication on the student's learning progress. By this means we would be able to confirm the presence of this basic pathology in education and its consequent cure.

Paul O'Leary claims that «individuals do not learn on their own by having a blank mind upon which the world writes clear messages»[31]. This contention is an evident confutation of accepting Locke's *tabula rasa* learning theory in educational speculation and implies that chil-

---

[30] Whenever I use the term «illness» I am not implying physical or psychological undertones but I am always referring to Wittgenstein's use of such word, i.e. the inability to engage in a healthy understanding – the lack of a perspicuous representation.

[31] P. O'LEARY, «The Concept of Learning», 224.

dren, on the inception of formal education, already possess a certain assortment of concepts. This statement posits that children evidently have not been raised in a vacuum.[32] Citing Cobb, Piaget and Vygotsky, John Bransford and others note, «In the most general sense, the contemporary view of learning is that people construct new knowledge and understandings based on what they already know and believe»[33]. Jerome Bruner seems to share this idea in *Child's Talk* when he points out that lexico-grammatical training is preceded by systematic and abstract prelinguistic forms of communication which together with certain cognitive endowments and suitable social encouragement provide the support needed for the child to develop linguistic skills.[34] This assertion helps us in developing our contention. The problem that concerns us, however, has nothing to do with the quantity and kind of concepts they have or the manner in which they are acquired but in how the meaning of these concepts is determined.

Most educationalists and philosophers of education would agree, we reckon, in affirming that children are prone to readily accept, granting the influence of ostensive teaching, the objective view of meaning. This standpoint claims that since in immediate, everyday experience, most especially in instrumental language, i.e. language of straightforward communication, which ensures the possibility of simple cooperation in a group, words almost always refer to things, there is an objective relationship between the meaning of the word and objects in the world. Wittgenstein observed this in *PI* §1:

> These words, it seems to me, give us a particular picture of the essence of human language. It is this: the individual words in language name objects – sentences are combinations of such names. – In this picture of language we find the roots of the following idea: Every word has a meaning. This meaning is correlated wit the word. It is the object for which the word stands.

---

[32] I am not asserting that this claim is comparable with the *nativist approach* which postulates that the human mind comes endowed with abstract representations and processing capacities or with *innatism* in the Cartesian tradition of concept formation. I am rather emphasizing the fact about the presence of *raw* concepts learned or experience acquired before the beginning of formal schooling.

[33] J. BRANSFORD – A. BROWN – R. COCKING, ed., *How People Learn*, 10. See also P. COBB, *Theories*; J. PIAGET, *Success and Understanding*, *The Grasp of Consciousness*; L.S. VYGOTSKY, *Thought and Language*.

[34] Cf. J. BRUNER, *Child's Talk: Learning to Use Language*.

To hold fast to this view would certainly lead us to confusion. As Wittgenstein has noted (and obviously we do too), there are words that have no objective reference in the world, for instance the term "pain". In this case then (to heed Wittgenstein's warning) there is a need for teachers to be careful with this particular point of view and endeavor to avoid its establishment as a plausible notion of determining the meaning of words.

These misunderstandings of meanings are often manifested in the questions posed by children. Although children don't make inquiries that are at par with those proposed by philosophers, they nevertheless have same tendency to ask strange questions. For instance, «is the verb "to sleep" active or passive?» [*PI* §47] or «where does the old moon go when we get a new one?» The grammatical constructions of these questions are evidently correct but they are conceptually muddled up. They are obviously due to the distortion of new information as it is assimilated into their cognitive structure and that such distortions result in various kinds of misconceptions. The misrepresentation of a concept due to the misunderstanding of how language is being used is evident and is not only limited to young children.

There may be varied factors that give rise to conceptual confusions manifested by children inside the classroom during instructions but we are concerned here with three prevalent types which are in affinity to Wittgenstein's proposed source of philosophical problems. They are: mistaken use of grammar, misleading analogies, and false generalizations.

Our reference to the mistaken use of grammar does not primarily indicate the common errors made by children in grammatical structures, for instance putting the Subject-Object-Verb pattern (or subject-verb agreement) wrongly or conjugating verbs erroneously. We are rather concerned here about a deeper implication of the misguided use of grammar (in the Wittgensteinian sense), i.e. following the rules of grammar speciously – a cogent disregard of the varied use of words in language.[35] In the case of the above example about active and passive verbs the immediate tendency of children is to apply one use of such

---

[35] Wittgenstein uses in an untraditional manner the traditional term 'grammar'. Wittgenstein's treatment of grammar becomes a wider network of rules, which determine what linguistic move is allowed as making sense and what is not. It describes the varied use of words in language particularly referring to *depth grammar*. Cf. G. HALLETT, *Wittgenstein's Definition of Meaning as Use*, 83ff. In this sense therefore reference to *grammar* confirms what it is to use or misuse language.

words into another field of reference – the verb *to sleep* – without ever considering whether the words *active* and *passive* are used differently. This also applies for the other example between the words *old* and *new*. Not only children but also adults are disposed to committing this simplification of grammatical rules. Studies have shown that children do, in fact, absorb a massive number of words, sentences and phrases but rather than parroting them back they abstract rules from them and create their own grammar which they then apply to create new utterances they have never heard before, for instance the phrase «doggie go walkies». In this regard, the inability to distinguish between the diverse uses of words distorts the grammatical consistency of language rules and obviously discriminates their meaning which consequently brings about conceptual confusion. This type of grammatical error(s) is often manifested by bilingual students due to the fact of the superimposition in one's consciousness particular features the foreign language on the overall order of his native language. This results in the interference of two language systems thus creating a partial fusion or contamination of language use.[36] As a result, misuse of grammar and the subsequent conceptual confusion are to be expected even after extensive language exposures.

Another factor that gives rise to conceptual puzzlements is the problem of misleading analogies. Indeed, some analogies are not false. It could certainly be argued that analogical reasoning is at the very foundation of all-formal, rational thought. Wittgenstein definitely does not deny this point in view of the fact that it allows us to generalize from specific instances to general forms of abstract principles. On the one hand, false analogies mimic formal reasoning, i.e. our way of thinking that is based in our ability to recognize relevant similarities and upon our highly valued tendency to draw conclusions derived from these resemblances. On the other hand, they really are manifestations of similitudes in verbal form which constantly beget mistaken notions of how similar terms work and therefore of actualities discussed by their means.[37] Usha Goswami and others have shown that even preschool children appear to engage in analogies.[38] Young children are likely to interpret analogies in terms of thematic connections or common object

---

[36] J.V. GORBYLEVA, «Dialectics of Internal & External», http://www.bu.edu/wcp/Papers/Lang/LangGorb.htm.

[37] GARTH HALLETT, «The Theoretical Content of Language», 312.

[38] Cf. U. GOSWAMI, *Analogical Reasoning*. See also D. GENTNER, «Analogy», 107-113.

properties. An example should drive home our point. The similarities between sentences like «I'll keep it in mind» and «I'll keep it in this box» can lead to think of the mind as a thing something like a box with contents of its own. The nature of this box and its mental contents can then seem very mysterious. The above-indicated paradigm (along with many others) evidently manifests the particular confusion that results from yielding to mistaken analogies. Students, especially grade school and elementary schoolchildren often assume, without any transition of explanation, that the same rules pertaining to one expression are generally true in application to other apparently similar expressions. Chiung-Chu Wang and Janet Gaffrey, based on the result of their study, assert that although children have insights into the use of analogy in deciding unfamiliar words, they might not be able to discriminate appropriate from inappropriate use of analogy.[39] Thus, false analogies clearly give rise to conceptual disorders.

The third factor we have indicated is the propensity to make false generalizations. It is an obvious fact that children, in their search to enrich their linguistic repertoire, frequently commit the mistake of overgeneralization, i.e. error in thinking that what works for one type of concept should work for another. This is manifested recurrently in learning a language. For example, a child learned the past tense of the words *break*, *fall*, and *take* as *broken*, *fallen*, and *taken*. Based on this observation he concluded that English past tenses end in «–en». He then invents the words *boughten*, *builden*, *ridden*, *gotten*, *cutten*, *touchen* and others. Here he obviously falsely generalized the rules of English past tenses. Our example manifestly illustrates that the child seduced by the uniform appearance of the verb ending «–en» in past tenses sought to apply it as something common to all verbs conjugated in that specific tense. Philosophically this inclination to make certain generalizations is either due to our conviction that something common exists between diverse instances or that our language seems to express the same range of things. Since children form concepts based on the general ideas they acquire from experience, unawareness of the diverse workings of language would apparently lead them to construct false generalizations which, when not corrected, would result in conceptual bewilderments.

How can these conceptual confusions affect the learning progress of children? Based on our discussion the presence of such conceptual per-

---

[39] See C-C. WANG – J. S. GAFFREY, «First Graders' Use of Analogy», 389-403.

plexities indicates a certain form of learning disability.[40] This type of impediment mainly concerns a child's inability to command a clear view of how language works. They are unaware of the relationships between their words used and their comprehension of the meaning of such words. They are unable to determine or distinguish the variations in the application of the concepts according to diverse language use. At the bottom of conceptual confusions lies the non-mastery of linguistic usage. Since such mastery is fundamental to the formation of concepts and the understanding of their meaning, misapplication of language use leads to the malformation of concepts. The aforementioned factors then aggravate the error and thus bring about conceptual confusions. Given that concepts are essential to learning, possession of incoherent conceptual framework due to such perplexities thus distorts the normal development of learning. This case is observed and manifested recurrently in classroom instruction. It is in this instance then that it can be considered as basic classroom pathology; *basic*, in the sense of its occurrence within every instructional situation especially among children; *pathological*, given that it is a sufficiently serious conceptual illness that may preclude meaningful learning. In this regard therefore, it is the educator's task to treat this kind of sickness. Since the factors we have indicated resemble that of the causes of philosophical problems according to Wittgenstein, then we reckon that his suggested therapeutic method could be used by the educator as a way to clear up the language-based conceptual muddle. We thus have an image of an educator as therapist.

2.2 *The Teacher/Educator as Therapist*

Gary Fenstermacher and Jonas Soltis in *Approaches to Teaching* indicate diverse types of procedures in the teaching practice, for instance what they termed the executive and the liberationist approaches. Among these they also include the therapist approach.[41] However, there is a difference between the purpose of their approach and ours. According to them «the purpose of teaching in the therapist approach is to enable the learner to become an authentic human being, a person capable of accepting responsibility for what he or she is and is becoming, a per-

---

[40] We are not here referring to any form of learning disability related to an organic cause but rather on difficulties in actually learning the meaning of concepts due to conceptual confusions or perplexities.

[41] G. FENSTERMACHER – J. SOLTIS, *Approaches to Teaching*. Chapter three of their book discusses the therapist approach, 23 – 35.

son able to make choices that define one's character as one wishes it to be defined»[42]. This image of the teacher as therapist is mainly concerned with the student's personal authenticity much in the vein of providing individualized psychosocial treatment. Our usage of the therapist image contrasts with the aforementioned view in the sense that we are not concerned with presenting the teacher as someone who seeks by means of psychotherapeutic sessions to cure the student's physical, social or psychological disorder. He rather endeavors to cure the problem, i.e. helping the child to overcome his language-based learning disorder primarily on the level of conceptual perplexities. The aim is indeed to restore intellectual health from the common conceptual pathology. In this sense, therefore, the teacher's task is akin to Wittgenstein's view of the philosopher's undertaking.

The teacher as therapist, given that he is aware of the particular conceptual impairment of the student, is involved, as Mihaly Csikszentmihalyi observes, in «changing the learner's cognitive structures».[43] However we have to stress that only the erroneous and distorted elements of that structure such as incorrect and malformed concepts due to the misuse of language are needed to be changed. As John Bransford and others observe

> A logical extension of the view that new knowledge must be constructed from existing knowledge is that teachers need to pay attention to the incomplete understandings, false beliefs, and the naïve renditions of concepts that learners bring with them to a given subject.[44]

Just as what Wittgenstein's philosopher-therapist would do, the teacher-therapist needs to prescribe and carry out some form of treatment for the student's conceptual sickness by way of a perspicuous representation, i.e. to achieve clarity by framing strategies of diagnostic-didactic moves in language-games in order to distinguish diverse uses of words or expressions in different perspectives. This means that for the teacher to be able to correct the misapplication of grammatical rules, the use of misleading analogies and the formulation of false generalizations, he needs to underscore the viewpoint wherein the student *sees*, i.e. the educator need not *show* anything to make one understand but making one see through description enables the understanding of diverse language use from various standpoints. This line of thought is consis-

---

[42] G. FENSTERMACHER – J. SOLTIS, *Approaches to Teaching*, 26.
[43] M. CSIKSZENTMIHALYI, «Intrinsic Motivation and Effective Teaching», 76.
[44] J. BRANSFORD – *al.*, *How People Learn*, 10.

tent with our claim of teaching, i.e. it aims at enabling the learner to take over and go on by himself – to bring the student to see for himself and to paraphrase Wittgenstein's assertion, be able to arrange what he has always known [*PI* §109].[45] In this sense his method would primarily be descriptive.

To be able to carry out this task, the teacher as therapist needs to have sufficient training and experience. He must be well trained and thoroughly educated especially in the use of language. His experience in the linguistic terrain must be at the degree wherein he is not in the main troubled by conceptual difficulties. He must be clearly attentive of the confines of language. He must be sensitive to the likelihood of conceptual entanglements and will not blame the students for their failure to comprehend the correct use of words or expressions but will rather try to analyze the sources of the errors and corrections. In this regard, he should make a concentrated effort to catch potential problems early by including, for instance, examples that show multiple meanings. He must also plan instructional strategies to describe the correct application of language. In this case, the teacher is not one who imparts knowledge and skill but one who helps the students to discover for themselves the multifarious workings of language, i.e. he should direct them towards the correct way of looking at language use so that they are thereby enabled to reach perspicuity – choosing the right usage in specific contexts and the consequent moves from the mastery of such use. Problems arising from conceptual confusions are more difficult when not prevented or remedied properly. Thus, it is the key objective for the teacher as therapist to bring the students to a level of awareness of the diverse uses of words and expressions in language, i.e. to command a clear view of the terrain – to help each student achieve a more mature understanding. Success in such a method, i.e. restored health from conceptual neurosis is achieved when the student is able to use and look at language correctly.

We have endeavored in this section to apply Wittgenstein's therapeutic approach to education. In doing this, we demonstrated the occurrence of language-based conceptual confusions particularly within the context of classroom instruction. These conceptual perplexities, we have noted, may arise from three factors, viz. mistaken use of grammar, misleading analogies and false generalizations. These aspects are clearly akin to Wittgenstein's sources of philosophical problems. Such

---

[45] See Chapter III section 5 of this work.

predicaments are evidently considered under the aspect of learning disability since it distorts the development of the student's learning capacity, i.e. the ability to distinguish variations in language use. Thus, it is regarded as a basic pathology which fortunately can be treated with the help of the teacher-therapist by bringing the student to a level of perspicuity that would enable him to see the diversity of language use. However, our task does not end here. We still need to determine whence these apparent misuses of language originated. Our query leads us to the most evident candidate –the community and communal practices.[46]

3. The Community: Positive and Negative Contributions to Language Use

It is important, we reckon, to open this section with an elucidation about our argument. We are not attributing full culpability to the community regarding the issue of linguistic misuse or the misunderstanding of the workings of language. We are rather concerned with the fact that the community and communal practices play an inevitable part in the development of knowledge as well as the occurrence of error in understanding, in other words conceptual errors. As we indicated in chapter two of this work, it is within the community that an individual can have most experiences and perform various activities which are important for him. As Anthony Paul Cohen notes, the community «is a source and repository of meaning, and a referent of [...] identity»[47]. According to Janine Nahapiet and Sumantra Ghoshal, we can find in the community «those resources providing shared representations, interpretations, and systems of meanings».[48] It is within this context that the community becomes a major influencing factor in one's concept formation which eventually includes his employment of language. We have to admit though that theoretical and polemical diversity makes incisive analysis into the key features of the community that affects our perception of the various uses of words in language difficult. Nevertheless, in this seg-

---

[46] See Chapter II, section 4 of this work. See also D. R. WILLIAMS, «Re-embedding Community», 90-101.

[47] A.P. COHEN, *The Symbolic Construction of Community*, 118. This book is an outstanding exploration of *community* that focuses on it as a cultural phenomenon. Cohen looks at the ways in which the boundaries to communities are symbolically defined and how people become aware of belonging to a community.

[48] J. NAHAPIET – S. GHOSHAL, «Social Capital, Intellectual Capital», 244.

ment we shall argue that there is sufficient evidence that demonstrates that indeed a certain degree of accountability can be attributed to the community and shared customs in the way the aims of education are achieved but more specifically on how we use or misuse our language.

3.1 *Dual-Benefit from an Interaction with the Community in Education*

Let us start with the positive contribution. Indeed, there are wide-ranging advantages that we can obtain from interacting with the community. However, we are concerned here with those that are significant to the educational enterprise. This relates to those which affect the teaching and learning processes. In this regard, we shall argue that our contact or connection with the community manifests two educationally important benefits: i) it enhances the students' learning capabilities and competence and ii) it facilitates the realization of the outcomes of school-based learning and supports the development of educational performance.

The framework of our claim accommodates the understanding that we form part of a particular community and the factors that describe it can have an impact not only on our affective growth but also more importantly on our cognitive development.[49] This contention echoes the work of John Dewey over a century ago that connected learning with the social and physical environment of the child. How can then a relationship with the community improve the learning potentials of students?

Communities not only provide the structures that facilitate learning but they also shape and determine what learning is valued. Etienne Wenger states that, «If learning is a matter of engagement in socially defined practices, the communities that share these practices play an important role in shaping learning»[50]. This means that in maintaining the shared *practices* of the members, i.e. the knowledge that is employed by the community members, the community, for instance in terms of the linguistic aspect, helps shape the actual terminologies used by the members in everyday life. This means that experiences of students from collaboration with out-of-school contexts become valuable

---

[49] These factors are represented by what is called *commonality* or *interlocking* or *integrated functional subsystems* within communities. Cf. U. BRONFENBRENNER – P. MOEN – J. GARBARINO, «Children, Family, & Community», 286.

[50] E. WENGER, «Communities of Practice», 20-26: 24. See also S. STANAGE, «Meaning & Value», 53.

materials in the progress of their abilities and skills for learning. For example, providing them with opportunities to exhibit the full range of either their cognitive strategies or the ways in which they have transferred knowledge into new contexts. According to Stephen Small and Andrew Supple, «the communities in which children and adolescents live can have important influences on their well-being and development»[51]. This goes along with the assertion of Meredith Honig, Joseph Kahne and Milbrey McLaughlin that «Many of the factors that shape students' opportunities to learn and teachers' opportunities to teach are beyond the purview of schools»[52]. They argue that community connections such as integrated services programs have often been constructed as vehicles through which the barriers to learning are removed thus promoting success in schools.[53] This shows that the major forces shaping children and young people in the process of education are the same as those that shape or direct all learners, namely, the structures and processes of the entire socio-cultural life going on around them, i.e. the community.

Another advantage with interacting with the community is the facility by which we realize the outcomes of school-based learning. This involves principally how we conceptualize and measure transfer of what one learns in school to everyday settings of the community. The sense of this benefit lies in the fact that such connection allows the application, the improvement and the broadening of what the students have learned in schools. For instance, in the context of linguistic competence, a child comes to recognize after being taught properly in school about the workings of language, his ability to understand language use when he is engaged in actual linguistic activities within the community. Such endeavor given the right conditions and reactions will undoubtedly contribute to the development of one's performance in schooling. We gain educational growth by means of this link with our community. Unfor-

---

[51] S. SMALL – A. SUPPLE, «Communities as systems», http://www.uwex.edu/ces/flp/resources/community.pdf.

[52] M. HONIG – J. KAHNE – M. McLAUGHLIN, «School-community connections», 999.

[53] Students and community members are often unable to learn because of complex social, emotional, health and developmental problems. These are barriers to their learning and prevent their involvement in community affairs. Community Schools bring a range of health, social, counseling, justice, personal support and recreation services to the school, or provide individuals and families with a link to these services. Examples of Integrated Service Programs may include: Conflict resolution programs, addiction programs, integrated team approach, counseling programs and others.

tunately, what has been discussed so far is only one side of the coin. We have indeed stressed the fact that the involvement with the community brings educationally valuable benefits. However, on the other side of the coin lies the negative impact of communal practices. We shall elaborate on this issue in the succeeding segment.

3.2 *Negative Impact of Communal Practice on Language Use*

We have underlined in the previous section that available evidence suggests that one of the most important influences on a child's cognitive, social-emotional and language development is the relationship with the community. Such is the case because each particular community performs and follows its own traditions, customs and practices. Communities have their own, as Wittgenstein would say *forms of life*. As there are various types of benefits one can obtain from an interaction with the community so too can there be diverse negative implications. Since space does not allow us to develop a thorough investigation of such consequences, we shall dwell on the main interest of this work and that concerns how the aspect of communal practices, i.e. *regularity* can produce an unconstructive outcome in the use of language.

Wittgenstein's arguments regarding «forms of life» strongly suggest that our concepts are not based on individual private experience, but are rooted in our social life which of its nature is shared publicly, i.e. the rules for using expressions must have anchors in the public world. He says: «What has to be accepted, the given, is – so one could say – a *form of life*» [*PI* §226]. Roger Trigg notes that «"practices", "forms of life" and "language-games" are all terms bearing witness to the intimate mutual dependence of language and other forms of acting»[54]. He furthers says, «It is through the participation in a society that we learn to use language and hence to think»[55]. This claim agrees with our contention that we learn the use of language in a public context. As Shirley Brice-Heath notes there are socially learned and culturally patterned use of language.[56] In this sense, an individual can institute a particular usage only under the condition that it is accepted as a social practice. It is important to stress that the *community* or *practice* view of language use does not confine us to speaking only of consensus and

---

[54] R. TRIGG, «Wittgenstein and Social Science», 212.

[55] R. TRIGG, «Wittgenstein and Social Science», 212-213.

[56] See S. BRICE-HEATH, *Ways with words*. See also R. L. SCHIEFELBUSCH – J. PICKAR, ed., *Acquisition of communicative competence*.

conformity in giving an account on meaning and understanding. Even if the only thing that determines what an expression or word means is the general practice in the use of that expression in the community it does not follow that to say what it means is to say only that it has a use in the community, or that everyone uses it in the same way. Nonetheless, this precise idea presupposes that the understanding of language itself follows the path of custom and habit, or rules and regularities. The point is clearly visible in *PI* §142:

> It is only in normal cases that the use of a word is clearly prescribed; we know, are in no doubt, what to say in this or that case. The more abnormal the case, the more doubtful it becomes what we are to say. And if things were quite different from what they actually are – if there were for instance no characteristic expressions of pain, of fear, of joy... - this would make our normal language-games lose their point. – The procedure of putting a lump of cheese on a balance and fixing the price by the turn of the scale would lose its point if it frequently happened for such lumps to suddenly grow or shrink for no obvious reason.

As Wittgenstein says, «The regularity of our language permeates our lives»[57]. Then it is this aspect of communal practices based on regularity which makes us believe that what is done and said by the community results in something determinate and absolute to the extent of considering that, as Rudolf Haller notes, «a change in conceptual scheme brings with it a change in the form of life»[58]. Our arguments direct our attention to the effectiveness of practices. The totality of rules and practices pervades our lives so much that we gain not only the use of language but also the conviction that it is not necessary to question beyond the forms of life embedded in it. However, it is inevitable that we can go wrong within a practice. This is so in view of the fact that, according to Barry Stroud, «only particular applications can be said to be correct or incorrect, and that there must be some standard or practice or pattern of behavior for there to be such thing as correctness or incorrectness at all»[59]. This argument seems to insinuate that communal practices set the standard for which members should follow. Because of their regularity we are led to think that our compliance to such standard makes our performance correct. This is evidently misleading since conformity to an incorrect standard does not make one's actions correct. Eva Brann

---

[57] L. WITTGENSTEIN, *Remarks on Colours*, 303.

[58] R. HALLER, *Questions on Wittgenstein*, 122.

[59] B. STROUD, *Meaning, Understanding and Practice*, 93.

cautions us that commitment to a public practice without entertaining doubts about it can border on ideology or close-mindedness.[60] Thus, given the cogency of the concept of regularity, the negative impact of communal practices lies in the fact that once they are recognized as providing the standard of correctness of our use of language we are drawn into the belief in a certain community-specific *mind map* which filters and transforms our employment of a word. Such would basically be considered correct only if it conformed to the use it then had in the community. In this case we can suppose that whatever mistakes and conceptual confusions teachers find in children's use of language are presumably a result of the negative impact of communal practices.

In this section we have highlighted the prevailing interaction between the community and the educational enterprise and we have come to notice the vital influence that the community has on the progress of education. The stress given to its positive and negative contributions of the community enabled us to see the aspects the affects the learning process. Thus we came to the reckon that the community is a resource of language use and a determinant of its misuse, i.e. although we can learn the use of language in the community, it is also from the impact of communal practices based on their regularity that certain misuse or misconceptions of language use stem from. It is in this standpoint then that the therapeutic approach in teaching is considered valuable.

4. The Significance of the Therapeutic Method in the Educational Enterprise

We have already accentuated in the previous sections some aspects of the therapeutic method, which are in actual fact substantial in the field of education such as the recognition of the importance of children's pre-classroom experiences, the vigor and solidity of communal practices and others. Not much however has been discussed regarding its importance in our conception of teaching. We shall thus investigate in this segment how Wittgenstein's view of the therapeutic approach affect our notion of teaching, i.e. its pedagogical implications and what aspect of such influence manifests congruency to the conception of teaching proposed in the third chapter of this work, i.e. that teaching aims at normalization.

---

[60] Cf. E.T.H. BRANN, *Paradoxes of Education in a Republic.*

4.1 *The Impact of the Therapeutic Approach on the Concept of Teaching*

We have indicated in the third chapter of this work that teaching considered as an activity which involves the element of intention to achieve learning is the most diffused and widely accepted conception. We are not going to disprove this claim nor are we going to offer any modification of such viewpoint. What we are concerned here is to investigate on the impact of the therapeutic method modeled from Wittgenstein's idea of philosophical therapy on our prevailing understanding of the teaching practice.

As we have previously discussed the therapeutic approach in Wittgenstein's philosophy primarily consists of the process of description which aims at dissipating the mist of philosophical confusions that one has. By this method one mainly intends to uncover «one or another piece of plain nonsense and of bumps that the understanding has got by running its head against the limits of language» [*PI* §119] by means of unmasking the differences and dissimilarities of the diverse uses of words in order to reveal conceptual confusions and eventually dissolve what Wittgenstein calls philosophical problems. The success of such a process does not rest upon any theoretical or speculative foundation but is based upon the awareness of and reference to varied language uses in diverse forms of life. The most significant characteristic of such an approach is the attention given to a description of particular instances in order to understand fully and correctly the logic of the entire case to which they belong. This is reflected from Wittgenstein's claim that describing instances of using language enables one to understand correctly the logic of language. In this sense then such a method is by nature inconclusive, i.e. it needs to keep on ferreting out new methods to deal with new problems. If we juxtapose these features to our conception of teaching we can observe three notable consequences: first, it affects our understanding of the task of teaching, secondly, it characterizes teaching not as an activity determined by one-approach descriptions such as «teaching as problem-solving», «teaching as showing», «teaching as communication» and the like, and third, it impugns the predominant presupposition of teaching as a knowledge-input from teachers.

4.1.1 On the Task of Teaching

The teaching task is commonly considered as consisting of the intention to bring about learning. Such an undertaking is actually indisputable in educational studies. However, some educational philosophers such as Allen Pearson, Peter Jarvis and others have accentuated the significance of extending the goal of the enterprise of teaching from just achieving learning to a concern for the appropriate employment of what has been learned in real life.[61] If we take a closer look, the therapeutic method as proposed by Wittgenstein evidently contributes to this change of viewpoint. How? First, since such a method puts emphasis on the importance of diverse practices and particular cases, which allow the individual to have a certain perspicuity, it empowers the person to consider their value in one's teaching. This leads to the extent that teaching will no longer be contented with a mere manifestation that one has learned but rather how one successfully applies what is learned in practice. Secondly, such an approach highlights the cogency of the form of life. It is, we might say, an ineluctable factor which renders the therapeutic method efficient. In like manner, this preoccupation with the form of life enables teaching to look beyond the horizon of merely achieving learning for the sake of learning towards the applicability and value of that learning in a form of life. It implies that diverse sociological variables are not disregarded in teaching since they are salient elements which when given proper recognition could lead to its success. Practically, teaching aims at normalization – a transformation to a form of life. This means that in teaching one strives not only to let the child learn but more importantly enable him to use that learning in whatever he does within the community - «What *we* do is to bring words back from their metaphysical to their everyday use» [*PI* §116].

The aforementioned argumentation indicates that it is undeniable that in some way or another teaching attempts to alter students. In Wittgenstein's words, «A present-day teacher of philosophy doesn't select food for his pupil with the aim of flattering his taste, but with the aim of changing it» [*CV* 17e]. The change we are referring here points to a transformation of children's understanding which is determined by the community-based background beliefs and practices. Teaching should be more concerned with helping the students undergo a slow reforma-

---

[61] Allen Pearson claims that «teaching is a tentative act», i.e. it steps towards the community. See A. T. PEARSON, «Teaching, Reason and Risk», 110; PETER JARVIS, *The Theory and Practice of Teaching.*

tion to a form of life. If we make a closer analysis of this claim we become aware of a notable impact, i.e. we are able to see from this perspective the value of having within the range of teaching the proper functioning of students within the community. By unmasking conceptual confusions, the child will grow towards a form of life that is more efficient within the objective constraints of human life; more efficient, i.e. than the form of life the child inherited at home. For instance, understanding the moon as the same object even though we use *old* and *new* helps the child to live better (in a general sense) because he now is able to connect this understanding with that which he has learned from science class. In this manner teaching becomes beneficial both theoretically and practically for the child.

4.1.2 On Teaching Methods

Generally, teaching is characterized by most educationists or educationalists in a single-approach description for instance, «teaching as communication», «teaching as problem-solving», «teaching as showing», and the like. These descriptions fail to take account the reality that teaching is described by and involves more than just one specific approach.[62] Wittgenstein's idea of the therapeutic method helps us to highlight this fact – «There is not *a* philosophical method, though there are indeed methods, like different therapies» [*PI* §133].

We have indicated in the preceding section that teaching should aim at learning which is linked to a form of life, i.e. to enable the students to blend in the form of life to which they belong with the aid of teaching. However, each form of life possesses its peculiar (communal) practices. This then implies that in order for teaching to achieve its goals particular attention should be given to these diverse practices. To facilitate in doing this, the teacher must adopt the appropriate method which (when employed properly) will successfully transform the student's outlook and obtain correct understanding so as to be able to effectively integrate himself within the particular form of life to which he is incorporated and participate actively in the various communal practices.

The one that carries some weight here is how we approach the subject matter. This idea prompts us to refrain from qualifying, describing, and labeling the teaching activity as if it consisted of only one ultimate

---

[62] I also think that accent on its polymorphous character would help drive home the point. Cf. R.F. DEARDEN, «Instruction and Learning by Discovery», 269.

approach which in such a peculiar way may be convertible with and equal to teaching itself. Although Wittgenstein does not directly address this issue, it may be safe to speculate that based on the therapeutic method he would contend that teaching should put into practice a certain form of flexibility of methods which are capable of coping with the exigency of the actual subject matter, for instance, the real functioning of linguistic expressions in their natural environment. In so doing, teaching might dissipate whatever problems found in the educational experience. The ideal of education is not to impart facts, but to create permanent interests, so that the student ultimately becomes his own teacher – «in this case the instructor *imparted* the meaning to the pupil – without telling him it directly; but in the end the pupil is brought to the point of giving himself the correct ostensive definition» [*PI* §362].

4.1.3 On Knowledge-Input and Teaching

The traditional image of the teacher is someone who tells students what to learn and persuades them to learn and run through what they have been taught. It has been they, so to say, who have mediated knowledge to children and adult learners alike.[63] In this regard, teaching seems to be a sort of monopoly of transmitting knowledge. This gives us the implication that in teaching others one is in fact just passing on possessed knowledge.

The problem we are dealing with here does not concern the issue regarding the notion of knowledge-base for teaching since it is evidently indisputable that teachers should, in some way or another, possess certain type of knowledge in order to be effective in their task.[64] However, what we do want to give focus is the claim that teaching is predominantly an endeavor of knowledge-input.[65] The crucial aspect of this as-

---

[63] Mark Mason seems to agree with this idea in his article which considers the question of the role of teachers with respect to knowledge and defends the view of teachers' role as *critical mediators* of knowledge, which describes them both as *mediators* of knowledge, and as *socio-cultural critics*. For further discussion see M. MASON, «Teachers as Critical Mediators of Knowledge», 343-352.

[64] Robert Orton in his article examines the questions that arise regarding the notion of teacher knowledge. He bases the development of his discussion upon the arguments presented by Lee S. Shulman and develops an analysis of the *tacit* and *situated* problems of teacher knowledge. For further discussion see R. E. ORTON, «Two Problems», 365-373.

[65] Michael Oakeshott expresses a similar assertion in his statement that «All teaching has a component of instruction, because all knowledge has a component of infor-

sertion is the idea of replication. If we assume teaching to consist basically of conveying knowledge to students then the result would fundamentally be centered upon the reproduction of knowledge input with memory storage and emphasized only on subsequent accuracy of knowledge input retrieval. In this case then it appears equivalent to the idea of photocopying and saving the photocopy of knowledge input into a parallel file in the brain for subsequent retrieval. An educational analogue of this imagery is the view that students learn by passively sitting still and absorbing knowledge rather than by actively manipulating things and testing the results of their inquiries[66] - in other words children are left with no space to work their problems out, e.g. conceptual defects/deformities and find answers and correction.[67] Although this claim may appear plausible it has lost its charm in educational studies in recent years since teachers now do not assume that their learners know nothing about the subject that they teach but must learn to build on knowledge acquired by their learners from variety of sources especially from communal practices.[68] This aspect illustrates the impact of the therapeutic method in teaching in the sense that it principally gives value to one's knowledge from various practices, i.e. it is not reductive – it accepts matters of fact and acknowledges salient sociological variables as vital elements in the process of learning. Although we are not denying that teaching does involve *to some extent* the conveying of knowledge, to consider it, as knowledge-input *sine qua non* is misleading since rigidly bound knowledge implied by such a description tends

---

mation. The teacher as instructor is the deliberate conveyor of information to his pupil» see M. OAKESHOTT, «Teaching», 15. Although his position does contain some truth about the teaching activity, we are apprehensive about the implication of such a claim since one might haphazardly conclude that teaching consists of no more than just transmission of knowledge or information.

[66] See J. DEWEY, *Democracy and Education*.

[67] Teaching should not include an imposition of the teacher's agenda upon the students. Ronald Strickland's discussion regarding confrontational pedagogy illustrates the point we are making here. Cf. R. STRICKLAND, «Confrontational Pedagogy», 291-300.

[68] Although this may seem to be in the vein of the constructivist epistemological position I want to emphasize that the assertion being proposed here is not intended to be explicitly affiliated to such a claim. What I endeavor to stress is the fact that teaching should not be absolutely considered as knowledge-input process. For further discussion on the constructivist's epistemological stance see R. MILLAR – R. DRIVER, «Beyond Processes», 57; R. NADEAU – J. DÉSAUTELS, *Epistemology*; R. DRIVER – V. OLDHAM, «A Consructivist Approach», 105-122; E. VON GLASERSFELD, «Cognition», 121-140.

to restrict meaning and right action. It is rather that teaching should be an activity which initiates the transportability of knowledge, i.e. when students are able to see connections between different aspects of the subject matter that contents of which become valuable in one's everyday living.

The magnitude of Wittgenstein's therapeutic method enhances the traditional understanding of teaching by i) extending its task from a mere achievement of learning to an effort that effects a transformation to a form of life, ii) by proposing that teaching should incorporate flexibility of methods in dealing with diverse subject matters and finally iii) by reproaching the radical claim of teaching as knowledge-input.

We have demonstrated in this section the significance of the therapeutic method and its impact on the concept of teaching. However, just like any other tool we can appreciate its value based on its utility. Evidently, its usefulness is found in its capability to unmask conceptual deformities or confusions from community-based background practices and putting them aright. Thus, we shall attempt in the succeeding segment to discuss possible remedies for such a conceptual illness produced by the negative influence of communal practices encountered in the classroom.

4.2 Possible Remedy for Conceptual Confusions brought about by the Negative Influence of Communal Practices

We have indicated in the preceding sections that a germane element in Wittgenstein's discussion of philosophy as therapy is the existence of diverse communal practices. We have also acknowledged that such practices are in fact capable of producing a strong influence upon an individual's concepts, beliefs and understanding some aspects of which are beneficial but some also yield negative effects noticeably manifested by conceptual errors. Thus, we shall attempt in this section to propose steps for a possible remedy of what Wittgenstein might call an *illness*, which might be of use for the teacher in situations wherein these types of perplexities of understanding are encountered. We shall put forward three phases of our proposed remedy. First is the design and implementation of a curriculum that is characteristically perspicuous, i.e. it must include a vision of wholeness. To follow this, the teacher should undertake a deliberate application of illustrations and examples as valuable devices. Thirdly, teaching should include a methodic-pedagogical adaptation. We shall elaborate these stages in the succeeding paragraphs.

4.2.1 Design and Implementation of a Perspicuous Curriculum

Generally, a school-based conception of educational objectives claims that it is by means of a significant curriculum that particular aims in education are realized. It then follows from this argument that in designing a core curriculum the fact that the child's existence in the community depends upon the values promoted by education should not be jettisoned but must be given emphasis. The perspicuity that this curriculum should possess springs from the fact that the nature of the child and his community primarily has some bearing on and determines the subject matter of what is or will be taught. This means that teaching must include a vision of wholeness, i.e. it must take into consideration that which happens beyond the classroom and the formal process of teaching, for instance communal practices or community-based beliefs.[69] This specific type of curriculum aims to develop the *whole* child and this incorporates, when formulated and implemented properly, a way of dissolving conceptual errors acquired by children through contact with the prevalent communal practices. However, this does not encompass a complete cure to such an illness. We still have to proceed onto another step if we are to strengthen the effectiveness of the remedy, i.e. the deliberate use of illustrations and examples in teaching to complement our first move.

4.2.2 Deliberate Use of Illustrations and Examples

The value of illustrations and examples in teaching are oftentimes underestimated in the sense that they are thought of mostly merely as devices utilized in cases where the student does not understand the subject matter, i.e. what is taught in the first instance. In other words, they are viewed as second-rate tools of the trade. This is certainly not the case if we look at Wittgenstein's procedure in the process of therapy. According to Alice Ambrose, «Wittgenstein did recognize the need of

---

[69] Donald Morton and Mas'Ud Zavandeh state that specific desires, forms of reflection, and concrete social practices within an interface of subject positions are significant in restructuring how we can know what we can know. Cf. D. MORTON – M. ZAVADEH, *Texts for Change.*

"hints" and "pointers"».[70] The sense of using them intentionally in one's teaching is to achieve refinement or even completing the system of rules for diverse subject matters. Although Wittgenstein's use of an illustration is unique to his philosophy, i.e. within a persistent discussion of the same point from various perspectives, it still can be considered as effective in a pedagogical endeavor.[71] Using an illustration implies that teaching endeavors to make the students *see*, i.e. it does not only help the child visually or imaginatively as what common understanding of an illustration implies but it motivates him to make connections of what is presented and from there begin to discover or rediscover by themselves the sense of what has been taught. This seeing consists of an appreciation of the whole. According to Ali Allmaker, «the "dialectic-by-illustrations" is not only suitable for the humanities but perhaps equally adaptable to many aspects of the social and natural sciences».[72] We are not insinuating that illustrations and examples should be indispensable elements in teaching. However, a deliberate and correct use of them would positively improve and produce relevant student learning and would most likely prevent misunderstandings in practice if not completely cure us from conceptual errors.

4.2.3 Continuous Methodic-Pedagogical Adaptation

The third but not the least step is an engagement of what we can call a continuous methodic-pedagogical adaptation. One of the aims of this phase is to maintain the functionality of the previous stages. By this we mean that in teaching one should consider the factors that affect the learning process of children such as what Wittgenstein refers to, viz., use, form of life, diverse communal practices and others which are often disregarded in formal education. This involves a constant didactic variation which enables the identification of seemingly invisible constraints in shared practices that bring us all towards the *normal* range of such practices. Within this particular undertaking teachers should realize that it is damaging to students when they try to directly impose

---

[70] A. AMBROSE, «Moore and Wittgenstein», 112.

[71] Cf. *PI* §§ 152-154, 321, 396, p. 182e regarding Wittgenstein's discussion of the concept of *understanding*. What is important here to observe is how he develops and presents his claim that understanding refers to behavior and not to a mental state and that application is a criterion of understanding. This case in point can be considered as Wittgenstein's most perfect demonstration of the use and effectiveness of illustrations.

[72] A. ALLMAKER, «*Wholeness*», 188.

judgments of the falseness of their perceptions and understanding without conscientiously taking into account the aspects from which these are set in motion. However, through frequent adjustment or should we say modification of pedagogic approach which includes a relentless uncovering of conceptual errors through illustrations and examples within a well formulated and implemented perspicuous curriculum, a remedy for the errors of our understanding and conception is not too far at hand.

Based on the above discussion, the Wittgensteinian analysis of the therapeutic method does serve the point of providing us a whole new approach in looking at the fundamental elements of the educational enterprise such as teaching and learning. We every so often disregard the aspects, which Wittgenstein holds essential in his idea of philosophy as therapy, within education to the extent that we underestimate (at times) the influence that comes from practices within the community – practices, which do not allow us to see the differences and dissimilarities and consequently lead us in committing conceptual errors and misunderstanding. Nonetheless, it is a reconsideration of the Wittgensteinian therapeutic process that enabled us to devise a possible remedy/cure for conceptual illnesses brought about by the negative influence of community-based practices and background beliefs.

5. Conclusion

The main aim of this chapter has been to demonstrate how Wittgenstein's idea of philosophy as therapy succeeds in underscoring the prevailing interaction between the community, together with its communal practices and background beliefs, and the educational enterprise. We endeavored to extract and make evident from the fundamental elements of Wittgenstein's view of the therapeutic method the particular function and contribution of the community in the sphere of education. We proceeded with this undertaking by first elaborating on the import of Wittgenstein's idea of *philosophy as therapy*. We have given attention in this segment the major elements of his idea and its relevance as a method by which we are able to cure conceptual errors. In our discussion we have seen that Wittgenstein considers philosophical problems, which arise basically out of the misleading features of our language, as intellectual illnesses, which fundamentally impairs an individual from engaging in a normal and healthy intellectual activity. As a cure to this particular pathology he encourages us to strive for a perspicuous representation, which he considers as fundamental in obtaining clarity. In this sense we are led to regard the task of a philosopher as specifically aimed at restoring intellectual health not by always striving to teach new facts but also by means of a method of perspicuous description.

After laying out the key concepts of Wittgenstein's idea of philosophy as therapy we proceeded on to apply the relevant features of the therapeutic method to education. Here we have specifically emphasized that, based on the recognition of various conceptual confusions – intellectual diseases and the employment of the descriptive method, there is a kind of illness that students generally experience within a typical classroom instructional situation. We classified this as a language-based conceptual confusion in the sense that since language is a pre-eminent venue through which formal education is conducted we assumed that it is within language-based activities that particular confusions with and errors in one's comprehension of the workings of language arise. This particular aspect allows us to recognize the fact that in every formal education one is always confronted with this basic classroom pathology. Faced with this problem the educator's task then should be designed to solve or dissolve it but more importantly he should not fail, to be consistent with Wittgenstein's idea of therapy, to consider the source whence these complexities in one's understanding arise. It is in this perspective where we are able to see clearly the function and contribution of the community.

We have indicated in the third section the positive and negative contributions of the community specifically to language use. Here we intended to highlight the fact that aside from the beneficial aspects we obtain from our interaction with the community, for instance the enhancement of the student's learning capacities, the realization of the outcomes of school based learning and the support for the development of educational performance, there are also diverse negative implications specifically those that we get from community-based practices. From our discussion we have not only demonstrated the role of the community in education but we have also concluded that we should not disparage the influence of one's form of life in every aspect of the educational experience, i.e. formal education from its inception should not be considered as independent from the social variables which are prevalently enclosed within the structure of a community but should rather take them into account as determinant and vital for the progress in education. If this were the case then the idea that learners come to be formally educated as *tabula rasa* is evidently ungrounded and misleading.

The overall argument laid down in this chapter has been to prove that Wittgenstein's comprehension of philosophy as therapy could be used as a model in evaluating the function and responsibility of the community in the educational enterprise. Formal education with a well-rounded perspicuous curriculum, then, in this sense, should possess a therapeutic character that would enable teachers as well as learners to achieve that state of intellectual health, to be cured from conceptual confusions and consequently to preserve such health in understanding. A successful application of this approach in the educational system will undoubtedly be capable of producing a well-formed, educated person. All these assessments were made possible with the help of Wittgenstein's idea of philosophy as therapy.

GENERAL CONCLUSION

The major impetus of our investigation has been to establish plausible line of reasoning upon which the claim that Wittgenstein's fundamental philosophical ideas are valid theoretical foundations for a clarification of the basic concepts of philosophy of education, viz., teaching, learning and the community, could be defended. In order to articulate this contention, we have drawn essential claims mostly from Wittgenstein's later writings principally from the *Philosophical Investigations*, as well as from significant studies in philosophy of education. In this concluding section, we shall first recapitulate succinctly the main lines of our arguments, then demonstrate the aspects that support our claim that Wittgenstein's ideas are legitimate basis in clarifying the above-mentioned educational concepts by way of indicating the relevant discoveries of our research and as a final point, mention some supplementary remarks on the implications of our study for further research concerning a relation of Wittgenstein's thoughts and philosophy of education.

1. A Recapitulation

In this thesis we attempted to show that Wittgenstein's philosophical thoughts are valid theoretical basis for a clarification of the basic concepts in the philosophy of education, namely, *teaching*, *learning*, and the *community*. Our first approach to the problem was to indicate and elaborate on the ideas contained in Wittgenstein's philosophy that are pertinent to the educational enterprise. We have pointed out in the first chapter that his thoughts on *meaning as use, rule-following* and *philosophy as therapy* are relevant to education primarily because of their evident didactic and pedagogical characteristics. By looking closely at how he develops his ideas about meaning and following a rule, on the one hand, we have discovered that particular use of educational concepts specifically that of *teaching* and *learning* is not only apparent but also fundamental. His view of philosophy as therapy, on the other hand, shows how the descriptive nature of philosophy untangles the conceptual confusions that we encounter because of our bewitchment in language. This perspective not only underlines the relationship between the community and the educational enterprise but also is valuable in evaluating the proficiency of children within particular instructional situations.

After a critical assessment of the fundamental themes in Wittgenstein's philosophy we then proceeded on to discuss and examine the rudiments of the basic concepts in the philosophy of education. It was the crucial task of the second chapter to delineate the essentials of their respective natures. However, before we advanced on a theoretical analysis of these concepts we attempted to clarify the nature of philosophy of education in order to delimit the scope of our discussion about the historical development of philosophy of education based on ideas of philosophers regarding the nature and purpose of education. This perspective was laid down not only to justify the status of the discipline itself but also to make us clearly understand the peculiar characteristics of our present day educational system.

Subsequent to a concise yet notable overview of the historical progress of philosophy of education we then continued to elucidate the concepts of teaching, learning and community respectively. An important aspect of this exposition was to delineate the significant features of each concept which are crucial in our later investigations. In this regard, we tried to avoid arguments which are in themselves noteworthy yet not pertinent to our study, such as debates concerning teaching as act or enterprise, teacher accountability, taxonomy of learning strategies, and others. The integral part of the chapter was intended to give us an idea about the established understanding of the nature of these basic concepts in philosophy of education.

Chapters three, four and five were considered as the core segments of this dissertation. They basically consisted of an undertaking to relate the central themes of Wittgenstein's philosophy to teaching, learning and community as basic concepts in philosophy of education.

We aimed in the third chapter to discover whether the conceptualization of teaching within Wittgenstein's treatment of meaning adheres to or is consistent with the established understanding of teaching in educational philosophy and whether or not his analysis of *meaning as use* provides an innovative outlook that would suggest a reconsideration of our present conception of teaching. In order to achieve this goal we looked into the interest of Wittgenstein in teaching and the rationale behind utilizing the concept in his investigations, we exposed the character of «teaching» by extracting its features from his later writings, we illustrated the existing logical connection between the concepts of *meaning* and *teaching* by referring to the notions of intention, context and practice(s) contained in his philosophical arguments, and finally following this line of reasoning we demonstrated how teaching possesses an indispensable role in Wittgenstein's analysis of meaning. Based on these considerations we were able to assess whether Wittgenstein's treatment of teaching in his analysis of meaning deviates or adheres from the accepted view of teaching and discover an innovative view of the concept based on his investigations.

A scrutiny of the learning process in the light of Wittgenstein's idea of rule-following was the main case of the fourth chapter. Here we argued that his idea of following a rule provides a unique view of understanding the learning process without falling into the predicament of the perennial dichotomy between cognitivism and behaviorism. We proceeded with our discussion by first providing an account of the character of the *process of learning* in the later works of Wittgenstein. Specific attention was given to his account of language learning in order to determine the significance of rules and rule-following in such process. We included in this section a differentiation of his views regarding the concepts often confused and interchanged with learning, namely, *understanding* and *knowing*. Since Wittgenstein's argument on *rule-following* is not immune to attacks, we elaborated on the skeptical point contained in his idea. We have taken into account an examination of the Kripkean position and determined the points which showed how his reading (although some of it are relevant to Wittgenstein's philosophy) deviates from that of Wittgenstein's idea. After this has been done, we then discussed the fundamental features that constitute his thoughts concerning *rule-following*. Based on these accounts we have discovered that the learning process manifests a feature that is comparable to following a rule. Thus, we proceeded to make an exposition of the rule-following character of the learning process. We concluded the chapter by discussing the impact of our claim to the psychological learning theories and its pedagogical implication.

The final section of this work, chapter five, was concerned with an investigation of the relevance of his thought regarding the nature of *philosophy as therapy* in the field of education. We specifically argued that such point of view is valuable in assessing the linguistic competence of children in classroom situations and the function and influence of the community within the educational enterprise. We have demonstrated with our arguments that, although Wittgenstein's idea of philosophy as therapy is primarily situated in philosophical discourse, to claim that it is exclusively confined within such ambit should be considered with caution. His thoughts regarding philosophical problems as specific forms of intellectual diseases, the therapeutic method as a way of restoring conceptual malady, and the idea of a perspicuous representation, noticeably produce a significant impact in the domain of education. We have discovered in this segment that Wittgenstein's idea of *philosophy as therapy* highlights the prevailing interaction between communal practices and the educational system. It was through our investigation of the elements of his thoughts on the therapeutic nature of philosophy that we exposed the particular function and contribution of the community in the sphere of education. This has direct effect on the instructional approach of educators and downgrades the contention that learners come to be educated as *tabula rasa*.

2. **Wittgensteinian Themes as Valid Theoretical Foundations**

The above-indicated approach in our investigation was meant to provide arguments that would support the main premise of our study, that is to demonstrate that the fundamental Wittgensteinian themes, namely, *meaning as use*, *rule-following*, and *philosophy as therapy*, are valid theoretical foundations for a clarification of the basic concepts of philosophy of education, viz., *teaching*, *learning* and the *community*. We shall deal specifically with the outcome of our research in this section.

It is not unusual that philosophers of education, when confronted with questions concerning the theoretical footing of educational concepts, have ample variety of philosophical ideas and views at their disposal to choose from. This is due to the fact that each philosophical thought is capable of providing, in its own right, a potential framework for a particular claim, i.e. it could be considered as a source of rational argumentation and explanation that supports an assertion. The logical context surrounding the philosophical thought maintains the cogency of a specific line of argument. In this regard, we examined Wittgenstein's most significant philosophical ideas and endeavored to demonstrate that they are valid theoretical frameworks for clarifying the aforementioned concepts of educational philosophy. However, in order for us to see clearly the central theme which we want to uphold with our contention, it is fitting to point out some of the noteworthy discoveries we arrived at by relating his ideas of meaning as use, rule-following and philosophy as therapy respectively to teaching, learning, and community.

Based on a general consideration of Wittgenstein's later analysis of meaning we found out that: a) the recognition of the relationship between the two phases of teaching, viz., training and explanation, is significant to a didactic endeavor, i.e. it accounts for the occurrence of a continuous progression from a *mechanical/practical* type of teaching to a *rational* one in a particular pedagogical experience. Anchored in Wittgenstein's ideas we concluded that appropriate *training* and *explanation* (as evident phases of teaching) can occur – or may even need to take place – at all stages in one's educational career. The only difficulty that can be encountered with this assertion is the identification of the specific instance wherein teaching shifts from training to explanation. Nevertheless, the presence of such phases is considerably evident; b) Teaching functions as a means of *normalization* in education. This signifies that teaching not only aims at the achievement of learning *per se* but also intends to enable the learner to take over and go on by himself. *Normality* here does not take any psychological connotation. It basically applies to the way one behaves, acts and participates within particular practices. This shows that teaching not only endeavors and makes possible that the students learn but also that it would enable them do what other "normal" members in a particular form of life would do – that they would become an independent individual, i.e. not only one who understands what has been taught but also able to make judgments that are accepted and considered normal within a particular community of practice. In this context, we may stress that the gauge of successful teaching does not only depend on the results of examinations or grades but how ultimately students are able to effectively deal with the challenges of living within a specific community. These innovative viewpoints do not only help us clarify the concept of the process of teaching within formal and academic education but also the broader aspects of the teaching concept generally comprehended.

Our study concerning the learning process brought us to the awareness that there has been more psychological attention, less interest in educational literature, and scant philosophical concern in working out extensive conceptual investigations about such a phenomenon. Although learning, as we have noted, is an integral part of the educational enterprise, psychologists carry out most of the studies undertaken about its development. The issue concerning the learning progress has been considered as one of the major preoccupations of psychologists when it comes to a study on the subject of children's intellectual growth. However, investigations of such a phenomenon have become, we might say, exceedingly scientific in the sense that explanations of the learning process have been characterized by a certain kind of experimental exactitude. This consequently gave rise to what we now know as the cognitive and the behaviorist theories of learning. It is, however, presumptuous to conclude that such viewpoints have nothing to contribute to the area of philosophy or education. To be more precise, it is basically the results of these studies that propel us to evaluate their relevant pedagogical impact. Since we are here primarily involved with a philosophical argumentation regarding the basic educational concepts, it is in this regard that we have undertaken a conceptual analysis of *learning* against the backdrop of Wittgenstein's idea of rule-following.

Although Wittgenstein never made explicit his ideas about the concept of learning, we were convinced that his thoughts concerning rule-following provide a unique perspective in understanding such phenomenon. In fact, founded on our research, we have discovered that the *process of learning* possesses a character comparable to following a rule. How did we come about such a finding?

Since Wittgenstein's later writings were not meant to offer a pedagogical theory, the first thing we did was to point out the nature of the process of learning based on his thoughts regarding *language learning*. Central to this idea are the concepts of knowing and understanding in view of the fact that both are oftentimes interchanged with, or mistaken for the phenomenon of learning. Based on the ideas extracted from Wittgenstein's later writings and the distinction made regarding the concepts of learning, knowing and understanding we have found out that: a) as a *process*, learning does not involve a preoccupation with reflection, reasons, and justifications; b) the underpinning grounds that effectively shape the character of the learning process are training (teaching) and ordinary practices; c) learning takes precedence in the order of occurrence and thus is considered as a foundation of competence for knowing and understanding. These perspectives directed us to regard learning as akin to rule-following.

However, before we were able to ascertain their affinity it was crucial for us to elaborate on the fundamental features that constitute Wittgenstein's idea of rule-following. We began our exposition with an evaluation of whether or not abiding by a rule is determined by recognition of a rule prior to its application. It was necessary to engage in such investigation in order to support our assertion that there is more to rule-following than just mere identification of a particular rule formulation and that in obeying a rule we primarily act without reasons, i.e., according to the *Investigations*, our moves are *uninformed* by an appreciation of facts about what the rules require. This led us to affirm that rule-recognition does not necessarily condition one's following a rule. In this case then, we have established the fact that in conforming to a particular rule one's actions are *usual*, *automatic*, and *unreflective*. According to Wittgenstein's considerations these characteristics of rule-following are results of *practice* and *training* (teaching). The integration of both concepts practically provides us with a clear view of the basic constituents of Wittgenstein's notion of rule-following.

Anchored in our previous discussions, we noted two points that appear vital to both the process of learning and rule following. First is the cogency of training and practice. Second, both processes are not *ultimately* based upon reasons, i.e. they are usual and unreflective. These aspects bring about a view that in participating with the established practice(s) and enduring suitable training we are able to undergo the process of learning and rule-following without the guidance of reason, i.e. they become immediate, automatic and unreflective activities. Hence, founded on these ideas we discovered that the process of learning is comparable to rule-following. In this sense, therefore, we can say that learning as a process, like following a rule, is described as an unreflective and natural activity of an individual based on his participation in practice(s), training and the inherent ability for learning.

Our consideration of the learning process under the perspective of rule-following has yielded two noticeable consequences. First, it has dissolved the prevalent dichotomy between the two major psychological theories of learning, namely, the cognitive and the behaviorist standpoints by means of integrating the fundamental points of both views. Second, the significance given to training and practice provides an impetus to establish better teaching designs that facilitate the learning process.

The final noteworthy upshot of our research came from our application of Wittgenstein's idea of the nature of philosophy to the concept of the *community* within the educational context. We have discovered that his thought of philosophy as therapy not only provided us with plausible views upon which to base our assessment of the linguistic abilities of children manifested within formal instruction but also it succeeded in underscoring the prevailing interaction between the community and the educational enterprise.

Wittgenstein's notion of philosophical problems as symptomatic of an intellectual disease provided us with a consistent source of argumentation which plausibly accounts for the detection of a basic pathology manifested by children within language-based activities undertaken in a classroom (instructional) situation. Students undoubtedly encounter conceptual puzzlements in the process of learning due to some factors which are situated beyond the boundaries of the school. This is observable especially among grade school pupils. Teachers are not often aware of the occurrence of such a problem due to the fact that some (if not most) of them hold the idea that children come to be educated as empty buckets, slates, containers, etc. waiting to be filled. It is precisely through our analysis of Wittgenstein's ideas regarding philosophy as therapy that we have come to know and ascertained that students have not been raised in vacuity. Each didactic occurrence obtained from ordinary experience could become a determining factor in the child's educational performance. The dynamic interchange between the individual and the situation with which he is confronted should not be bypassed. Thus, in this sense teachers and educators, based on Wittgenstein's views of the therapeutic endeavor of a philosopher to untangle himself (an others) from the web of intellectual confusions, should make an effort to help the child to overcome conceptual perplexities by way of a perspicuous representation, i.e. unmasking, divulging, or exposing the errors of one's understanding. In this line of thought, Wittgenstein's therapeutic view of philosophy presented two aspects which manifest its pertinence to the field of education. They are the recognition of various conceptual confusions (intellectual illnesses) and the employment of the *descriptive method* contained within his view of a perspicuous representation, which is considered as a cure for conceptual diseases.

In view of the aforementioned facts we were able to accentuate the relevance of the *community* in conjunction with its communal practices as the elemental source not only of the development of knowledge but also of the apparent errors in understanding that children, as well as adults, have. This is due to the fact that, in congruence to Wittgenstein's idea of *practice*, there is a strong influential factor in the concept of *regularity* consequential to the community's shared beliefs, communication, interaction and mutual dependence, that concerns the individual's educational progress. Based on this point, it is categorical that in education we should not jettison the fact that the community performs functions important both to the individual and to society. In this case then, teachers should have no disregard for the impact of communal practices in their pedagogical endeavors. They should not ignore the diverse sociological variables which are evidently critical in the formulation of educational policies. In this sense, teaching aims at normalization – a transformation to a form of life. The teacher/educator strives not only to let the student learn but more importantly enable him, through the unmasking of conceptual confusions, to use that learning in his involvement with the community. In this perspective and based on Wittgenstein's proposed method we were able to derive three steps to a possible remedy, they are: a) the design and implementation of a *perspicuous* curriculum, b) the deliberate use of illustrations and examples in every didactic undertaking, and c) to engage in a continuous methodic-pedagogical adaptation. The success of this suggested remedy hinges on the individual's conviction of the presence and constraints of conceptual errors to the learning progress of children and the recognition of the vital influence of the community in educational advancement.

We have shown thus far the significant results of our research based on an application of Wittgenstein's fundamental themes to teaching, learning, and community. Now, could these findings support the main question of our study, i.e. can Wittgenstein's ideas be considered legitimate theoretical foundations?

Anchored upon our arguments we conclude and attest that they are valid conceptual frameworks in clarifying and explaining these basic concepts in educational philosophy. They are valid theoretical foundations in the sense that the abovementioned Wittgensteinian ideas, a) conspicuously hold a correlation to educational notions, b) manifestly stress on the relevance of the basic concepts of educational philosophy specially *teaching* and *learning*, c) distinctly shed light on the conditions/contexts upon which these concepts are used and applied and d) have the capability to ensure distinctions concerning matters of teaching, learning and the community, i.e. they can be used as tools to examine the premises on which educational conclusions rest, to analyze the language of education, and to look at the kind of evidence which can be used to confirm or refute educational propositions.

However, although they provide a logical structure, we have found out a particular difficulty. This pertains to their inadequacy in supplying an *absolute* representation of the essentials for a definitive elucidation. They are insufficient for the reason that since these concepts, especially teaching and learning, are evidently multifaceted, they cannot completely disclose the necessary elements that would comprise the ultimate clarification of such concepts. If, however, such an undertaking were possibly obtained, it would consequently end all debates arising from the perplexities in understanding them. Nevertheless, the insufficiency of these Wittgensteinian themes as means for a complete clarification should not be considered as detrimental to their philosophical integrity considering that it is evidently a consequence of Wittgenstein's philosophical claim itself, i.e. that there is no single, specific, and unique meaning for every word. Accordingly, the meaning of every educational concept depends on its various uses according to diverse contexts (language-games). Thus, founded on this argument we should not expect or pretend to maintain that every philosophical thought could fully exhaust *all* the requisites for a particular explanation.

3. Further Remarks

The endeavor undertaken in this dissertation has been mainly a conceptual analysis of the fundamental Wittgensteinian themes and its relation to the basic concepts of educational philosophy. In a sense, therefore, this thesis represents an interdisciplinary investigation. As we have stated at the outset, Wittgenstein possessed no explicit theory of education or any kind of Wittgensteinian philosophy of education. To claim that it exists would be misleading. Nonetheless, this aspect does not curb the pertinence of his philosophical ideas to philosophy of education, which has been appropriately demonstrated in this dissertation. However, our study does not end here. Since there are still other areas in the philosophy of education which need further conceptual analysis, the result of our investigation can greatly contribute to its development. Let us cite some themes or future studies which can be derived from the findings of our dissertation.

One significant issue that could be developed based on this thesis concerns the responsibility and sensitivity of teachers to children's meaning constructs. We have dealt in chapter three of this study the logical connection between the concepts of meaning and teaching. Anchored on this aspect, a study on the teacher's task of knowing whether students have learnt or understood what is taught through a perceptive observation of their meaning constructs and the way they make connections could be a very insightful area for further research.

Another subject matter that could use our investigation as point of departure touches on the impact of the concept of rule-following to the curriculum formulation and the improvement of researches on learning disabilities. A satisfactory curriculum includes more than just the courses for study, timeframe, instructional materials and accountability. It should also consist of the underlying philosophy, goals, objectives, strategies, and assumptions. The elements of Wittgenstein's idea of following a rule and its relation to the learning process as discovered in this thesis serve, we reckon, as valuable line of reasoning for an assessment of adequate and acceptable curricula.

Learning disabilities refer to disorders that affect such processes as reading, writing, listening, speaking, and that cause a discrepancy in student potential and actual achievement. It is unknown exactly what causes learning disabilities, but most researchers believe that factors such as genetics, pregnancy or birth complications, and childhood trauma could lead to learning disabilities. With the presentation of the relation between rule-following and the process of learning in our study, a relevant ground for a philosophical investigation concerning the problem of learning disorders is offered. We do not presume however that it would be sufficient. At least a new perspective other than the psychological and scientific could be undertaken.

The most recent subject matter that could utilize the fruits of our research deals with the concept and the role of the community in education within this *globalized* networking era. Advancement of computer technology has evidently altered the concept of community from a localized perception to a worldwide vision through the Internet. Now, this manifestly affects the educational enterprise. The point regarding the influence and the control of the community in educational development dealt with in our study could help in distinguishing the effects and benefits of a local versus a global community in the progress of education with reference to the notion of "community of practice".

Educational discourse is permeated with concepts and generalizations which have not been adequately analyzed. Educators and educational philosophers risk the danger of becoming unnecessarily divided over issues because they are not aware of the necessity for clarifying the expressions and concepts they are conveying. In our study we have attempted to wrestle with Wittgenstein's fundamental philosophical ideas with the aim of justifying their validity as logical frameworks in clarifying the basic concepts of educational philosophy, viz., teaching, learning and the community. It is my hope that through our investigation we have demonstrated that Wittgenstein's thoughts are not in any way unrelated and irrelevant to the area of philosophy of education. The techniques he specifically developed may well be very valuable in helping educational theorists, philosophers, and practitioners deal with important concepts in educational theory and practice.

ABBREVIATIONS

1. Abbreviations of Wittgenstein's Books

BB	*The Blue and Brown Books*, Oxford 1958.
BT	*Big Typescripts* (TS 213)
CV	*Culture and Value*, London 1998
LCA	*Lectures and Conversations on Aesthetics, Psychology and Religious Belief*, Oxford 1966.
LWII	*Last Writings on the Philosophy of Psychology vol. II: The Inner and the Outer, 1949-1951*, Oxford 1992.
OC	*On Certainty*, Oxford 1969.
PG	*Philosophical Grammar*, Oxford 1974.
PI	*Philosophical Investigations*, Oxford 1958.
PO	*Philosophical Occasions 1912-1951*, Indianapolis 1993.
PR	*Philosophical Remarks*, Oxford 1975.
RFM	*Remarks on the Foundation of Mathematics*, Oxford 1978.
RPPI	*Remarks on the Philosophy of Psychology*, Vol. I, Chicago 1988.
RPPII	*Remarks on the Philosophy of Psychology*, Vol. II, Chicago 1988.
TLP	*Tractatus Logico-Philosophicus*, London 1981.
Z	*Zettel*, Oxford 1967.

2. Other Abbreviations

AcMRev	*Academy of Management Review*
al.	*alii* (others)
ArPh	*Archives de Philosophie*
AWL	Wittgenstein's Lectures Cambridge 1932-1935, New York 2001.
cf.	confer
CJP	*Canadian Journal of Philosophy*

ColEng	*College English*
ed.	*edidit, ediderunt* (editor or editors)
e.g.	*exempli gratia* (for example)
EdPsych	*Educational Psychology*
EducPhilTheor	*Educational Philosophy and Theory*
EducStud	*Educational Studies*
EducTheor	*Educational Theory*
etc.	*et cetera*
ff.	following
fn.	footnote number
Fs.	Festschrift (written in honour of, etc.)
Gr.	*Gregorianum*
HEdRev	*Harvard Educational Review*
HEJ	*History of Education Journal*
HFJ	*Healthcare Forum Journal*
ibid.	*ibidem*
i.e.	*id est* (that is)
JGE	*Journal of General Education*
JLR	*Journal of Literacy Research*
JOrgC	*Journal of Organizational Change*
JPhilEduc	*Journal of Philosophy of Education*
JPhilR	*Journal of Philosophical Research*
MJE	*McGill Journal of Education*
MWL	Wittgenstein' Lectures in 1930-31, London 1959.
p.	page
PhilEduc	*Philosophy of Education*
PhilInvest	*Philosophical Investigations*
PhRev	*Philosophical Review*
PolTheor	*Political Theory*
pp.	pages
RIPh	*Revue Internationale de Philosophie*
SPE	*Studies in Philosophy and Education*
SSEd	*Studies in Science Education*
TColRec	*Teachers' College Record*
TeachPhil	*Teaching Philosophy*
trans.	translation, translations
viz.	*videlicet* (namely)
WVC	Wittgenstein and the Vienna Circle (1929-1932), Oxford 1979.

BIBLIOGRAPHY

1. Works by Wittgenstein

WITTGENSTEIN, L., *Culture and Value: A selection of Posthumous Remains (1914-51)*, ed. G.H. von Wright, rev. ed. A. Pichler, trans. P. Winch, London 1998.

———, *Eine Philosophische Betrachtung [1936]*, ed. R. Rhees, Frankfurt 1970.

———, *Geheime Tagebücher 1914-1916*, ed. W. Baum, Wien 1992.

———, *Last Writings on the Philosophy of Psychology II: The Inner and the Outer, 1949-1951*, ed. G.H. von Wright – H. Nyman, trans. C.G. Luckhardt – M.A.E Aue, Oxford 1992.

———, *Lectures and Conversations on Aesthetics, Psychology and Religious Belief*, compiled from Notes taken by Y. Smythies, R. Rhees, and J. Taylor, ed. C. Barrett, Oxford 1966.

———, *Letters to Russell, Keynes, and Moore*, ed. G.H. von Wright, trans. B.F. McGuinness, Oxford 1974.

———, *Notebooks 1914-1916*, ed. G.H. von Wright – G.E.M. Anscombe, Oxford 1961.

———, «Notes for Lectures on "Private Experience" and "Sense Data"», ed. R. Rhees, *PhRev* 77 (1968) 275-320.

———, *On Certainty [Über Gewissheit]* (1950-51), ed. G.E.M. Anscombe – G.H. von Wright, trans. D. Paul – G.E.M. Anscombe, Oxford 1969.

———, *Philosophical Grammar*, ed. Rush Rhees, trans. A.J.P. Kenny Oxford 1974.

———, *Philosophical Investigations* (German-English parallel text), trans. G.E.M. Anscombe, Oxford 1958.

———, *Philosophical Occasions 1912-1951*, ed. J. Klagge – A. Nordmann, Indianapolis 1993.

————, *Philosophical Remarks*, ed. R. Rhees, trans. R. Hargreaves – R. White, Oxford 1975.

————, «*Philosophie* §§86-93 (S. 405-435) aus dem sogenannten Big Type-script (Katalognummer 213)», ed. H. Nyman, *RIPh*, 43, 169 (1989) 175-203 trans. C.G. Luckhardt – M.A.E. Aue, «Philosophy: Sections 86-93 (405-435) of the so-called "Big Typescript" (Catalog Number 213)», *Synthese* 87, 1 (1991) 3-22.

————, *Remarks on Colours*, ed. G.E.M. Anscombe, Oxford 1977.

————, *Remarks on Frazer's the Golden Bough*, ed. R. Rhees, trans. C. Miles, Atlantic Highlands, N.J. 1979.

————, *Remarks on the Foundation of Mathematics*, ed. G.H. von Wright – R. Rhees – G.E.M. Anscombe, trans. G.E.M. Anscombe, Oxford 1978.

————, *Remarks on the Philosophy of Psychology*, I (1946-49), ed. G.E.M. Anscombe – G.H. von Wright, trans. G.E.M. Anscombe, Chicago 1988.

————, *Remarks on the Philosophy of Psychology*, II (1947-48), ed. G.E.M. Anscombe – G.H. von Wright, trans. C. G. Luckhardt – M. A. E. Aue, Chicago 1988.

————, «Some Remarks on Logical Form», *ArSoc* 9 (1929) 162-171.

————, *The Blue and Brown Books*, Oxford 1958.

————, *Tractatus Logico-Philosophicus* (German-English parallel text), trans. C.K. Ogden with an introduction by Bertrand Russell, London 1981.

————, *Wörterbuch für Volksschulen*, ed. W. Leinfelner – E. Leinfelner – A. Hübner, Vienna 1977.

————, *Zettel*, ed. G.E.M. Anscombe – G.H. von Wright, trans. G.E.M. Anscombe, Oxford 1967.

2. Other Works Cited

ACERO, J.J., «Wittgenstein, la Definicion ostensiva y los Limites del Lenguaje», *Teorema* 18, 2 (1999) 5-17.

ADDIS, M., *Wittgenstein: Making sense of other minds*, Brookfield 1999.

AGGARWAL, J.C., *Theory and Principles of Education: Philosophical and Sociological Bases of Education*, New Delhi 1985.

AKMAN, V. – *al.*, ed., *Modeling and Using Context* - Proceedings of the Third International and Interdisciplinary Conference on Modeling and Using Context (CONTEXT 2001) Lecture Notes in Computer Science, 2116, Dundee 2001.

ALLMAKER, A.L., *«Wholeness» in the Philosophy of the Later Wittgenstein and its Applicability to the Philosophy of Education*, New York 1972.

AMBROSE, A., ed., *Wittgenstein's Lectures Cambridge 1932-1935*, New York 2001.

———, «Moore and Wittgenstein as Teachers», *TeachPhil* 12, 2 (1989) 107-113.

AMBROSE, A. – LAZEROWITZ, M., ed., *Ludwig Wittgenstein: Philosophy and Language*, London 1972.

ANDERSON, A.B., «Teaching Children: What Teachers Should Know», in *Teaching Academic Subjects to Diverse Learners*, ed. M. Kennedy, New York 1991, 203-217.

ANSCOMBE, G.E.M., *An Introduction to Wittgenstein's Tractatus*, Pennsylvania 1971.

AQUINAS, T., *Quaestiones disputatae de veritate: quaestio XI*, art. 1, ed. A. Dyroff, Bonn 1918 (1921 printing)

———, *Summa Theologiae*, London 1964-1981.

ARENSBERG, C. – KIMBALL, S.T., *Culture and Community*, New York 1965.

ARISTOTLE, «The Politics», in *Cambridge Texts in the History of Political Thought: Aristotle The Politics*, ed. S. Everson, New York 1988, 7-200.

———, *Nichomachean Ethics*, trans. ed. R. Crisp, Cambridge 2000.

ARNSTINE, B., «To whom it may concern? A review of philosophy and education: 18th Yearbook of the National Society for the study of education», *EducTheor* 31, 1 (1981) 17-22.

ARRINGTON, R., – GLOCK, H.J., ed., *Wittgenstein's Philosophical Investigations: Text and Context*, London 1991.

ARRINGTON, R., «Mechanism and Calculus: Wittgenstein on Augustine's Theory of Ostension», in *Wittgenstein: sources and perspectives*, ed. C.G. Luckhardt, Ithaca, New York 1979.

ATKINSON, R. L. – al., *Introduction to Psychology*, Fort Worth – London 1993.

AUGUSTINUS, A., *Against the Academics (Contra Academicos)*, trans. J. O'Meara, London 1951.

———, *City of God (De Civitate Dei)*, trans. ed. R.W. Dyson, Cambridge 1998.

———, *Confessions*, trans. H. Chadwick, Oxford 1998.

BAKER, G.P. – HACKER, P.M.S., *An Analytical Commentary on Wittgenstein's Philosophical Investigations. I. Understanding, and Meaning. II. Rules, Grammar, and Necessity*, Oxford – Cambridge M.A. 1992, 1994.

BANNER, J.M. JR., – CANNON, H.C., *The Elements of learning*, New Haven – London 1999.

————, *The Elements of Teaching*, London 1997.

BARROW, R., «Misdescribing a Cow: The question of conceptual correctness», *EducTheor* 33, 2 (1983) 205-207.

BARRY, D., *Forms of Life and Following Rules: A Wittgensteinian Defence of Relativism*, Netherlands 1996.

BARTH, R.S., *Learning by Heart*, San Francisco 2001.

BARTLEY, W.W. III, *Wittgenstein*, London 1974.

BAUMLIN, J.S. – WEAVER, M.E., «Teaching, classroom authority, and the psychology of transference», *JGE* 49, 2 (2000) 75-87.

BEARN, G.C.F., *Walking to Wonder: Wittgenstein's existential Investigations*, Albany 1997.

BECHTEL, W. – GRAHAM, G., ed., *A Companion to Cognitive Science*, Oxford 1998.

BECK, C.R., «A taxonomy for identifying, classifying, and interrelating teaching strategies», *JGE* 47, 1 (1998) 37-62.

BECK, R.H., «Plato's views on teaching», *EducTheor* 33, 2 (1983) 119-134.

BECKE, C.P., «Ostensive Teaching from the Phenomenological Point of View», in *Analyomen 2. II. Philosophy of Language, Metaphysics*, ed. G. Meggle, Berlin – New York 1997, 22-28.

BELL, R.H., «On becoming a teacher of teachers», *HRE* 69, 4 (1999) 447-455.

BELL-GREDLER, M.E., *Learning and Instruction: theory into practice*, New York 1986.

BENNE, K.D., *A Conception of Authority: an Introductory Study*, New York 1943.

————, *Education in the Quest for Identity and Community*, Columbus, Ohio 1961.

BERGEN, T.J. JR., «The greeks and the education of humanity», *JGE* 43, 1 (1994) 32-43.

BERGER, M.I., «Philosophizing about Teaching: Some Reconsiderations on Teaching as Act and Enterprise», *SPE* 6, 3 (1968) 282-292.

BERLINER, D.C., «Comments on the NSSE Yearbook Philosophy and Education», *EducTheor* 31, 1 (1981) 31.

BESS, J.L., ed., *Teaching Well and Liking it*, Baltimore, Maryland 1997.

BIGGE, M., *Educational Philosophies for Teachers*, Columbus, Ohio 1982.

BLAKE, N. – al, ed., *The Blackwell Guide to the Philosophy of Education*, Oxford 2003.

BLITS, J.H., «*Self*-knowledge and the modern mode of learning», *EducTheor* 39, 4 (1989) 293-300.

BLOCK, I., ed., *Perspectives on the philosophy of Wittgenstein*, Cambridge 1981.

BLOOR, D., *Wittgenstein, Rules and Institutions*, London – New York 1997.

BLUE, T.W., *The teaching and learning Process (with emphasis on identification)*, Washington, D.C. 1981.

BOGHOSSIAN, P.A., «Analyticity», in *A Companion to the Philosophy of Language*, ed. B. Hale – C. Wright, Oxford 1999, 331-368.

BOHL, R.F. JR., «Something in the Tractatus Wittgenstein did not reject in Language», *Logic & Philosophy:* Proceeding of the 4th International Wittgenstein Symposium, Vienna 1979, 217- 219.

BOLTON, D., *An Approach to Wittgenstein's Philosophy*, New Jersey 1979.

BOSSING, N. L., *Teaching in Secondary Schools*, Boston 1952.

BOURDIEU, P., *Outline of a Theory of Practice*, Cambridge 1977.

BOURDILLON, H. – STOREY, A., *Aspects of Teaching and learning in Secondary Schools*, London 2002.

BOYD, W., *Emile for Today. The Emile of Jean Jacques Rousseau selected*, trans. W. Boyd, London 1956.

BRANN, E.T.H., *Paradoxes of Education in a Republic*, Chicago – London 1979.

BRANSFORD, J. – BROWN, A., – COCKING, R., ed., *How People Learn: Brain, Mind, Experience and School* (Commission on Behavioral and Social Sciences and Education, National Research Council), Washington, D.C. 2000.

BRICE-HEATH, S., *Ways with words: Language, life, and work in communities and classrooms*, New York 1983.

BRONFENBRENNER, U., – MOEN, P. – GARBARINO, J., «Children, Family, & Community», in *The Family: Review of Child Development Research* 7, ed. R. Parke, Chicago 1984, 283-328.

BROOM, L. – SELZNICK, P., *Sociology: A Test with Adapted Readings,* New York 1968.

BROPHY, J. – EVERTSON, C., *Learning from Teaching: A Developmental Perspective*, Boston 1976.

BROSE, K., «Pedagogical Elements in Wittgenstein's late work, On Certainty», in *Meaning and the Growth of Understanding: Wittgenstein's Significance for Developmental Psychology*, ed. M. Chapman – R. Dixon, London 1987, 408-411.

BRUMBAUGH, R.S., «Plato's Ideal Curriculum and Contemporary Philosophy of Education», *EducTheor* 37, 2 (Spring 1987) 169-178.

BRUNER, J., *Child's Talk: Learning to Use Language*, New York 1983.

BRYK, A.S. – LEE, V.E. – HOLLAND, P.B., *Catholic Schools and the Common Good*, Cambridge, MA 1993.

BURBULES, N., «Wittgenstein, Styles, and Pedagogy», in *Wittgenstein: Philosophy, Postmodernism, Pedagogy: Critical Studies in Education and Culture*, ed. M. Peters – J. Marshall, Connecticut 1999, 152-173.

BURNS, H.W. – BRAUNER C.J. – BECK, R.H., *Philosophy of Education: Essays and Commentaries*, New York 1962.

CAHN, S.M., *Classic and Contemporary Readings in the Philosophy of Education*, New York 1997.

CAMPBELL, J., *Understanding John Dewey: nature and cooperative intelligence*, Chicago, Illinois 1995.

CANFIELD, J. V., ed., *Meaning*, New York 1986.

———, *The early philosophy – Language as Picture*, New York 1986.

CANFIELD, J.V. – SHANKER, S.G., *Wittgenstein's Intentions*, New York 1993.

CARUANA, L., *Holism and the Understanding of Science*, Aldershot 2000.

CATO, D., «Teaching as tacit integration», *MJE* 29 (1994) 15-30.

CAVELL, S., «Notes and Afterthoughts on the Opening of Wittgenstein's Investigations», in *The Cambridge Companion to Wittgenstein*, ed. H. Sluga – D. Stern, Cambridge 1996, 261-295.

———, *The Claim of Reason: Wittgenstein, Skepticism, Morality and Tragedy*, Oxford 1979.

CHADWICK, H., *Augustine*, Oxford 1986.

CHAPMAN, M. – DIXON, R., *Meaning and the Growth of Understanding: Wittgenstein's Significance for Developmental Psychology*, London 1987.

CHARLES, D. – CHILD, W., ed., *Wittgensteinian Themes*, Fs. D. Pears, Oxford 2001.

CHRISTENSEN, C. A. – al., «Toward a Sociological perspective of learning disabilities», *EducTheor* 36, 4 (1986) 317-331.

CLARKE, A. – ERICKSON, G., ed., *Teacher Inquiry: Living the research in everyday practice*, London 2003.

COBB, P., *Theories of Mathematical Learning and Constructivism: A Personal View*, Klagenfurt 1994.

COCHRANE, D., «Teaching and creativity: a philosophical analysis», *Educ Theor* 25, 1 (1975) 65-73.

COGGI, R., *S. Tommaso D'Aquino: Pagine di Filosofia*, Bologna 1988.

COHEN, A.P., *The Symbolic Construction of Community*, London 1985.

COLLINS, E., *Paulo Freire: His Life, Works and Thought*, New York 1977.

CONKLIN, K.R., «Knowledge, proof and ineffability in teaching», *EducTheor* 24, 1 (1974) 61-67.

CRANSTON, M., *John Locke*, London 1969.

CRARY, A, *The New Wittgenstein*, London 2000.

CRITTENDEN, B., «Aims, Intentions and purposes of teaching and educating», *EducTheor* 24, 1 (1974) 47-51.

CROUSE, R., «Paucis Mutatis Verbis: St. Augustine's Platonism», in *Augustine and his Critics*, ed. G. Lawless – R. Dodaro, New York 2002, 37-50.

CSIKSZENTMIHALYI, M., «Intrinsic Motivation and Effective Teaching: A Flow Analysis», in *Teaching Well and Liking it*, ed. J. L. Bess, Baltimore, Maryland 1997, 72-91.

DAVIS, B., «Why teaching isn't possible», *EducTheor* 27, 4 (1977) 304-309.

DEARDEN, R.F., «Instruction and Learning by Discovery», in *Philosophy of Education: Major Themes in the Analytic Tradition. IV. Problems of Educational Content and Practice*, ed. P. Hirst – P. White, London 1998.

DELANEY, D. M., *The Philosophical Presuppositions of the Theory of Education of the «Later» John Dewey*, New York 1984.

DENNIS, R., «Phenomenology: philosophy, psychology and education», *EducTheor* 24, 2 (1974) 142-154.

DENT, N., «Rousseau, Jean-Jacques», in *Oxford Companion to Philosophy*, ed. T. Honderich, Oxford 1995, 780.

DEWEY, J., *Democracy and Education*, New York 1916.

———, *Experience and Nature*, New York 1929.

———, *How We Think*, Lexington, MA 1910.

———, *Moral Principles in Education*, New York 1959.

DIAMOND, C., ed., *Wittgenstein's Lectures on the Foundations of Mathematics Cambridge 1939*, Ithaca New York 1976.

DILLON, J.T., «Student questions and individual learning», *EducTheor* 36, 4 (1986) 333-341.

DILMAN, I., *Wittgenstein's Copernican Revolution: the questions of linguistic Idealism*, New York 2002.

DOLHENTY, J., *Philosophy of Education: an Example of Applied Philosophy*, [accessed: November 27, 2003], http://www.radicalacademy.com/philapplied2.htm.

DRIVER, R. – OLDHAM, V., «A Consructivist Approach to Curriculum Development in Science», *SSEd* 13 (1986) 105-122.

DRURY, M.O'C., *The Danger with Words*, Bristol – Washington DC 1996.

DUCKWORTH, E., *The Having of Wonderful Ideas and other Essays on Teaching and Learning*, New York 1991.

DUMMETT, M., *Frege, Philosophy of Language*, London 1973.

DUPUIS, A., *Philosophy of education in historical perspective*, Chicago 1966.

DURKHEIM, E., *Division of Labor in Society,* New York 1984; 1933.

DYKHUIZEN, G., *The Life and Mind of John Dewey*, Carbondale, IL 1973.

EDWARDS, A.D. – FURLONG, V.J., *The Language of Teaching: Meaning in Classroom Interaction*, London 1978.

EGIDI, R., ed., *Wittgenstein e Il Novecento: Tra filosofia e psicologia*, Roma 1996.

ELDRIDGE, R., *Leading a Human Life: Wittgenstein, Intentionality and Romanticism*, Chicago 1997.

ENNIS, R. H., «Is answering questions teaching?», *EducTheor* 36, 4 (1986) 343-347.

ERICSON, D. P. - ELLET, F. S. JR., «Teacher Accountability and the Causal Theory of Teaching», *EducTheor* 37, 3 (1987) 277-294.

ESFELD, M., «Rule-Following and the Ontology of the Mind», in *Metaphysics in the Post-Metaphysical Age* VII (1), ed. U. Meixner – P. Simons, Kirchberg am Wechsel 1999, 191-196.

ESSIEN, F. S., «Callan and Dewey's conception of education as growth», *Educ Theor* 33, 2 (1983) 195-199.

EVERSON, S., ed., *Cambridge Texts in the History of Political Thought: Aristotle The Politics*, New York 1988.

FENSTERMACHER, G. – SOLTIS, J., *Approaches to Teaching*, New York 1986.

FIDDLER, M. B., «Teaching to competence: enhancing the art of teaching (adults)», *JGE* 43, 1 (1994) 289-303.

FINCH, H.L.R., *Wittgenstein – The Early Philosophy*, New Jersey 1971.

———, *Wittgenstein – The Later Philosophy*, New York 1977.

FINDLAY, J.N., *Wittgenstein: a Critique*, London 1984.

FINE, M. – WEIS, L. – POWELL, L. C., «Communities of difference: a critical outlook at desegregated spaces created for and by youth», *HEdRev* 67, 2 (1997) 247-284.

FITZGERALD, A. D., – *al.*, ed., *Augustine through the Ages: An Encyclopedia*, Cambridge 1999.

VAN FLETEREN, F., «Plato, Platonism», in *Augustine through the Ages: An Encyclopedia*, ed. A. D. Fitzgerald – *al.*, Cambridge 1999, 651-654.

FODOR, J. – LEPORE, E., *Holism*, Oxford 1992.

FOGELIN, R. J., *Wittgenstein: the arguments of the philosophers*, ed. T. Honde, New York 1987.

FREGE, G., *Die Grundlagen der Arithmetik*, Breslau 1884.

FREIRE, P., *Pedagogy of the Oppressed*, trans. M.B. Ramos, New York 1989.

———, «The Adult Literacy Process as Cultural Action for Freedom», *HEdRev* 68 (1998), 480-498.

FRENCH, P., UEHLING – T. JR., – WETTSTEIN, H., ed., *Midwest Studies in Philosophy Volume XVII: The Wittgenstein Legacy*, Notre Dame, Indiana 1992.

FRÖBEL, F., *The Education of Man*, trans. J. Jarvis, New York 1885.

FRONGIA, G., *Wittgenstein, Regole e Sistema*, Milano 1983.

FUJIMOTO, T., «The Notion of Erklärung», in *Ludwig Wittgenstein: Philosophy and Language*, ed. A. Ambrose – M. Lazerowitz, London 1972, 222-232.

GADOTTI, M., *Pedagogy of praxis: a dialectical philosophy of education*, Preface by Paulo Freire, trans. J. Milton, Albany 1996.

GAGE, N.L., *The Scientific Basis of the Art of Teaching*, London 1980.

GAGNÉ, R., *The Conditions of Learning and Theory of Instruction*, New York 1985.

GARGANI, A., ed., *Ludwig Wittgenstein e la cultura contemporanea*, Ravenna 1983.

———, «Wittgenstein on Intentional acts», in *Wittgenstein: Critical Assessments*, I, ed. S. Shanker, London 1986, 287-295.

GEFWERT, C., *Wittgenstein on Thought, Language and Philosophy*, Burlington 2000.

GEMIE, S., «What is a school? Defining and controlling primary schooling in early nineteenth-century France», *HEJ* 21, 1 (1992) 129-148.

GENOVA, J., *Wittgenstein: A way of seeing*, New York 1995.

GENTNER, D., «Analogy», in *A Companion to Cognitive Science*, ed. W. Bechtel – G. Graham, Oxford 1998, 107-113.

GIBBS, R. W. JR., *Intentions in the experience of meaning*, Cambridge 1999.

VON GLASERSFELD, E., «Cognition, Construction of Knowledge, and Teaching», *Synthese* 80, 1 (1989) 121-140.

GLOCK, H.J., *Wittgenstein: A Critical Reader,* Massachusetts 2001.

GOLDBERG, B., «Mechanism and Meaning», in *Investigating Psychology: Science of the mind after Wittgenstein*, ed. J. Hyman, London 1991, 48-66.

GOLDFARB, W., «Wittgenstein on Understanding», in *Midwest Studies in Philosophy. XVII. The Wittgenstein Legacy*, ed. P. French – T. Uehling Jr. – H. Wettstein, Notre Dame, Indiana 1992.

GOLDSTEIN, L., *Clear and Queer Thinking: Wittgenstein's development and his relevance to Modern Thought*, London 1999.

GOODLAD, J. I., *In Praise of Education*, New York 1997.

GORBYLEVA, J. V., «Dialectics of Internal & External: Structure & Speech Contamination», [accessed: April 8, 2002], http://www.bu.edu/wcp/Papers/Lang/LangGorb.htm.

GOSWAMI, U., *Analogical Reasoning in Children*, Hillsdale, New Jersey 1992.

GRAHAM, P.A., «Comment on Philosophy and education», *EducTheor* 31, 1 (1981) 29-30.

GRAYLING, A.C., «Wittgenstein's Influence: Meaning, Mind and Method», in *Wittgenstein Centenary Essays*, ed. P. Griffiths, New York 1991.

GRAYLING, A.C. – WEISS, B., «Frege, Russell and Wittgenstein», in *Philosophy 2: further through the subject*, ed. A.C. Grayling, Oxford 1998, 705-792.

GREELEY, K., *Why Fly that Way? Linking Community and Academic Achievement*, New York 1986.

GREEN, J., «Wittgenstein's influence on philosophy of education», *EducStud* 8 (1977) 1-20.

GREEN, T. F., «A Topology of the Teaching Concept», in *Concepts of teaching: philosophical essays*, ed. C.J.B. Macmillan – T.W. Nelson, Chicago 1968, 28-62.

GRIFFITHS, P., ed., *Wittgenstein centenary essays*, New York 1991.

HACKER, P.M.S., *Wittgenstein: On Human Nature*, London 1997.

———, *Analytical Commentary on the Philosophical Investigations.* III. *Meaning and Mind.* IV. *Mind and Will*, Oxford 1993, 2000.

HAGBERG, G.L., *Art as Language, Wittgenstein, Meaning and Aesthetic Theory*, Ithaca – London 1995.

HALE, B., «Rule-following, Objectivity and Meaning», in *A Companion to the Philosophy of Language*, ed. B. Hale – C. Wright, Oxford 1999, 369-396.

HALE, B. – WRIGHT, C., ed., *A Companion to the Philosophy of Language*, Oxford 1999.

HALLER, R., *Questions on Wittgenstein*, London 1988.

HALLETT, G., *A Companion to Wittgenstein's Philosophical Investigations*, Ithaca – London 1977.

———, *Wittgenstein's Definition of Meaning as Use*, New York 1967.

———, «The Theoretical Content of Language», *Gr.* 54, 2 (1973) 307-337.

HAMLYN, D.W., «Education and Wittgenstein's philosophy», *JPhilEduc* 23, 2 (1989) 213-222.

HAMM, C. M., *Philosophical Issues in Education: An Introduction*, Philadelphia 1989.

HANFLING, O., *Wittgenstein's Later Philosophy*, London 1989.

HANSEN, D. T., «Was Socrates a "Socratic teacher"?», *EducTheor* 38, 2 (1988) 213-224.

HARDIE, C.D., «Inductive Learning», *EducTheor* 25, 1 (1975) 40-44.

HARDWICK, C. S., *Language learning in Wittgenstein's later Philosophy*, Paris 1971.

HARE, W., «Reason in teaching: Scheffler's Philosophy of Education. A maximum vision and a Minimum of mystery», *SPE* 16, 1-2 (1997) 89-101.

———, «Teaching and the barricades to inquiry», *JGE* 49, 2 (2000) 88-109.

HAROUTUNIAN-GORDON, S., «Teaching in an "ill-structured" situation: the case of Socrates», *EducTheor* 38, 2 (1988) 225-238.

HARRIS, R., *Language, Saussure and Wittgenstein: How to play with words*, New York 1988.

HARTLEY, J., *Learning and Studying: A Research Perspective*, London 1998.

HARTNACK, J., *Wittgenstein and Modern Philosophy*, trans. M. Cranston, New York 1965.

HATIVA, H. – MARINOVICH, M., ed., *Disciplinary differences in teaching and learning: Implications for practice*, San Francisco 1995.

HAWLEY, A.H., *Human ecology: a theory of community structure*, New York 1950.

HAYEK, F. A., *The Sensory Order: An Inquiry into the Foundations of Theoretical Psychology*, London 1952.

HEATON, J. M., *Postmodern Encounters: Wittgenstein and Psychoanalysis*, Duxford, Cambridge 2000.

————, *Wittgenstein and Psychoanalysis*, Duxford, Cambridge 2000.

HEINKE, D., *Verstehen fremder Kulturen: Die Relevanz des Spätwerks Ludwig Wittgensteins für die Sozialwissenschaften*, Frankfurt 1997.

HERGENHAHN, B.R. – OLSON, M., *An Introduction to Theories of Learning*, New Jersey 1993.

HESLEP, R. D., *Philosophical Thinking in educational practice*, Westport, Connecticut 1997.

HEYTING, F. – LENZEN, D. – WHITE, J., ed., *Methods in Philosophy of Education*, London 2001.

HILLS, P., *Teaching and Learning as a communication process*, London 1979.

HILMY, S. S., *The Later Wittgenstein: The emergence of a new philosophical method*, New York 1987.

HINTIKKA, M. B. – HINTIKKA, J., *Investigating Wittgenstein*, New York 1986.

HIRST, P., «The logical and psychological aspects of teaching a subject», in *The Concept of Education*, ed. R.S. Peters, London 1967, 44-60.

HIRST, P. – WHITE, P., ed., *Philosophy of Education: Major Themes in the Analytic Tradition. IV. Problems of educational content and practice*, London 1998.

HOGAN, P. – SMITH, R., «The Activity of Philosophy and the Practice of Education», in *The Blackwell Guide to the Philosophy of Education*, ed. N. Blake – *al.*, Oxford 2003, 165-180.

HOLTZMAN, – LEICH, ed., *Wittgenstein: To Follow a Rule*, London 1981.

HONDERICH, T., *Oxford Companion to Philosophy*, Oxford 1995.

HONIG, M. – KAHNE, J. – MCLAUGHLIN, M., «School-community connections: Strengthening Opportunity to Learn and Opportunity to Teach», in *Handbook of Research on Teaching 4th edition*, ed. V. Richardson, Washington, D.C. 2001, 998-1028.

HOSPERS, J., *An introduction to Philosophical Analysis*, London 1990.

HOUGH, J. B. – DUNCAN, J. K., *Teaching: Description and analysis*, Reading, M.A. 1970.

HOUSTON, J., *Fundamentals of Learning*, New York 1976.

HOWIE, G., *Educational Theory and Practice in St. Augustine*, London 1969.

————, *St. Augustine: On Education*, South Bend, Indiana 1969.

HUNTER, J.F.M., *Wittgenstein on Words as Instruments*, Edinburgh 1990.

HYMAN, J., *Investigating Psychology: Science of the mind after Wittgenstein*, London 1991.

HYMAN, R. T., ed., *Contemporary Thought on Teaching*, New Jersey 1971.

ISHIGURO, H., «The So-called picture theory: language and the world in *Tractatus Logico-Philosophicus*», in *Wittgenstein: Critical Reader*, ed. H-J. Glock, Massachusetts 2001, 26-46.

————, «Use and Reference of Names», in *Studies in the Philosophy of Wittgenstein*, ed. P. Winch, London 1969.

JACKSON, P. W., *The Practice of Teaching*, New York 1986.

JACOBS, R. M., OSA, «Augustine's Pedagogy of Intellectual Liberation: Turning Students from "Truth of Authority" to "Authority of Truth"», in *Augustine and Liberal Education*, ed. K. Paffenroth – K. L. Hughes, Hants 2000, 111-123.

JARVIS, P., *The Theory and Practice of Teaching*, London 2002.

JESSEN, R. – RAMETTE, C. – BALSHEM, M., «Practices for engaging student learning: classroom observations», *JGE* 48, 2 (1999) 82-89.

JOHNSON, M., *The body in the Mind: the bodily basis of meaning, imagination and reason*, Chicago 1987.

JOHNSTON, H., *A Philosophy of Education*, New York 1963.

JONES, B. – HALLIWELL, S. – HOLMES, B., *You speak, they speak: focus on target language use*, London 2002.

JOYCE, B. R. – HAROOTUNIAN, B., *The Structure of Teaching*, Chicago 1967.

KAHNE, J., *Reforming Educational Policy: Democracy, Community, and the Individual*, New York 1996.

KASPIRIN, L., «Teaching – the institutionalization of a concept: response to Kazepides' Wittgenstein and rationalists on learning and teaching», *PhilEduc* 42 (1986) 335-339.

KAZEPIDES, T., «Wittgenstein and the rationalists on learning and teaching», *PhilEduc* 42 (1986) 323-334.

KAZMI, A. A., ed., *Meaning and reference: Canadian Journal of Philosophy Supplementary Series* 23, Calgary 1997.

KENNEDY, M. M., ed., *Teaching Academic Subjects to Diverse Learners*, New York 1991.

KERR, D. – SOLTIS, J., «Locating Teacher Competency: An Action Description of Teaching», *EducTheor* 24, 1 (1994) 3-10.

KERR, F., *Theology after Wittgenstein*, Oxford 1986.

KEVANE, E., *Augustine the educator: a study in the fundamentals of Christian formation*, Westminster 1964.

KIDD, J. R., *How Adults Learn,* New York 1973.

KIMBLE, G. A., *Hilgard and Marquis Conditioning and Learning*, New Jersey 1961.

KOETHE, J., *The continuity of Wittgenstein's Thought*, Ithaca – London 1996.

KOLB, D. A., *Experiential Learning*, Englewood Cliffs, New Jersey 1984.

KOMISAR, P. B., «Teaching: Act and Enterprise», *SPE* 6, 2 (1968-69) 168-193.

KRAMER, S., «Education and Digressions in Plato's *Theaetetus*», *EducTheor* 26, 4 (1976) 388-394.

KRENTZ, A., «Play and Education in Plato's *Republic*», [accessed: April, 10, 2002], http://www.bu.edu/wcp/Papers/Educ/Edukren.htm.

KRIES, D., «De Magistro», in *Augustine through the Ages: An Encyclopedia*, ed. A. D. Fitzgerald – *al.*, Cambridge 1999, 519-520.

KRIPKE, S., *Naming and Necessity*, Cambridge, MA 1972.

——, *Wittgenstein on Rules and Private Language*, Oxford 1982.

KYRIACOU, C., *Effective Teaching in Schools*, Hemel Hempstead, Herts 1986.

LAMPERT, M., «Knowing Teaching: the intersection of research on teaching and qualitative research», *HEdRev* 70, 1 (2000) 86-99.

LAPP, D. – *al.*, *Teaching and Learning: Philosophical, Psychological, Curricular Applications*, New York 1975.

LARDIZABAL, A. S.– *al.*, *Principles and Methods of Teaching*, Quezon City, Philippines 1977.

LAUGIER, S., «Où se trouvent les règles?», *ArPh* 64, 3 (2001) 505-524 .

LAVE, J. – WENGER, E., *Situated Learning: Legitimate peripheral participation*, Cambridge 1991.

LAWLESS, G. – DODARO, R., *Augustine and his Critics*, New York 2002.

LEACH, J. – MOON, B., ed., *Learners and Pedagogy*, London 1999.

LEE, P., «Language in thinking and learning: pedagogy and the new Whorfian framework», *HEdRev* 67, 3 (1997) 430-471.

LEHMAN, H., «Conditioning and Learning», *EducTheor* 24, 2 (1974) 161-169.

LINSKIE, R., *The Learning Process: Theory and Practice*, New York 1977.

LLOYD, D.I., ed., *Philosophy and the Teacher*, London 1976.

LOCKE, J., *An Essay Concerning Human Understanding*, New York 1959.

——, *Some Thoughts Concerning Education*, Oxford 1990.

——, *Two Treatises of Government*, New York 1965.

LOWENKRON, B., *Joint Control and Rule Following: An analysis of purpose*, [accessed: August 10, 2003], http://www.calstatela.edu/faculty/zlowenk/abal1999/rulefollowing.html.

LUCKHARDT, C.G., ed., *Wittgenstein: sources and perspectives*, Ithaca, New York 1996.

LUGG, A., *Wittgenstein's Investigations 1-133: a guide and interpretation*, New York 2000.

MACKIE, M., *Educative Teaching*, Sydney 1968.

MACMILLAN, C.J.B., «Rational Teaching», *TColRec* 86, 3 (1987) 411-422.

MACMILLAN, C.J.B. – NELSON, T.W., ed., *Concepts of Teaching: Philosophical Essays*, Chicago 1968.

MACMURRAY, J., *Person in Relation*, Atlantic Highlands, N.J. 1966.

MALCOLM, N., *Ludwig Wittgenstein: a Memoir*, Oxford 1984.

———, *Nothing is Hidden*, Oxford 1986.

———, *Wittgenstein: A Religious Point of View?*, Ithaca, New York 1994.

———, *Wittgensteinian Themes: Essays 1978 – 1989*, ed. G.H. von Wright, Ithaca – London 1995.

VAN MANEN, M., *The Tact of Teaching: the meaning of Pedagogical Thoughtfulness*, Canada 1991.

MACONI, D., ed., *Guida a Wittgenstein: Il «Tractatus», dal «Tractatus» alle «Ricerche», Matematica, Regole e Linguaggio privato, Psicologia, Certezza, Forme di Vita*, Roma – Bari 1997.

MARCUSCHI, L.A., *Die Methode des Beispiels: Untersuchungen über die methodische Funktion des Beispiels in der Philosophie, ins besondere bei Ludwig Wittgenstein*, Erlangen 1976.

MARÍAS, J., *History of Philosophy*, trans. S. Appelbaum – C. C. Strowbridge, New York 1967.

MARSHALL, J., «I am LW: Wittgenstein on the Self», *EducPhilTheor* 20 (1988) 7-11.

MARUYAMA, Y., *Wittgenstein on Teaching and Otherness: Toward an Ethic of Teaching*, Florida 2000.

MASON, M., «Teachers as Critical Mediators of Knowledge», *JPhilEduc* 34, 2 (2000) 343-352.

MAYER, F., *Philosophy of Education for our time*, New York 1958.

McCARTHY, T. – STILD, S. C., ed., *Wittgenstein in America*, Oxford 2001.

McCARTY, L.P. – McCARTY, D.C., «Reading in the darkness: Wittgenstein and indoctrination», *PhilEduc* (1990) 383-395.

———, «Semantic Physiology: Wittgenstein on Pedagogy», *PhilEduc* (1989) 231-243.

———, «Wittgenstein on the Unreasonableness of Education: Connecting Teaching and Meaning», in *Philosophy of Education: Accepting*

Wittgenstein's Challenge, ed. P. Smeyers – J. Marshall, Dordecht 1995, 63-76.

MCCULLAGH, M., «Wittgenstein on Rules and Practices», *JPhilR* 27 (2002) 83-100.

MCGINN, C., *Wittgenstein on Meaning*, Conley Rd., Oxford 1984.

MCGUINNESS, B., *Approaches to Wittgenstein*, New York 2002.

MCHOUL, A., *Wittgenstein on Certainty and the Problem of Rule in Social Science*, Toronto 1986.

MCLAUGHLIN, T., «Wittgenstein, Education, and religion», *SPE* 14, 2-3 (1995) 295-311.

MCMAHON, M., « Social Constructivism and the World Wide Web – A paradigm for Learning », [accessed: June 12, 2002], http://www.ascilite.org.au/conferences/perth97/papers/Mcmahon/Mcmahon.html.

MCNEILL, J., «Recognizing Teaching and some Related Acts», *PhilEduc* (1975) 90-100.

MEIXNER, U. – SIMONS, P., ed., *Metaphysics in the Post-Metaphysical Age*, Papers of the 22nd International Wittgenstein Symposium. Contributions of the Austrian Ludwig Wittgenstein Society, VII (1), Kirchberg am Wechsel 1999.

MERRELL, F., *Peirce, Signs and Meaning*, Toronto 1997.

MERZ, C. – FURNAM, G., *Community and Schools*, New York 1997.

MILLAR, R. – DRIVER, R., «Beyond Processes», *SSEd* 14 (1987) 33-62.

MOLLANEDA, R. P., *Concrete Approach and Therapeutic Activity: G. Marcel and L. Wittgenstein On Doing Philosophy*, Manila 1976.

MONK, R., *Ludwig Wittgenstein: The Duty of Genius*, London 1991.

MOON, B. – ANN MAYES, S. – HUTCHINSON, S., ed., *Teaching, Learning and the Curriculum in Secondary Schools: A reader*, London 2002.

MOORE, A., *Teaching and Learning: Pedagogy, Curriculum and Culture*, London 2000.

MOORE, G.E., *Philosophical Papers*, London 1959.

———, «Wittgenstein's Lectures in 1930-31», in *Philosophical Papers*, ed. G.E. Moore, London 1959, 252-324.

MOORE, T.W., *Philosophy of education: an introduction*, London 1982.

MORAN, G., *Showing How: the Act of Teaching*, Valley Forge, Pennsylvania 1997.

MORAWETZ, T., *Wittgenstein and Knowledge: the importance of On Certainty*, Amherst 1978.

MORTON, D. – ZAVADEH, M., *Texts for Change: Theory/Pedagogy/Politics*, Urbana 1991.

NADEAU, R. – DÉSAUTELS, J., *Epistemology and the Teaching of Science*, Ottawa 1984.

NAHAPIET, J. – GHOSHAL, S., «Social Capital, Intellectual Capital, and the Organizational Advantage», *AcMRev* 22, 2 (1998) 242-266.

NELSON, J.O., «Is Pears-McGuiness Translation of the Tractatus really superior to Ogden's and Ramsey's?», *PhilInvest* 22, 2 (1999) 165-175.

NETTLESHIP, R.L., *The Theory of Education in Plato's Republic*, London 1935.

NICHOLS, M., «Rousseau's Novel Education in the *Emile*», *PolTheor* 13 (November 1985) 535-558.

NISBET, R, A., *The Sociological Tradition*, New York 1966.

NODDINGS, N., *Philosophy of Education*, Colorado 1995.

NORDBERG, R. B., «Is Education real? A reply to Robin Barrow», *EducTheor* 33, 2 (1983) 201-203.

O'DONNELL, J. J., «De Doctrina Christiana», in *Augustine through the Ages: An Encyclopedia*, ed. A. D. Fitzgerald – al., Cambridge 1999, 279-280.

O'LEARY, P., «The Concept of Learning», in *Teaching, Schools and Society*, ed. E. Orteza y Miranda – R. F. Magsino, London 1990, 214-230.

OAKESHOTT, M., «Teaching», in *Contemporary Thought on Teaching*, ed. R. T. Hyman, New Jersey 1971, 13-19.

OGBONNAH, C.C., *The Problems of Learning and the Teaching Profession in the Nigerian Context*, Roma 1986.

ORNSTEIN, A. – al., *An Introduction to the Foundations of Education*, Boston 1981, 112-113.

ORTEZA Y MIRANDA, E. – MAGSINO, R.F., ed., *Teaching, Schools and Society*, London 1990.

ORTON, R. E., «Two Problems with Teacher Knowledge», *PhilEduc* (1994) 365-373.

OZMON, H. A. – CRAVER, S. M., *Philosophical foundations of education*, New York 1990.

PAFFENROTH, K. – HUGHES, K. L., ed., *Augustine and Liberal Education*, Hants 2000.

PARKE, R., ed., *The Family: Review of Child Development Research*. VII, Chicago 1984.

PARSONS, T., *The Social System*, Glencoe, Illinois 1955.

PASSMORE, J., *The Philosophy of Teaching*, London 1980.

PATANÈ, L.R., *Il Pensiero Pedagogico di S. Agostino*, Bologna 1967.

PEACOCKE, C., «Holism», in *A Companion to the Philosophy of Language*, ed. B. Hale – C. Wright, Oxford 1997, 227-247.

PEARSON, A.T., *Teaching, Learning and Ontological Dependence*, Philosophy of Education Proceedings of the 45th annual meeting of the philosophy of education society, Urbana Illinois 1989.

———, «Teaching, Reason and Risk», *SPE* 16, 1-2 (1997) 103-111.

———, *The Teacher: theory and practice in teacher education*, New York 1989.

PEKARSKY, D., «The Aristotelian principle and education», *EducTheor* 30, 4 (1980) 281-292.

PENCO, C., «Local Holism», in *Modeling and Using Context*, Proceedings of the Third International and Interdisciplinary Conference on Modeling and Using Context (CONTEXT 2001), ed. V. Akman – *al.*, Lecture Notes in Computer Science 2116, Dundee, UK 2001, 290-303.

PENDLEBURY, S., «Teaching: Response and responsibility», *EducTheor* 36, 4 (1986) 349-354.

PERRY, J., «Davidson's Sentences and Wittgenstein's Builders», *Proceedings and Addresses of the American Philosophical Association* 68, 2 (1994) 23-37.

PESTALOZZI, J.H., *How Gertrude Teaches her Children*, trans. L. E. Holland – F. C. Turner, ed. E. Cooke, London 1894.

PETERMAN, J., *Philosophy as therapy: An Interpretation and Defense of Wittgenstein's Later Philosophical Project*, New York 1992.

PETERS, M. – MARSHALL, J., *Wittgenstein: Philosophy, Postmodernism, Pedagogy: Critical Studies in Education and Culture*, ed. H.A. Giroux, Connecticut 1999.

PETERS, R.S., ed., *Authority, Responsibility and Education*, New York 1960.

———, *John Dewey reconsidered*, London 1977.

———, *The Concept of Education*, London 1967.

PETTIT, P., «The Reality of Rule-Following», *Mind* 99 (1990) 1-21.

PHILLIPS, D.C. – SOLTIS, J., *Perspectives in learning*, New York 1985.

PIAGET, J., *Success and Understanding*, Cambridge, M.A 1978.

———, *The Grasp of Consciousness*, London 1977.

PIAGET, J. – GARCIA, R., *Toward a logic of meaning*, ed. P M. Davidson – J. Easley, Hillsdale, New Jersey 1991.

PITKIN, H.F., *Wittgenstein and Justice*, Los Angeles 1972.

PITMAN, M.A., – EISIKOVITS, R.A. – DOBBERT, M.L., *Culture Acquisition: A holistic approach to human learning*, New York 1989.

PLATO, *Republic*, ed. G.R.F. Ferrari, trans. T. Griffith, Cambridge – N.Y. 2000.

POLANYI, M., *The Tacit Dimension*, London 1966.

POLE, D., *The Later Philosophy of Wittgenstein*, London 1958.

POPP, J. A., *Naturalizing Philosophy of education: John Dewey in the postanalytic period*, Carbondale – Edwardsville 1998.

POUNDS, R. L. – GARRETSON, R. L., *Principles of Modern education*, New York 1962.

POWER, E. J., *Philosophy of Education: Studies in Philosophies, Schooling, and Educational Policies*, New Jersey 1982.

PRICE, K., «On Education as a species of Play», *EducTheor* 27, 4 (1977), 253-260.

PROEFRIEDT, W.A., «The significance of the teacher's work», *EducTheor* 31, 3-4 (1981) 341-350.

QUINTON, A., *From Woodhouse to Wittgenstein: Essays*, Manchester 1998.

RAMSEY, B., «De Catechizandis rudibus», in *Augustine through the Ages: An Encyclopedia*, ed. A. D. Fitzgerald – al., Cambridge 1999, 144-145.

RAO, P.A., *A survey of Wittgenstein's theory of meaning*, Calcutta 1965.

RAYWID, M.A., «Community and schools: a prolegomenon», *PhilEduc* 1988, 2-17.

REINSMITH, W. A., *Archetypal forms in teaching: A continuum*, New York 1992.

REISS, T. J., *The uncertainty of analysis: Problem in truth, meaning and culture*, Ithaca – London 1988.

RICHARDSON, V., ed., *Handbook of Research on Teaching*, 4th edition, Washington, D.C. 2001.

RIEGLE, R. P., «The Concept of "Learning"», *PhilEduc* (1973) 77-85.

RING, M., «"Bring me a slab!": meaning, speakers and practices» in *Wittgenstein's Philosophical Investigations: Text and Context*, ed. R. Arrington – H.J. Glock, London 1991, 12-34.

RIST, J., *Augustine: Ancient Thought Baptized*, New York 1994.

RIZVI, F., «Wittgenstein on grammar and analytic philosophy of education», *EducPhilTheor* 19 (1987), 33-46.

ROUSSEAU, J. J., *Emile*, trans. A. Bloom, New York 1979.

RUBENSTEIN, D., *Marx and Wittgenstein: social praxis and social explanation*, London 1981.

RUNDLE, B., «Meaning and Understanding», in *Wittgenstein: A Critical Reader*, ed. H-J. Glock, Massachusetts 2001, 94-118.

RYLE, G., *The Concept of Mind*, London 1949.

SAVICKEY, B., «Philosophical and Pedagogical Beginnings: *Philosophical Investigations* §1», [accessed: May 13, 2002], http://www.bu.edu/wcp/Papers/Cont/ContSavi.htm.

VON SAVIGNY, E., *The social foundations of meaning*, Berlin 1988.

SCHATZKI, T. R., *Social Practices*, Cambridge 1996.

SCHEFFLER, I., «A concept of Teaching», in *Concepts of Teaching: Philosophical Essays*, ed. C.J.B. Macmillan – T.W. Nelson, Chicago 1968.

———, «The Concept of Teaching», in *Philosophy of Education: Major Themes in the Analytic Tradition, IV. Problems of educational content and practice*, ed. P. Hirst – P. White, London 1998.

———, *Reason and Teaching*, London 1973.

SCHIEFELBUSCH, R. L. – PICKAR, J., ed., *Acquisition of communicative competence*, Baltimore, M.D. 1984.

SCHILPP, P.A., ed., *The Philosophy of John Dewey*, 2nd Edition. New York 1951.

SCHOFIELD, H., *The Philosophy of Education: An introduction*, London 1972.

SCHULTE, J., *Wittgenstein: an Introduction*, trans. W. H. Brenner – J. F. Holley, New York 1992.

SCHULTZ, F.M., *Social-philosophical Foundations of Education*, Iowa 1977.

SERGIOVANNI, T. J., *Building Community in Schools*, San Francisco 1994.

SHANKER, S., ed., *Ludwig Wittgenstein: Critical Assessments* 1, London 1986.

———, «The Enduring Relevance of Wittgenstein's Remarks on Intentions», in *Investigating Psychology: Science of the mind after Wittgenstein*, ed. J. Hyman, London 1991, 67-94.

SHUELL, T. J., «Toward an Integrated Theory of Teaching and Learning», *EdPsych* 28, 4, 1993, 291-311.

SICHEL, B. A., «Correspondence and contradiction in Ancient Greek society and education: Homer's epic poetry and Plato's early dialogues», *EducTheor* 33, 2, 1983, 49-60.

SIEGEL, H., «The future and purpose of philosophy of education», *EducTheor* 31, 1, 1981, 11-15.

SILVERMAN, J., «The aesthetic experience of learning: sketching new boundaries», *JGE* 46, 2 (1997) 73-95.

SKORUPSKI, J., «Meaning, use, verification», in *A Companion to the Philosophy of Language*, ed. B. Hale – C. Wright, Oxford 1997, 29-59.

SLUGA, H. – STERN, D., ed., *The Cambridge Companion to Wittgenstein*, Cambridge 1996.

SMALL, R., «Educational praxis», *EducTheor* 28, 3 (1978), 214-222.

SMALL, S. – SUPPLE, A., «Communities as systems: Is a Community more than the sum of its parts?», [accessed: January 27, 2003], http://www.uwex.edu/ces/flp/resources/community.pdf.

SMEYERS, P., «Assembling Reminders for Educational Research: Wittgenstein on Philosophy», *EducTheor* 48, 3 (1998) 287-308.

————, «Some radical consequences for Educational Research from a Wittgensteinian point of view or does almost anything go?», *PhilEduc* (1994) 139-147.

SMEYERS, P. – MARSHALL, J., ed., *Philosophy of Education: Accepting Wittgenstein's Challenge*, Dordecht 1995.

————, «The Wittgensteinian frame of reference and Philosophy of Education at the end of the twentieth century», *SPE* 14, 2-3 (1995) 127-159.

SMITH, F., *The Book of Learning and Forgetting*, New York 1998.

SMITH, O. B., «On the Anatomy of Teaching» in *Contemporary Thought on Teaching*, ed. R. T. Hyman, New Jersey 1971, 20-27.

SMITH, P. G., «A response to President Soltis», *EducTheor* 25, 3 (1975) 223-225.

SMITH, R., *Learning How to Learn: Applied Theory for Adults*, Milton Keynes 1983, Originally published: Chicago 1982.

SOAMES, S., «Skepticism about Meaning: Indeterminacy, Normativity, and the Rule-Following Paradox», in *Meaning and reference: Canadian Journal of Philosophy Supplementary Series*, XXIII, ed. A. A. Kazmi, Calgary 1998.

SOLTIS, J. F., «Philosophy of education: retrospect and prospect», *EducTheor* 25, 3 (1975) 211-222.

SPECHT, E.K., *The Foundations of Wittgenstein's late philosophy*, trans. D.E. Walford, Manchester 1969.

SPENDER, J.C., «Organizational Knowledge, learning and memory: Three concepts in search of a theory», *JOrgC* 9, 1 (1996) 63-78.

STANAGE, S., «Meaning & Value: Human action and matrices of relevance in philosophies of education», *EducTheor* 26, 1 (1976) 53-71.

STEINBERG, L., *Beyond the Classroom*, New York 1996.

STEINER, R., *Toward a grammar of abstraction: modernity, Wittgenstein and the paintings of Jackson Pollock*, University Park, Pennsylvania 1992.

STERN, D., *Wittgenstein on Mind and Language*, Oxford 1995.

STEWART, W.A. – McCANN, W. P., *The Educational Innovators*. I, London 1967.

STOKHOF, M., *World and Life as One: Ethics and Ontology in Wittgenstein's early thought*, California 2002.

STONE, L., «Disavowing Community», *PhilEduc* (1992) 93-101.

STOUT, M., «Response to "Disavowing Community"», *PhilEduc* (1992) 102-104.

STRAUGHAN, R., – WILSON, J., *Philosophers on Education*, London 1987.

STRICKLAND, R., «Confrontational Pedagogy and Traditional Literary Studies», *ColEng* 52 (March 1990) 291-300.

STROLL, A., *Wittgenstein*, Oxford 2002.

STROUD, B., «Mind, meaning, and practice», in *The Cambridge Companion to Wittgenstein*, ed. H. Sluga – D. Stern, Cambridge 1996, 296-319

———, *Meaning, Understanding and Practice: Philosophical Essays*, Oxford 2000.

SUGRUE, C. – DAY, C., *Developing Teachers and Teaching Practice: International research perspectives*, London 2002.

SUTER, R., *Interpreting Wittgenstein: A Cloud of Philosophy, A Drop of Grammar*, Philadelphia P.A. 1989.

TARCOV, N., *Locke's Education for Liberty*, Chicago 1984.

THORNDIKE, E., *Human Learning*, Cambridge 1966.

TING, F-N., *Wittgenstein's Descriptive Method*, Hong Kong 1989.

TÖNNIES, F., *Community and Society Gemeinschaft und Gesellschaft*, trans. ed. C. Loomis, New York 1957.

TRAVIS, C., *The Uses of Sense*, Oxford 1989.

TRIGG, R., «Wittgenstein and Social Science», in *Wittgenstein centenary essays*, ed. P. Griffiths, New York 1991, 209-222.

TROXELL, E.A., «Teaching Wittgenstein's later philosophy: noticing what is always before one's eyes», *TeachPhil* 19, 1 (1996) 3-29.

ULJENS, M., *School Didactics and Learning: a school didactic model framing an analysis of pedagogical implications of learning theory*, East Sussex, UK 1997.

VOLTOLINI, A., *Guida alla Lettura delle Ricerche Filosofiche di Wittgenstein*, Roma 1998.

VYGOTSKY, L.S., *Thought and Language*, Cambridge, MA 1962.

WAISMANN, F., *Wittgenstein and the Vienna Circle (1929-1932)*, ed. B. McGuiness, trans. J. Schulte – B. McGuiness, Oxford 1979.

WALLER, W., *The sociology of teaching*, New York 1967.

WANG, C-C. – GAFFREY, J. S., «First Graders' Use of Analogy in Word Reading», *JLR* 30, 3 (1998) 389-403.

WARD, S. A., «The philosopher as synthesizer», *EducTheor* 31, 1 (1981) 51-72.

WARMINGTON, E. H. – ROUSE, P.G., *Great Dialogues of Plato*, trans. W.H.D. Rouse, New York 1956.

WARREN, R.L., *Community in America*, Chicago 1963.

WENGER, E., «Communities of Practice: The Social Fabric of a Learning Organization», *HFJ* 39, 4 (July-August 1996) 20-26.

WETTSTEIN, H. K., *Has semantics rested on a mistake? (And other essays)*, California 1991.

WHITE, A. M., ed., *Interdisciplinary Teaching*, San Francisco 1981.

WILLIAMS, D. R., «Re-embedding Community», *PhilEduc* (1993) 90-101.

WILLIAMS, M., «The Significance of Learning in Wittgenstein's Later Philosophy», *CJP* 24, 2 (1994) 173-203.

————, *Wittgenstein, Mind and Meaning: toward a social conception of mind*, London 1999.

WILSON, B., *Wittgenstein's Philosophical Investigations: a Guide*, Edinburgh 1998.

WILSON, J., «The inevitability of certain concepts (Including education): A reply to Robin Barrow», *EducTheor* 33, 2 (1983) 203-204.

WINCH, C. - GINGELL, J., *Key Concepts in the Philosophy of Education*, London, 1999.

WINCH, C., *The philosophy of Human Learning and theory instruction*, New York 1998.

WRIGHT, C., «What is Wittgenstein's point in the rule-following discussion?», [accessed: March 6, 2003], http://www.nyu.edu/gsas/dept/philo/courses/rules/papers/Wright.pdf.

WRIGHT, C., «Rule-Following, Objectivity and the Theory of Meaning», in *Wittgenstein: To Follow a Rule*, ed. Holtzman, – Leich, London 1981.

VON WRIGHT, G.H., «The origin and composition of Wittgenstein's Investigations» in *Wittgenstein: sources and perspectives*, ed. C.G. Luckhardt, Ithaca, New York, 1979.

————, «A Biographical Sketch», in *Ludwig Wittgenstein: a Memoir*, ed. N. Malcolm, Oxford 1984, 1-22.

WRINGE, D.S., «The teacher's task», in *Philosophy and the Teacher*, ed. D.I. Lloyd, London 1976, 6-18.

YOLTON, J.W., *John Locke and the Way of Ideas*, Oxford 1968.

ZAJDA, J., ed., *Learning and Teaching*, Australia 1997.

ZEMACH, E.M., *The reality of Meaning the meaning of "Reality"*, Hanover – London 1992.

ZHANG, Y., «Why the Tractarian Object Cannot be Properties and Relations», [accessed: May 16, 2002], http://www.bu.edu/wcp/Papers/Onto/ OntoZhan.htm.

INDEX OF AUTHORS

TABLE OF CONTENTS

STAMPA: Marzo 2005

presso la tipografia
"Giovanni Olivieri" di E. Montefoschi
ROMA • tip.olivieri@libero.it

TESI GREGORIANA

Since 1995, the series «Tesi Gregoriana» has made available to the general public some of the best doctoral theses done at the Pontifical Gregorian University. The typesetting is done by the authors themselves following norms established and controlled by the University.

Published Volumes [Series: Philosophy]

1. HERRERÍAS GUERRA, Lucía, *Espero estar en la verdad. La búsqueda ontológica de Paul Ricoeur*, 1996, pp. 288.

2. CLANCY, Donal, *Valor y Razón. La constitución de la moralidad en Joseph de Finance y Giuseppe Abbà*, 1996, pp. 276.

3. SALATIELLO, Giorgia, *L'autocoscienza come riflessione originaria del soggetto su di sé in San Tommaso d'Aquino*, 1996, pp. 152.

4. CASTILLO, Martín Julio, *Realidad y transcendentalidad en el planteamiento del ploblema del mal según Xavier Zubiri*, 1997, pp. 348.

5. NAICKAMPARAMBIL, Thomas, *Through Self-Discovery to Self-Transcendence. A Study of Cognitional Self-Appropriation in B. Lonergan*, 1997, pp. 296.

6. FINAMORE, Rosanna, *B. Lonergan e* L'Education: «l'alveo in cui il fiume scorre», 1998, pp. 344.

7. ŚLIWIŃSKI, Piotr, *Il ragionamento per analogia nella filosofia analitica polacca*, 1998, pp. 192.

8. KOBYLIŃSKI, Andrzej, *Modernità e postmodernità. L'interpretazione cristiana dell'esistenza al tramonto dei tempi moderni nel pensiero di Romano Guardini*, 1998, pp. 560.

9. MÁRCIO, Antônio de Paiva, *A liberdade como horizonte da verdade segundo M. Heidegger*, 1998, pp. 216.

10. DA SILVA, Márcio Bolda, *A filosofia da litertação a partir do contexto histórico-social da América Latina*, 1998, pp. 336.

11. PARK, Byoung-Jun Luis, *Anthropologie und Ontologie. Ontologische Grundlegung der transzendetal-anthropologischen Philosophie bei Emerich Coreth*, 1999, pp. 292.

12. LUCHI, José Pedro, *A superação da filosofia da consciência em J. Habermas. A questão do sujeito na formação da teoria comunicativa da sociedade*, 1999, pp. 538.

13. BIDERI, Diogène, *Lecture blondélienne de Kant dans les principaux écrits de 1893 à 1930: Vers un dépassement de l'idéalisme transcendantal dans le réalisme intégral*, 1999, pp. 236.

14. TOTI, Daniela, *Franz Rosenzweig. Possibilità di una fondazione della nuova filosofia nella storia*, 2000, pp. 284.

15. DI NAPOLI, Roselena, *Il problema del male nella filosofia di Luigi Pareyson*, 2000, pp. 332.

16. NDAYE MUFIKE, Jérôme, *De la conscience à l'amour. La philosophie de Gabriel Madinier*, 2001, pp. 368.

17. MUHIGIRWA RUSEMBUKA, Ferdinand, *The Two Ways of Human Development According to B. Lonergan. Anticipation in* Insight, 2001, pp. 200.

18. CALDERÓN CALDERÓN, Jaime, *La libertad como fundamento de configuración de la personalidad en Xavier Zubiri*, 2002, pp. 470.

19. BŪGAITĖ, Elena, *Linguaggio e azione nelle opere di Paul Ricoeur dal 1961 al 1975*, 2002, pp. 404.

20. SANABRIA CEPEDA, Víctor Hugo, *La metafísica de la muerte según Maurice Blondel*, 2002, pp. 438.

21. VITOR DE OLIVEIRA, Ibraim, *Arché e telos. Niilismo filosófico e crise da linguagem em Fr. Nietzsche e M. Heidegger*, 2004, pp. 324.

22. APARECE, Pederito A., *Teaching, Learning and Community. An Examination of Wittgensteinian Themes Applied to the Philosophy of Education*, 2005, pp. 238.